In memory of our esteemed colleague and coeditor
Carolyn Galerstein

Feminine Concerns in Contemporary Spanish Fiction by Women

Scripta humanistica

Directed by
BRUNO M. DAMIANI
The Catholic University of America

ADVISORY BOARD

Samuel G. Armistead
University of California
(Davis)

Juan Bautista Avalle-Arce
University of California
(Santa Barbara)

Theodore Beardsley
The Hispanic Society of
America

Giuseppe Bellini
Università di Milano

Giovanni Maria Bertini
Università di Torino

Heinrich Bihler
Universität Göttingen

Harold Cannon
National Endowment
for the Humanities

Michael G. Cooke
Yale University

Dante Della Terza
Harvard University

Frédéric Deloffre
Université de Paris-
Sorbonne

Hans Flasche
Universität Hamburg

Robert J. DiPietro
University of Delaware

Giovanni Fallani
Musei Vaticani

John E. Keller
University of Kentucky

Richard Kinkade
University of Arizona

Myron I. Lichtblau
Syracuse University

Juan M. Lope Blanch
Universidad Nacional
Autónoma de México

Leland R. Phelps
Duke University

Martín de Riquer
Real Academia Española

Joseph Silverman
University of California
(Santa Cruz)

John K. Walsh
(Berkeley)

Feminine Concerns
in Contemporary Spanish Fiction by Women

Edited by
Roberto C. Manteiga
Carolyn Galerstein
and
Kathleen McNerney

Scripta humanistica

44

Feminine concerns in contemporary Spanish fiction by women/edited by
Roberto C. Manteiga, Carolyn Galerstein, and Kathleen McNerney.
p. cm. — (Scripta Humanistica; 44)
Bibliography: p.
Contents: Rewriting myth and history / Elizabeth Ordóñez — Historial novel from a feminine perspective—Urraca / Biruté Ciplijauskaité — Personal and public history in Laforet's long novels / Roberta Johnson — Portraits of the femme seule by Laforet, Matute, Soriano, Martín Gaite, Galvarriato, Quiroga, and Medio / Janet Pérez — Self-discovery in Quiroga's Presente profundo / Carolyn Galerstein — The challenge of Martín Gaite's woman hero / Joan Lipman Brown — The feminist message / Eunice Myers — The dilemma of the modern woman / Roberto Manteiga — A feminist literary renaissance in Catalonia / Kathleen McNerney — The renewal of the quest in Esther Tusquet's El mismo mar de todos los veranos / Lucy Lee-Bonnano — Montserrat Roig / Catherine Bellver.
©Scripta Humanistica, R. Manteiga, C. Galerstein, K. McNerney
ISBN 0-916379-49-3 : $35.00
1. Spanish fiction—20th century—History and criticism.
2. Spanish fiction—Women authors—History and criticism. 3. Women in literature. I. Manteiga, Robert C. II. Galerstein, Carolyn L., 1931-   . III. McNerney, Kathleen. IV. Series: Scripta Humanistica (Series); 44.
PQ6144.F36   1988   87-36776
                                                                                                CIP

Publisher and Distributor:
SCRIPTA HUMANISTICA
1383 Kersey Lane
Potomac, Maryland 20854 U.S.A.

©Scripta Humanistica, R. Manteiga, C. Galerstein, K. McNerney
Library of Congress Catalog Card Number 87-36776
International Standard Book Number 0-916379-49-3

Printed in the United States of America

Acknowledgments

The authors wish to thank the University of Texas at Dallas for contributing toward the institutional support required for the publication of this book.

Contents

Introduction 1
Rewriting Myth and History: Three Recent Novels by Women 6
    ELIZABETH ORDOÑEZ
Historical Novel from a Feminine Perspective: *Urraca* 29
    BIRUTE CIPLIJAUSKAITE
Personal and Public History in Laforet's Long Novels 43
    ROBERTA JOHNSON
Portraits of the *Femme Seule* by Laforet, Matute, Soriano,
    Martín Gaite, Galvarriato, Quiroga, and Medio 54
    JANET PEREZ
Self-Discovery in Quiroga's *Presente Profundo* 78
    CAROLYN GALERSTEIN
The Challenge of Martín Gaite's Woman Hero 86
    JOAN LIPMAN BROWN
The Feminist Message: Propaganda and/or Art?
    A Study of Two Novels by Rosa Montero 99
    EUNICE MYERS
The Dilemma of the Modern Woman: A Study of the
    Female Characters in Rosa Montero's Novels 113
    ROBERTO MANTEIGA
A Feminist Literary Renaissance in Catalonia 124
    KATHLEEN MCNERNEY
The Renewal of the Quest in Esther Tusquets'
    El mismo mar de todos los veranos 134
    LUCY LEE-BONANNO

Montserrat Roig: A Feminine Perspective and a
   Journalistic Slant   152
   CATHERINE BELLVER
Bibliography   169
Feminine Concerns in Contemporary Spanish Fiction
   by Women   184

Introduction

As several critics have already pointed out, the feminine presence has never been lacking in Spanish literature. But, with relatively few exceptions, the fictional woman character has been the product of a masculine mentality. La Celestina, la Lozana andaluza, Pepita Jiménez, Fortunata y Jacinta, la Hermana San Sulpicio, and la Regenta are but a few of the examples we could cite. It is not until the 20th Century—more specifically, the post-Civil War period—that we find a significant departure from this deeply rooted tradition. The awarding of the Nadal Prize for literature to Carmen Laforet for her 1944 novel, *Nada*, opens the doors to an influx of "female" raconteurs on the Spanish literary scene. Throughout the forties, fifties and early sixties, generally considered the years of the novel of social realism in Spain, writers like Ana María Matute, Elena Quiroga, Mercè Salisachs, Eulalia Galvarriato, and the aforementioned Laforet direct their literary efforts toward the concerns of women. Their protagonists, almost always women, usually adolescents—and the majority of these orphans or social outcasts—confront the problems of what it means to be a woman growing up in a society which seems alien to them. Theirs is both a struggle for acceptance as well as a search for authenticity. Despite the imposing censorship of the Franco-regime, many of these women writers find the courage to speak to certain controversial issues like suicide, divorce and women's rights. Quiroga's highly acclaimed 1954 novel, *Algo pasa en la calle*, addresses all three issues. In her 1962 novel, *La Plaça del Diamant*, Mercè Rodoreda attacks the traditionally patriarchal Spanish society for its lack of concern for women, while, at the same time, criticising women themselves for their passive acceptance of their own subjugation.

Martín Gaite and several other more contemporary women writers have taken the novel in a new direction. Treating the literary text as more than a mere social document, they speak to women's issues as they relate to other overriding textual concerns. In the case of Martín Gaite, it is an interest in rhetoric (the author's preoccupation with the acts of writing and speaking) which determines the focus of several of her more popular novels, and which prompts her appeal for the destruction of certain traditional social barriers which make open and honest communication between men and women impossible.

One of the outstanding features of the literature produced in Spain since the death of Franco has been the growing prominence of female writers. Nowhere is this more apparent than in Catalonia which has experienced a cultural renaissance, and with it the appearance on the literary scene of an entourage of very successful women writers like Montserrat Roig, Carme Riera, and Esther Tusquets, all effective spokeswomen for the women's cause.

With the threat of censorship removed, today's Spanish woman writer has the freedom to express her concerns openly. All too often, however, these expressions of concern fall on deaf ears. The burden of tradition continues to weigh heavily on Spanish society, and the Spanish woman still finds herself in what appears to be a never-ending struggle to secure an identity.

Criticism has responded slowly to the new women's literature. While there have been many interviews and book reviews, until very recently, few substantial articles of scholarly criticism have appeared, and even fewer full-length studies. What *has* been written tends to dwell all too often on the personal lives of the authors and not enough on their work. It is assumed that everything the writer says is autobiographic and that, once she has related her own experiences, there is nothing left to say. Worse still is the tendency to trivialize the life experiences of women as addressed by these writers. In the prologue to her *Novelistas femeninas de la postguerra española*, Janet Pérez cites some alarming statistics. Of the 1,145 doctoral dissertations from 1972-1977 only 21 deal with the literary work of Spanish women writers. Fewer still address the concerns of women. The situation has improved somewhat. In addition to an increase in the number of dissertations on women writers, there has appeared a handful of important collections: the aforementioned book by Janet Pérez; Beth Miller's, *Women in Hispanic Literature;* Gloria Waldman's and Linda Gould Levine's *Feminismo ante el franquismo;* and Lucía Fox-Lockert's, *Women Novelists in Spain and Spanish America*. The Waldman/Levine book is a collection of interviews with Spanish feminists, not critical essays per se. Miller's work does not deal specifically with literature by women, rather with the female character in Spanish literature. Peréz's collection of essays is, by the author's own admission, not intended to present a particularly feminine perspective, but to treat certain literary issues in a broader philological sense. Fox-Lockert's book does examine the fiction of Hispanic women authors from a feminine point of view, but the focus of the book is extremely broad. There have been recent attempts to provide a thorough bibliography of Hispanic women writers. Efforts by the Modern Language Association Division of Women's Studies in Languages and Literatures have seen the publication of Margery Resnick and Isabelle de Courtivron's, *Women Writers in Translation: An Annotated Bibliography, 1945-1980* (New York: Garland Press, 1981) and *Towards a Bibliography of Women Writers in Spain* prepared and distributed among Hispanic scholars by Diane Marting of Rutgers University. In addition a number of Hispanic scholars have contributed to Carolyn Galerstein's *Women Writers of Spain: An Annotated Bio-bibliographical Guide* (Westport, Connecticut: Greenwood Press, 1986).

The aforementioned collections notwithstanding, to date there has been no major study written which deals specifically with the concerns of women as presented in the works of a particular group of Hispanic women writers. The present volume is an attempt to do precisely that. The scope of this study has been limited to those novelists who are women, who are from Spain, and whose literary careers began after the Spanish Civil War. While it is impossible for a collection such as this to be all inclusive, we have made an attempt to include as many of the major women novelists as possible. Still there are many worthy of mention like Teresa Barbero, María Luz Melcón, Concha Alós, Soledad Puértolas and Mercè Salisachs, to name only a few, who have not found their way into this collection. We find this regrettable, and hope that today's marketplace will encourage critics to take more interest in the literary production of these and other women novelists.

The present collection includes eleven essays by a number of already well established scholars in the fields of Contemporary Spanish Literature and Women's Studies. Each deals with typically feminine concerns as revealed in the novelistic production of one or more contemporary Spanish women writers. Elizabeth Ordóñez demonstrates how recent Spanish narrative texts by women authors like Riera, Ojea and Ortiz actually rewrite history, displacing previous constrictive patriarchal mythical and historical accounts of women that have deprived women of their autonomy. Following along similar lines, Ciplijauskaité singles out Lourdes Ortiz's novel *Urraca* as a prime example of a novel which attempts to present a more intimate portrayal of a historical female figure than the distorted mythical view presented by historians. Roberta Johnson finds that Carmen Laforet departs radically from many of the male novelists who, like her, embody history in their novels. Laforet's is an inductive rather than a deductive approach to history. There is no preconceived moral viewpoint and no attempt to interpret historical events, only the day to day minutia of individual lives in a well-defined historical circumstance. Janet Pérez studies the character of the single woman as treated in the fiction of several post-Civil War women authors, revealing a portrait that is very different from the one we find in fiction by men. In her analysis of Elena Quiroga's *Presente profundo*, Carolyn Galerstein notes that the two female protagonists of the novel, while coming from very different backgrounds, actually have a great deal in common. Victims of the traditionally patriarchal Spanish society, both seek liberation through the only option open to them, suicide and death. For Joan Lipman Brown, Carmen Martín Gaite's novels offer an unparalleled source for learning about the lives of Spanish women. Her study shows how Martín Gaite's women characters reflect the changing social climate of contemporary Spain. Eunice Myers and Roberto Manteiga examine the narrative works of Rosa Montero from two rather different, almost contradictory, perspectives. Myers sees Montero's message as clearly feminist while Manteiga insists that the author's concerns are not exclusively feminist and that concealed in her novels is an implied criticism of certain aspects of the feminist movement. Kathleen McNerney presents an overview of contemporary Catalan literature by women, focusing on important works by Riera and Rodoreda, two of Catalonia's most widely acclaimed women novelists. Lucy Lee-Bonanno discovers the feminist theme of self-actualization (a rebirth of faculties stifled by a lifelong adherence to patriarchal dictates) in Esther Tusquet's novel *El mismo mar de todos los veranos*. Like many women today, her middle-aged protagonist rediscovers the possibilities of growth and freedom left behind in the green world of her youth. Finally, Catherine Bellver suggests that the differences among individual women may, in fact, be greater than those between men and women. Montserrat Roig, Bellver argues, is a case in point. Her works deviate significantly from the standard autobiographical mold of those of other women writers. Rather than present a purely sociological view of things, Roig documents the features of the world around her as they relate to the psychological struggles of women.

    This collection is not intended to present any particular viewpoint. The essays are as rich in their diversity as the novels they address. They explore a variety of issues, thereby bringing us much closer to an understanding of what it is like to be a woman struggling to find her place in the very difficult social climate of contemporary Spain.

Rewriting Myth and History:
Three Recent Novels by Women

Elizabeth J. Ordóñez

> Woman must write herself: must bring women to their
> senses and to their meaning in history.
> Helene Cixous, "The Laugh of the Medusa"

Following its adolescence of creativity in the sixties and seventies, a new generation of Spanish women writers is coming of age. Its workplace is a cultural context in which democratic and progressive ideals are taking root; its works display fresh theories and practices now able to grow and transform in their more fertile, open environment. And into this more receptive cultural climate has flowed feminist literature from abroad, bringing with its virtual ubiquity a tendency among young women writers to often identify more with foreign models than with their own Spanish literary foremothers.[1] Among those various trans-Pyrenean influences now making themselves felt are the innovative writings of French feminism. Their presence is plainly visible —

---

[1] Ymelda Navajo in her prologue to *Doce relatos de mujeres* (Madrid: Alianza Editorial, 1983), p. 12, assesses some influences on today's women writers: "In my opinion, the influence exercised by authors like Virginia Woolf, Simone de Beauvoir, Doris Lessing or Mary MacCarthy has contributed toward 'universalizing' to a certain extent the uneasiness or projects of the immense majority of women who are publishing at this time. I would even say, for example, that many of the narratives collected in this volume more closely approach the work of young American or British women writers than the feminine fiction of the Spanish postwar period." Translation is my own.

and articulated with direct relevance to our project of reading recent narrative texts by women — in a series of articles appearing during the early eighties in the literary journal, *Quimera*.[2] Through that medium, Hispanic writers and critics engage in dialogue about the question of difference in women's writing, and though there may be some dissent among them, one can still identify common threads in their discussions. Influenced by North American as well as by French feminist theory, these writers wonder about how to inscribe female desire into the text, how to reappropriate discourse, tell their own stories. Marta Traba discovers a relationship between women's and oral literature; Carme Riera seriously considers Helene Cixous' call for a language of the female body or another voice for women; Evelyn García calls for the creation of new myths, especially the myth of androgyne. All point toward the necessity of developing new ways of reading, perspectives which might unveil silences and establish a complicity between writer and reader or among women.

Hispanic perspectives such as these happily confirm my own thoughts and writings on the same subject. In the early eighties I, too, proposed a reading process at least receptive to the idea of difference, one which may better be able to discover the possible connections suggested by Sandra Gilbert between genre and gender, between textuality and sexuality.[3] Concurrently, difference in women's writing was coming to be viewed on both sides of the Atlantic as, what I have called, "self-defining not self-defeating."[4] Or, as Mary Jacobus has so ebulliently expressed, difference in women's writing was defining itself "not as male versus female — not as biologically constituted — but as a multiplicity, joyousness and heterogeneity which is that of textuality itself. Writing, the production of meaning, becomes the site both of challenge and Otherness."[5]

Jacobus's observation finally underscores the part of my earlier argument with most direct bearing upon the concerns of this study. There I sug-

---

[2] Marta Traba, "Hipótesis sobre una escritura diferente," *Quimera*, 13 (November 1981), pp. 9-11; Carme Riera, "Literatura femenina: ¿Un lenguaje prestado?" *Quimera*, 18 (April 1982), pp. 9-12; Evelyne García, "Lectura: N. Fem. Sing. ¿Lee y escribe la mujer en forma diferente al hombre?" *Quimera*, 23 (September 1982), pp. 54-57.

[3] See my "Reading Contemporary Spanish Narrative by Women," *ALEC*, 7 no. 2 (1982), pp. 237-51., and, Gilbert, "What Do Feminist Critics Want?; or, A Postcard from the Volcano," *ADE Bulletin* (Winter 1980), p. 19.

[4] Ordóñez, "Reading," p. 240.

[5] "The Difference of View," in *Women Writing and Writing About Women*, edited by Mary Jacobus (London: Croom Helm, 1979), p. 12.

gested that contemporary Spanish narrative texts by women share a common theoretical impulse: a tendency to demythify patriarchal or phallic myths that have bound or deprived women of being and autonomy, and a desire to free female discourse, and by extension female existence, from their historical constrictions. These moves are, of course, compensatory, as they serve to displace previously deficient or distorted mythical and historical accounts of women's lives. In the present analysis, I should like to further illustrate this theory by demonstrating the presence of these tendencies in three recent novels by writers of the new generation: Carme Riera, Carmen Gómez Ojea, and Lourdes Ortiz. *Una primavera para Doménico Guarini* (Riera, 1981), *Otras mujeres y Fabia* (Gómez Ojea, 1982), and *Urraca* (Ortiz, 1982) are excellent examples of this impulse toward change: each text interweaves a consciousness of the constrictive nature of certain mythical and/or historical accounts of women with a retelling, indeed a rewriting of myth and history. Sometimes overtly, sometimes more subtly and implicitly, these texts engage in a process of female mythmaking or mythopoesis.

All three novels exhibit a consciousness of the text as problem or challenge, and each of the protagonists is in some way reader, sifter, selector, and reshaper of a given textual and extratextual context — what Wolfgang Iser might call a "repertoire" or Michel Foucault an "archive."[6] Faced with a veritable library of accounting devices, each writer-protagonist must choose and mold according to her needs. But her needs are not always immediately apparent; in fact, her evolution as a writer is simultaneous to her growth as a woman. As she passes through a collection of hermeneutic and generative possibilities, she emerges at the other side of her book with a more decided notion of which of the discourses may serve her most effectively as a means of writing her self. As with the French feminists and other deconstructionists, each rewriting necessarily entails a certain degree of subversion and rupture from preceding models.

Thus each text manifests a certain restlessness or uneasiness with its intertext. In *Una primavera,* Clara's literary recollections during her train trip to Florence include flashes from the pages of Pardo Bazán, Galdós, Whitman, and Tolstoy, but she shamefully rejects the frozen literary references as "frívola pedantería" (frivolous pedantry) opting instead for a quest into her

---

[6] Iser, *The Act of Reading: A Theory of Aesthetic Response* (Baltimore: The Johns Hopkins Univ. Press, 1978); Foucault, *The Archaeology of Knowledge*, trans. A.M. Sheridan Smith (NY: Harper and Row, 1972).

personal memory.[7] If any text might be appropriate at the beginning of her journey, it would be the "novela rosa," for this popular genre's contrived turns of plot seem apt to explain Clara's sudden mission to investigate and write up the Guarini case. But subsequently, the journalistic project itself, with its initially febrile anxiety before erasures and ripped up pages, serves as a means and a central metaphor whereby the central "text" challenging Clara comes to be written: the text of her pregnant body. Fabia of *Otras mujeres*, a literature student and implied writer, reacts to several of the same texts or artists as Clara (Pardo Bazán, "la novela rosa," Botticelli), thus pointing to the challenges of a common generational intertext. Ever a reader, a decoder, Fabia also deciphers a multitude of other women in her cultural context, thus assessing which texts and contexts might best provide vehicles for self-expression and growth as a woman and a writer. Urraca reemerges from history to invent her own chronicle, to fill in the gaps from other accounts of her life with her own version of her existence. The flow and play and battles of her life and reign overlap with the shape of her narrative to create a text which seeks to assume the very shape of her female desire: provocative, surprising, improvisational, inventive. Gauging the mood of her interlocutor, Brother Robert, she may choose or reject diverse genres as vehicles for her story — fairy tale, horror story, naturalistic-realism. But her text never ceases being subversive, an affirmation of the claims of her body against the authority of man.

Una primavera is filled with the living history of this decade: terrorism, homosexuality, drug addiction, the clash between traditional and newly emergent values; but most important or most pivotal is the anguished searching of a young woman facing the question of whether or not to abort. Caught among various undesirable options, Clara becomes a sign for today's single professional woman: those around her espouse Marxism with its exploitation of woman as helpmate, still "reposo" (resting place) as under Falangist ideology; immature or misunderstood feminism, with its tendency to slip into self-righteous rhetoric and slogans; conservative traditionalism with its acceptance of female repression and suffering as the norm. Before such unsavory alternatives, Clara, as many of her contemporaries, finds herself obliged to invent her own responses to the challenges of her existence.

---

[7] Carme Riera, *Una primavera para Doménico Guarini*, trans. Luisa Cotoner (Barcelona: Montesinos Editor, S.A., 1981), p. 25. Hereafter all quotations from this work will be indicated by UP and the page number following the quote. All translations are my own.

To discover the means of articulating her life and her text, Clara must react to both contemporary and Renaissance ideologies and myths surrounding woman. As she covers the case of Doménico Guarini's act of vandalism against Botticelli's "Primavera" for a Barcelona newspaper, the events in her personal life become intertwined with the mysterious events she is reporting (particularly in Parts I and II of the novel); in Part III a lecture explicating the Botticelli painting elicits a series of recollections and reflections on Clara's past. The epilogue comes full circle, back to the train in which Clara returns to Spain and tentatively resolves her own dilemma as the Guarini case ironically concludes and the train emerges from a tunnel.

In Part II, as Clara follows and records the Guarini affair, she finds its details often couched within a labyrinthine variety of textual models: a lawyer calls the case a horror story fit for the nineteenth century "folletín" or the neorrealist cinema; leftists criticize it as a "western"; the Italian public is fascinated by its melodramatic and sensationalistic aspects. Immersed in this web of textual possibilities, Clara decides to experiment with form and literally write Guarini's text for him. She forges a well-wrought counterpoint of first and third person narration, revealing Guarini's obsessive attraction to Laura, his decision to "love" according to Neoplatonic, Petrarchan concepts, the futility of such an anachronistic posture, and Guarini's growing desire to destroy the Laura who resists insertion into the hyperbolic codes of his fantasy. This interpolated text in many ways echoes the psychotic intensity of Sábato's *El túnel* or even the obsessive violence of the film, *Taxi Driver*. However, its primary interest is situated not so much in its portrayal of yet another solitary man driven by angst and the mimetic grandeur of his anachronistic obsessions, as in the issues suggested by its reception.

Alberto, Clara's friend and former lover, reads the Guarini text with a critical eye. His precise analysis of the protagonist-narrator's degraded Neoplatonic "love" introduces to Clara the problem of her apparent identification as writer with the phallic imagination, that which seeks to make of woman its object. While Clara defends Guarini, the male projection of her imagination, as strong, good, and self-sacrificing, Alberto interprets Guarini as mythified, incapable of loving, dominating, possessive, paternalistic. Ironically influenced by Clara's third-person narrator, who has described Laura as changing codes to arrive at a more direct form of communication, Alberto defends Laura with an intensity absent in Clara, Laura's implied author. He thus responds negatively, as reader, to the conservative, traditional codes governing Guarini's behavior, even blasting, iconoclastically, Dante and Petrarch as men, too, who "buscaban el poder a través de su amada" (UP, p. 107) (sought power through their beloved). Alberto's reading, engaging as it does in dialogue with both the text and its implied author, achieves a goal envisaged by Bakhtin: "one would enter into dialogue with texts, open oneself to anachronisms and contemporary issues, and make the entire process an occasion for discovering ourselves and our world."[8] If Clara has identified too closely with the male discourse of her text, Alberto's more objective, indeed more "feminist," reading seeks to reveal to Clara how her preferred literary character is mystified, caught within patterns of an anachronistic discourse which today seeks to achieve with "palabras más inteligibles' (UP, p. 86) (more intelligible words) what Dante sought in the vernacular: "at one stroke, Love and women are both brought under control."[9] Clara's version of Guarini in fact pursues such complete control over Laura that when the latter defies his imaginary codes (quite innocently, quite spontaneously), he pierces the center of her being with the symbolic equivalent of his thwarted phallic authority: "el estilete penetró justo en el centro del pecho" (UP, p. 103) (the stiletto penetrated the exact center of her breast). So Alberto teases Clara's idealizing assimilation of the phallic principle in her text, her admiration of and identification with Guarini's obsessive behavior, as he echoes and inverts Flaubert's famous dictum: "Doménico Guarini c'est moi ..." (UP, p. 108) (Doménico Guarini is me). Through his spirited criticism and mocking responses, this reader within the text suggests the need for a displacement of myths of domination if Clara is to achieve her own textual/sexual identity.

Ironically, events do subsequently ally themselves with Laura's (or woman's) cause, figuratively freeing her from entrapment within or destruction by anachronistic male codes. Laura's mortal remains are not found on the site where Guarini affirmed he had buried them. Instead, police find a package of papers and other artifacts, including Petrarch's *Cancionero*. Thus what Clara was remiss to bury, Guarini buries for her. At the foot of a laurel tree (the tree into which the nymph, Daphne, was transformed to elude Apollo) Guarini's obsession is interred, and his imitation of Petrarch assumes its proper proportions as "un simulacro anacrónico y grotesco" (UP, p. 118) (an anachronistic and grotesque semblance) of life. Not insignificantly,

---

[8] Gary Saul Morson, "Who Speaks for Bakhtin?: A Dialogic Introduction, *Critical Inquiry*, 10, no. 2 (December 1983), p. 236.
[9] Gayatri Chakravorty Spivak, "Finding Feminist Readings: Dante-Yeats," in *American Criticism in the Poststructuralist Age*, edited by Ira Konigsberg (Univ. of Michigan: Michigan Studies in the Humanities, 1981). p. 54.

Daphne, in her human counterpart, Laura, survives unravished again, as her pursuer is forced to acknowledge his folly. Laura's implicit association with the myth of Daphne thus provides a provocative sign at a significant juncture in the text: the nymph's metamorphosis points unequivocally to contemporary woman's insistence on her inviolate autonomy.[10]

Part III of the novel is therefore especially revealing, for the interrelationship between the professorial exegesis of Botticelli's "Primavera" and the circumstances of Clara's past serves to underscore the vexing and confining aspects for women of both Renaissance mythology and traditional Spanish ideology. A slight digression into the background of the Renaissance painting will help place this concern into perspective. "Primavera" was originally painted for Lorenzo de Pierfrancesco, when this patron of Botticelli was a boy of some fourteen to fifteen years of age. And though, according to E.H. Gombrich, there are few, if any, fixed meanings in the painting, Gombrich's exegesis, as well as the one we find in the novel, make most sense when we know that the recipient of the painting and of its message was a boy.[11] Venus, "as a guide to the love of men," and the other mythological figures of her entourage were supposed to "speak" to the boy, provide an ambiguous, sometimes even arcane lesson in the practical and spiritual virtues of Renaissance manhood.[12] This suggests a problem in interpretation when the viewer or "reader" of the painting happens to be female. In the novel, this problem is projected through Clara's recollections of her youth, stimulated or elicited by the exegetical lecture she overhears while viewing the painting. Though Clara provides no explicit interpretation of her own, merely juxtaposing her memory with Neoplatonic myth, in the resulting contiguity of the two, we may read the silences, unveil another text.

Layers of myth and experience superimpose themselves as the professor explains the pursuit by Zephyr of Cloris, which recalls that of Daphne by Apollo, which recalls that of Laura by Guarini, which recalls that of Clara as a child by a pervert in the movie theater and demonic incubi in her dreams. Contemporary experience seems eminently more sordid than its mythological antecedents, yet Zephyr's pursuit is not without a certain ag-

---

[10] See Annis Pratt's pertinent consideration of the myth of Daphne and Apollo in *Archetypal Patterns in Women's Fiction* (Bloomington: Indiana Univ. Press, 1981), pp. 3-12.
[11] E.H. Gombrich, "Botticelli's Mythologies: A Study in the Neoplatonic Symbolism of his Circle," *Journal of the Warburg and Courtauld Institutes*, 8 (1945), pp. 7-60.
[12] Gombrich, p. 17.

gressive hostility. The once baleful wind god seeks to possess the nymph so that he may be reborn. In return he bestows upon her the gift of converting whatever she touches into flowers. Then disregarding the nymph's likely frustration from her having too much of a good thing, Zephyr transforms his beloved into Flora, causing her mouth to spew forth roses. Flowers, not words, are Flora's gift from her lover. She is conceded the power to transform him through her beautiful silence. Much like Beatrice in Dante's *La Vita Nuova*, "the woman's desire is nowhere in question, she remains mute, acts against her will."[13] An analogy between Renaissance myth and contemporary experience is then strikingly established in Clara's recollection of a youthful confession: there the girl was likewise mute (the confession is rendered in a priestly monologue). Even at home the words of others threatened the girl with ferocity, that if she were to masturbate she would be condemned to Hell where her mouth would spew forth toads and serpents and the only sound she would emit would be the bestialized language of brays. Autoeroticism (or the language of the girl's own body) would then be punishable by eternal verbal noncommunication, a terrifying and distorted extension of the fate of girls on earth. Schooled in silence ("nosotras hemos venido al mundo para sufrir y aguantar," UP, p. 139) (we have come into the world to suffer and endure), words for females were appropriate only for prayer or to pardon masculine libertines like Clara's father. Small wonder that Clara initially chooses a male voice for her text. She has never had another.

The professor's exegesis of Venus is hardly more gratifying for the woman in quest of her own text. Though in "Primavera" Venus may represent Venus Generatrix, goddess of fecundity — some viewers have detected a subtle abdominal protuberance in the painting's central figure — the explicator points out the higher status of Venus Humanitas and Venus Caelestis respectively.[14] Each manifestation of Venus ascends in superiority over the other as she transcends her corporeality, becomes increasingly spiritualized. The celestial Venus, born from the mutilated genitals of her father, Uranus, thus incorporates only the phallic principle; she has no mother. Or as the professor etymologically explains: "rechaza la materia, precisamente por el hecho de no tener madre. Pensad que las dos palabras 'mater' y 'materia' tienen la misma raíz ..." (UP, pp. 144-145) (she rejects matter, precisely

---

[13] Spivak, p. 51.
[14] Gombrich leans, for historical reasons, toward Venus Humanitas as the central figure of "Primavera." "Botticelli's Mythologies," p. 19.

because of the fact she had no mother. Remember that the two words 'mater' and matter' have the same root...). This symbolic affirmation of nonmaternal nonmateriality may provide an apt sign for a young man's spiritual development, his flight from the demands of the mother and what he may perceive as the threatening aspects of the female flesh. Indeed, for the abstract male or patriarchal spirit, Venus Caelestis may be preferable to Venus Generatrix; it effectively cancels out the maternal economy. But for a female, especially a pregnant one, such a rarefied, ethereal figure may provide little more than a cold and alienating indifference to her condition. Clara's memory proves that this is so, for cut off from communication with her mother, she longed as a child for the maternal intimacy of a teacher. But the latter rejected the girl's attempts at confidence, advising her to confide her plight to the Virgin (Christianity's version of the celestial Venus). The girl did direct her pleas heavenward. She spoke in prayer, but her tearful monologue was met with silence.

How to make the mother speak seems to be, then, a central challenge confronting Clara, or any woman writer for that matter. To co-opt the phallic Mother, to make her a "dissident," a renegade of the phallic order, would allow Clara/woman-writer to shape a discourse more resistant to the mystification of patriarchal beliefs and phallicization.[15] Clara does this through an imaginative recollection in which her masochistic mother momentarily claims a single defiant utterance.

Clara's mother, long suffering the humiliation of an unfaithful husband, was said to have challenged his faithlessness one evening. She was reported to have descended quite regally to where her guests were awaiting her. Accepting their flattery with dignity, she remained composed in the presence of her husband's latest lover. But before she excused herself to give orders to the servants, she made the following announcements and accompanying performance:

> "—Atención, amigos míos, escuchadme un minuto. Todos sabéis con quien me engaña Perico, ahora os enseñaré con quien le engaño yo.
> Con un gesto rapidísimo te arremangaste la falda, deslizaste hacia abajo las bragas de encaje y empezaste a acariciarte el sexo" (UP, p. 144).
> (—Attention, my friends, listen to me for a moment. You all

---

[15] See Jane Gallop, *The Daughter's Seduction: Feminism and Psychoanalysis* (Ithaca, NY: Cornell Univ. Press, 1982), pp. 113-21, for a discussion of the phallic Mother.

know with whom Perico is deceiving me, now I'll show you with whom I'm deceiving him.

With a rapid gesture you rolled up your skirt, slipped down your lace panties and began to caress your sex organ.)

Such a grandiose and subversive gesture seems incredible to Clara, and yet as she recounts it she affirms precisely its daring brilliance .. and, expectedly, its consequences: imprisonment of the mother ("te dejaron encerrada," UP, p. 144) (they locked you up) by the Fathers (husband and brother-in-law). Still, the affirmation of such a defiant posture subverts, at least momentarily, the authority of the libertine father. As the mother ascends the "pequeño estrado" (UP, p. 143) (little stage) for her brief but shocking performance, the father is simultaneously dethroned. The mother, fleetingly transformed into a provocative rebel against the phallic order, literally unveils a sign ("el sexo," autoeroticism) indicating woman's own rewriting of herself through her body.

Fittingly, this recollection is framed by references to Venus Generatrix, whose presence also elicits Clara's defense of her pregnancy. Both women, mother and daughter, are thus implicitly linked by the Goddess of fecundity, and as the professor might say: remember that "generatrix" and "genitals" share the same root. For both women, the genitals serve as metaphorical openings to their own discourse. Or as Jane Gallop discloses: "feminine discourse reveals the sex organ."[16] Furthermore, as Clara affirms the maternal — even matrilineal — identity of her future child ("quiero que lleve mis apellidos, no los de él," UP, p. 142) (I want it to carry my surname, not his), she begins to name her own text.

But before Clara can arrive at textual/sexual self-definition she must reject playing mother to her lover, Enrique, and writing his texts for him ("escribía ... unas crónicas ... que todo el mundo atribuía a Enrique," UP, p. 171) (I wrote ... some chronicles ... that everyone attributed to Enrique). She must come to terms with her own Three Graces, metonymic representations of other women and their diverse values: the missionary nun, the feminist, and the rebellious young freeloader. And she must accept the loss of her Mercury (Jaime), the only male, besides Alberto, who was capable of inhabiting a non-patriarchal, paradisiacal space where an untainted language could invent the world anew. As Clara reencounters these sources of pleasure, pain, and language in her past, much like the new French feminists she becomes more acutely aware of "una vida nueva [que] se está abriendo

---

[16] Gallop, p. 31.

camino en mi vientre" (UP, p. 178) (a new life [that] is opening its way in my womb).[17] Clara learns to read the mythological codes of "Primavera" for her own profit, discovering the hermeneutics of chrysalis, the signs of transformation. As she accepts her impending maternity she knows she will become "transformada" (UP, p. 196) (transformed). For now she accepts being completely alone, implicitly freer of the constraints of repressive myths, prepared to forge her own meanings in the manner of Kristeva's marginal "enceinte": "an 'enceinte' woman loses communital meaning, which suddenly appears to her as worthless."[18] Thus as Clara emerges from the train tunnel, her acceptance of pregnancy as a source of transformation, and her existential solitude as a source of independent meaning, confer upon her the potential to fulfill one of Riera's own fondest proposals for women: to cease being spoken and begin to speak.[19]

Though also a solitary woman in an urban context, Fabia of *Otras mujeres* looks toward that environment as the source of her myths and history. While perceptive of the ugliness and disquieting aspects of her neighborhood, she remains expectant, ready to discover the unforeseen: "sin embargo, a pesar de los ruidos, de las escenas costumbristas y de los tufos grasientos a bárbaros guisos, quizás aquella calle guardara algún encanto que ella no había sabido todavía descubrir" (nevertheless, in spite of the noises, the local color, and the greasy odors of barbarous concoctions, perhaps that street held some charm that she had not yet been able to discover).[20] As Milagros Sánchez Arnosi has pointed out in a recent review, in Fabia's "barrio," noises and smells even perform an evocative function.[21] And the "sin embargo" (nevertheless) along with a repeated use of "pero" (but) recurrently mark the tone of the text as compensatory: there is always another, and often more hopeful, side of female reality.

As a seeker of the hidden bounties of her environment, Fabia belongs to that class of single women in literature through whom authors, according to

---

[17] Interestingly apropos this character, Riera cites Annie Leclerc's attempts to invent new words "en mi vientre" (in my womb). Riera, "Literatura femenina," p. 10. Translation is my own.
[18] Julia Kristeva, *Desire in Language: A Semiotic Approach to Literature and Art*, edited by Leon S. Roudiez (New York: Columbia Univ. Press, 1980), p. 240.
[19] Riera, "Literatura femenina," p. 12.
[20] *Otras mujeres y Fabia* (Barcelona: Edited by Argos Vergara, 1982), p. 13. Hereafter all quotations from this work will be indicated by OM and the page number following the quote. All translations are my own.
[21] "El mundo de los libros," *Insula*, 37, no. 431 (October 1982), p. 8.

Annis Pratt, "seem to be clearing out a new space ... a place that, essentially apatriarchal, contains once-forgotten possibilities of personal development."[22] And as a rewriter of history, Fabia also participates in the quest for a woman-defined text which might "make the invisible visible, make the silent speak:"[23] "a través de esas voces acalladas de mujer —madres, abuelas — como la voz de una juglaresa anónima, no bajó a la tumba, junto con tantos cadáveres,. la historia no escrita, la historia no amanada, para que nadie pueda leerla torcidamente. Gracias a esas madres y abuelas, a través del cordón umbilical de sus palabras, los niños pueden hacer suyo el pasado ..." (OM, p. 80) (through those silenced voices of women — mothers, grandmothers — as through the voice of an anonymous minstrel, unwritten history, unskilled history did not descend to the tomb, along with so many cadavers, so that no one might read it deviously. Thanks to those mothers and grandmothers, through the umbilical cord of their words, the children can appropriate their past). Fabia becomes one of those children who recuperates a heretofore buried past, recording it now for future generations.

Otras mujeres bears out Virginia Woolf's maxim that "a woman writing thinks back through her mothers," and reconfirms my own observation that "in many [contemporary Spanish narrative] texts [by women], one encounters an exhilarating recurrence of female heroes embarking upon heroic quests for matrilinear identity" and myths for women.[24] One of the first moves in this direction in *Otras mujeres* is Fabia's discovery of a matrilineal chain reaching back to the Mother of mothers, passing backward in time through the Carlist Wars, the Enlightenment, the Conquest, the Inquisition, and the Jewish ghetto. The scope of such an undertaking is imposing: "si todas las mujeres de la línea materna se cogieran de la mano hasta llegar a esa Gran Madre común, ella sería la última de la fila y ni poniéndose de puntillas alcanzaría a verla bien" (OM, p. 17) (if all the women of the maternal line were to join hands until they arrived at that Great Mother of them all, she [Fabia] would be the last of the line and not even on tiptoe would she manage to see her [the Great Mother] well). These foremothers animate Fabia's room with their presence, their advice, even their reproaches for Fabia's childless state. Yet when she contemplates the imperative to pro-

---

[22] Pratt, p. 127.
[23] Elaine Showalter, "Feminist Criticism in the Wilderness," *Critical Inquiry*, 8, no. 2 (Winter 1981), p. 201.
[24] Woolf, *A Room of One's Own* (London: Hogarth Press, 1929), p. 146; Ordóñez, "Reading," p. 248.

create and the advantages and disadvantages of having children, she irreverently compensates for a patriarchal myth about procreation (Lao-Tze's birth from a virgin at the age of seventy-two) with her own demythifying candor: "que horror tener en la barriga, años y años, un viejo filósofo malhumorado" (OM, p. 20) (how horrible to have in one's belly, years and years, a badtempered, old philosopher). Rejecting guilt for her nongenerative body, she humorously turns to other voices, those of her Enlightenment foremothers who would likely have said: "es el colmo de los colmos que los ciclos periódicos de tu ovario te produzcan este tipo de desarreglos mentales" (OM, p. 21) (it's absolutely absurd that the periodical cycles of your ovary should produce this type of mental disorder).

History is imaginatively conjoined with myth to rewrite matrilineal endings for stories told quite differently (moralistically, punitively) by patriarchal myth and history: "lo grandioso hubiera sido que, por ejemplo, a Cleopatra la hubiese mordido la mismísima Isis, disfrazada de aspid, para llevársela a las moradas de la luz" (OM, p. 29) (the most magnificent thing would have been, for example, that Isis herself, disguised as an asp, would have bitten Cleopatra, in order to carry her off to the dwellings of light). The Church father, Saint Paul, is conjectured to have required women to cover their heads in Church because "había visto los ojos claros de la diosa de la Acropólis y se había estremecido, sin comprender la vieja sabiduría de su mirada" (OM, p. 44) (he had seen the clear eyes of the goddess of the Acropolis and he had trembled, not comprehending the ancient wisdom of her gaze). Fabia's grandmother leaps out from her portrait to speak with a tongue of fire and the spirit of a warrior (OM, p. 49).[25] Another character, Señora Efe, would be a hero if she could be Queen Urraca, daring to speak against her father, renting male political discourse with her protest: "a mí porque soy mugier, dejaisme desheredada" (OM, p. 78) (me, because I am a woman, you leave disinherited). But Señora Efe cannot find the denouement to her own plot ("faltaba el desenlace," OM, p. 79) (the ending was missing); she cannot name her emptiness, in spite of her degree in literature. Señora Efe can only blame men for her malaise and engage in a certain irascible and disruptive iconoclasm. Even Magdalena Pe, apparently practical, whole, in control — a teller of fairy tales with comfortable endings — is

---

[25] In my "Narrative Texts by Ethnic Women: Rereading the Past, Reshaping the Future," *MELUS*, 9 (1982), p. 26, I observe an aspect of Maxine Hong Kingston's *The Woman Warrior* which provides a suggestive analogy here: "the new Woman Warrior is a writer, a re-teller of ancient tales so that woman may emerge hero of her own destiny, her own text."

possessed by irrational fears of death and hypochondria. So Fabia must sift through the stories of these and other women's lives to discover a text able to reappropriate the mothers, the moon, and the potentially subversive intertext of "las pechugonas [que] tienen que comunicarse como sea" (OM, p. 75) (the big-bosomed women [who] have to communicate no matter what).

The word "pechugona" as sign expands and reverberates with meanings and connotations: big-bosomed, shameless, brazen, insolent, bold, single-minded women. If Señora Efe is brazen, she is not sufficiently single-minded and bold. It remains up to Fabia to be the woman who makes the bold and single-minded step toward linking up with the myths and texts of her foremothers and contemporaries. The word which signals her technique is metonymy (OM, p. 99). Each woman fans out, as it were, into a multitude. Through metonymy Fabia discovers how she can draw her inspiration from the world and words of women, present and past.

So Fabia becomes, as Sánchez Arnosi has indicated, "una especie de juglar, o mejor dicho de cronista objetivo de una historia anudada a su propia historieta individual"[26] (a kind of minstrel, or better said objective chronicler of a larger history tied in with her own personal tale). She searches not only through the intertext of Spanish foremothers but in the example of their lives for codes which may prove useful for her, her text, and others of her generation. The secret of Pardo Bazán, for example, was her practicality, a quality lacking in the scandalous Señora Efe, whose complicity in what she considered her unfortunate fate was at least partly to blame for her limitations, real or imagined. Instead of only disparaging the codes of courtly love and quoting from the classics, Señora Efe might have done well to also look toward the popular literature of housewives ("la novela rosa") for a fuller understanding of herself and other women. Fabia reads *Gone With the Wind* unabashedly, unapologetically. Like Carmen Martín Gaite in *El cuarto de atrás*, Gómez Ojea seems to indicate that the popular fiction of women may not only be an unjustly denigrated window to the female imagination, but may also provide a source of textual coding rich in pleasure and surprising sources of wisdom.[27] Beyond the popularized romantic image of Scarlett O'Hara is a strong woman; beyond a tearful sentimentality is the wisdom

---

[26] Sánchez Arnosi, p. 8.
[27] See my "Reading, Telling and the Text of Carmen Martín Gaite's *El cuarto de atrás*," in *From Fiction to Metafiction: Essays in Honor of Carmen Martín Gaite*, edited by Mirella Servodidio and Marcia L. Welles (Lincoln, Nebraska: The Society of Spanish and Spanish-American Studies, 1983), pp. 173-84.

that, though love may be fleeting and illusive, there is hope in change. And probably of key significance is *Gone With the Wind*'s evocative mythic ending: its "subdued autumnal promise" of transformation and rebirth.[28]

In the summer of her life, Fabia seeks to discover forms of discourse more appropriate for her development as a mature woman and implied writer. She finds that Botticelli's image of woman in "Primavera" is less valid for her now that it was in the past. Though once likened by a lover to Simonetta, Fabia can but vaguely recall traces of that youthful love and the idealized image she represented to that shadowy lover in the springtime of her life. This particular rendering of Neoplatonic Renaissance mythology can no longer encode the feelings and desires of her maturing generation, women and men who, like Tinkerbell, have lost their magical wings and from now on "sólo se arrugarían" (OM, p. 100) (would only grow wrinkled). Interestingly, Botticelli's pictorial language has fascinated and left its imprint on both Riera's Clara and Gómez Ojea's Fabia. Yet there is in both texts a certain uneasiness with this mythological inheritance; admiration turns to struggle as these writers and their protagonists similarly move beyond that given and largely fixed mythological medium toward a more fluid and capacious discourse of their own.

So Fabia finds herself beyond idealized love, beyond economic bondage — she has won the lottery and is temporarily liberated from economic concerns. As a maturing woman she can afford the luxury of reading, studying, and observing her neighborhood with its often hidden and unexpected qualities. And as she confronts the counterpoint of female figures which pass through her imagination and which speak to her in a variety of voices, Fabia's capacity for a broader spectrum of human relationships seems to grow. The wisdom of her grandmother's maternal discourse ("lo que me pasma de tus tiempos es ese remachar, dale y dale, sobre asuntos del sexo," OM, p. 53) (what astonishes me about your time is that stress, over and over again, on sexual matters) — strikingly similar to May Sarton's critique of the same subject ("but what is becoming tiresome now in the American ethos is the emphasis on sex")[29] — foretells Fabia's own movement, as a mature, single woman, toward widening circles of human interaction. As her street appears ever more "larga, larga" (OM, p. 109) (long, long), a seemingly endless road

---

[28] Helen Deiss Irvin, "Gea in Georgia: A Mythic Dimension in *Gone With the Wind*," in *Recasting: Gone With the Wind in American Culture*, edited by Darden A. Pyron (Miami: Univ. Press of Florida, 1983), p. 68.

[29] Pratt, p. 129, from *Journal of a Solitude* (New York: W.W. Norton, 1973), p. 113.

toward possibility, her relationships analogously promise to extend beyond the solely erotic ("no tenía amante," OM, p. 100) (she had no lover). And as she uncovers that which lies submerged in her "barrio," she recuperates her collective identity as woman and implied writer, discovering her capacity to invent and rewrite matrilineal or woman-defined myths and history.

Very little is known about the personal life of the twelfth century monarch, Queen Urraca. As Bernard F. Reilly has affirmed after minute and painstaking archival research: "the study of the reign of Urraca, for all her prominence, remains a study of her public acts and the public institutions of the realm itself. There is as yet no feasible method of penetrating her thoughts or her councils."[30] Unlike Reilly's meticulously documented approach, the accounts of earlier historians tend to reflect the points of view and prejudices of their authors more than a fidelity to observable fact. For example, nineteenth century Juan de Dios de la Rada y Delgado defends the Queen as weak, the object of manipulation, detractors, and false stories imputing her morality.[31] E.L. Miron, writing during the early years of this century, offers another apologia for the Queen: although acknowledging her strength as head of her troops, he also portrays her as the victim of a brutish husband, and insists on the Victorian view that Urraca and Count Pedro González de Lara were lawfully wed.[32] Before such partial views of this fascinating Castilian monarch, how does one create a narrative capable of compensating for partiality and omission? One makes the most of the least, as Urraca's author, Lourdes Ortiz, explains: "precisamente la escasez de referencias históricas verdaderamente documentadas era alicente para la invención?"[33] (precisely the scarcity of truly documented historical references was an incentive for invention). By taking advantage of the gaps in recorded history, Ortiz could invent a novelistic text free to recreate those psychological processes which are often veiled by the bare or insufficient facts of history. And since, as Jane Tibbets Schulenburg has pointed out, official chronicles of the twelfth century were extremely biased and narrow, and

---

[30] *The Kingdom of Leon-Castilla Under Queen Urraca: 1109-1126* (Princeton, NJ: Princeton Univ. Press, 1982), p. 353.

[31] *Mujeres célebres de España y Portugal* (Buenos Aires: Espasa Calpe, S.A. 1954), pp. 55-84.

[32] *The Queens of Aragon: Their Lives and Times* (N.Y. Kennikat Press, 1970), pp. 43-61. Reilly's more recent evidence cites the Count of Lara as Urraca's "lover and her companion until her death," *The Kingdom*, p. 353.

[33] As communicated to me in personal correspondence, October 13, 1983. Translation is my own.

woman's spheres of influence began to shrink, what better vehicle could today's woman writer choose for rewriting such exclusion and loss than a new chronicle, one written by woman herself?[34]

Queen Urraca narrates this new chronicle, one which clearly seeks to displace previously deficient accounts with her own voice: "ellos escribirán la historia a su modo; Urraca tiene ahora la palabra"[35] (they may write history in their way; it is now Urraca's turn to speak). Female authored, it thus becomes a compensatory text including elements usually omitted from traditional male-authored chronicles, such as a certain naturalistic sordidness which might demythify official accounts of male heroism or masculine myths about womanhood, or an affirmation of female eroticism and the female body. The tone of Urraca's new chronicle is thus intimate, sensual, yet subtly chronological without losing its air of spontaneity, its approximation to the flow of consciousness and natural, spoken discourse. Above all, Urraca's new chronicle is a daring attempt to reinvent and reconstruct a particular woman's history, while at the same time its implications reach beyond the confines of the individual.

In captivity as a result of the orders of her son, Urraca's sole interlocutor is a monk, Roberto. The context of the Queen's narration is already a sign for her existence in a broader sense: she must struggle to make her own word credible, a mark of authority in an environment largely shaped by a masculine drive for power and cultural-spiritual hegemony. Urraca's characteristically medieval world of Reconquest Spain is a vast field of shifting alliances, a world in which lovers kill each other with more than tender kindness. The characters of this world, as seen through the recollections of the Queen, are driven by intense passions: erotic, bellicose, religious. These three passions often overlap as the bed is recalled a battleground of aphrodisiac sin, a den of conspiracy; the battleground is remembered as the dust and sweat perfumed boudoir of the Queen's love of empire; the Church is evoked as the Bishop's bedroom and the planning chamber for intrigue and the satisfaction of his lust for power. In this context, Urraca reveals herself as no ordinary woman. Albeit a victim of her times, she also emerges

---

[34] "Clio's European Daughters: Myopic Modes of Perception," in *The Prism of Sex: Essays in the Sociology of Knowledge*, edited by Julia A. Sherman and Evelyn T. Beck (Madison: The Univ. of Wisconsin Press, 1977), p. 42.

[35] Lourdes Ortiz, *Urraca* (Madrid: Puntual Ediciones, 1982), p. 12. Hereafter all quotations from this work will be indicated by U and the page number following the quote. All translations are my own.

a hero, fighting indefatigably for her idea of Empire, premature by some four and a half centuries.

Urraca challenges official accounts of history by forcing us to view persons and events in a manner to which we are not ordinarily accustomed. For example, she flies in the face of a sacred cow like El Cid, calling him "un mercenario sin escrúpulos" (U, p. 135) (an unscrupulous mercenary). Though Urraca's view of Rodrigo Díaz is no doubt conditioned, in part, by her family ties, even if her perspective originates in her being her father's daughter, she ends up disclosing an important historical truth: "un guerrero metido a justiciero tiene siempre algo de buitre" (U, p. 136) (a warrior who takes up righteousness is always something of a vulture). In another retelling of historical events, as Urraca recounts the uprising of the burghers of Sahagún, her fantasy carries her from official versions of the royal-clerical alliance against the citizens to a vision of rebellion which we might name, borrowing from Roland Barthes, "doubly perverse."[36] Couching her narrative in the subjunctive mode, Urraca imagines herself as townswoman dancing frenetically "la danza loca de la libertad" (U, p. 186) (the mad dance of freedom). Recreating herself as rebel, she creates a subversive text which "simultaneously and contradictorily participates in the profound hedonism of all culture ... and in the destruction of that culture."[37] Along with a traditional historical account of Urraca's alliance with the abbot, such as the one we find in Reilly, the chronicle rewritten by Urraca dares to provoke, undermine, even overturn that alliance, as the Queen imagines herself participating in "la danza obscena de las mozas desnudas en la plaza, ... los sueños de ser libres" (U, p. 186) (the obscene dance of naked maidens in the square, ... dreams of freedom).[38] This new chronicle thus marks difference in the way noted by Mary Jacobus; that is, it challenges official historiography through multiplicity, joyousness, and heterogeneity. Finally, while her interlocutor might prefer accounts which speak only of honor and heroism, Urraca may insist on her own — more naturalistic — versions of events: "mi crónica es más sórdida" (U, p. 107) (my chronicle is more sordid). Part of her text's heterogeneity is even the Queen's willingness to expose her own cruelty and treachery, the dark side of her character, which though typical of her generic oppression as a woman, is generally atypical of traditional official chronicles

---

[36] Roland Barthes, *The Pleasure of the Text*, trans. Richard Miller (New York: Hill & Wang, 1975), p. 14.
[37] Barthes, p. 14.
[38] See *The Kingdom*, pp. 346-49.

which tend to filter out those less-than-heroic aspects of their royal protagonists.

Urraca's rewritten chronicle also transforms negative medieval beliefs about woman into images and accounts of events — at times of grandiose mythical proportions — which affirm a more positive view of female power. Of a statue portraying an adulteress with a close resemblance to the Queen, Urraca makes a deity affirming love and life. Throwing down her gauntlet before the Bishop, she affirms her own triumph in a blasphemous celebration of vitality: "la mujer adúltera reina en tu catedral; tu me has igualado al Altísimo, sin proponértelo" (U, pp. 130-31) (the adulterous woman reigns in your cathedral; you have made me an equal of the Almighty without intending to do so). Subsequently challenging Roberto's impossible desire for the solely symbolic woman — his Marianism — Urraca ironically proves his likewise irrestible need for "la madre, el cuerpo femenino. Yo, Urraca" (U, p. 153) (the mother, the female body. Me, Urraca). In these ways Urraca displaces the tendency of medieval man, along with multitudes of his descendants, to polarize woman into separate categories of good and evil, spiritual and corporeal.[39] The Queen also calls into question prevailing notions of the tainted nature of female sexuality by juxtaposing to them evidence of Alfonso's bloody cruelty to his subjects. The resultant irony is that monarchical cruelty was, of course, far filthier than any of the natural processes of the female body.

Urraca's sexual desires are potently exposed in her chronicle: first teasingly and temptingly ("no voy a hablarte de ellos todavía ... no son temas para una crónica," U. p. 47) (I won't talk to you about them yet ... they're not themes for a chronicle); then in a more direct and uncensored manner ("Pedro de Lara ... necesito esa borrachera del juego y del abrazo, cuando todo era posible. Mi garañón, es tu cuerpo lo que quisiera ahora, tu cuerpo y tus palabras obscenas," U, pp. 176-77) (Pedro de Lara ... I need that drunken playfulness and embrace, when everything was possible. My stud, it's your body that I desire now, your body and your obscene words). It is this playful game of words and bodies, this enjoyment "which exceeds exchange," that the Queen never ceases to remember.[40] Yet alongside it, she continuously juxtaposes the more Amazonian matters of political deeds,

---

[39] See Beth Miller,, "Introduction: Some Theoretical Considerations," in *Women in Hispanic Literature: Icons and Fallen Idols*, edited by Beth Miller (Berkeley: Univ. of Calif. Press, 1983), p. 8, for a succinct overview of the polarization of female characters in male-authored Hispanic literature.

[40] Gallop, pp. 49-50.

intrigue, and the machinations of war: "estas manos han sostenido la espada y han lanzado el dardo con precisión" (U, p. 146) (these hands have borne the sword and have hurled the dart with precision). Urraca's chronicle thus speaks against any unidimensional, partial, or gender stereotypical accounts of either her desires or her deeds. She discards, equally, popular laments of her marriage to Alfonso ("la desdicha de su reina, a quien llaman la malquerida," U, p. 80) (the wretchedness of his queen, whom they call the despised one), or fairy tale versions ("Érase una reina que quiso casar con el monarca de un país vecino," U,, p. 69) (There once was a queen who wished to marry the king of a neighboring country), or traditional historical accounts ("un rey déspota, un rey maricón que maltrató a su mujer," U, p. 80) (a despotic king, a pansy king who mistreated his wife). Urraca opts instead for her own self-defined version of her marital sexuality, of her stormy relations with Alfonso. So, even though tradition would teach her to recognize that "una crónica debe ser elegía, canto, glosa triunfal" (U, p. 99) (a chronicle should be elegy, song, triumphant gloss), she chooses to explore the erotic eccentricities of Alfonso, his irresistible taste for menstrual blood: "Alfonso acudía especialmente a mí en esos días para bañarse en la impureza, para extraer vigor de lo que más le repelía: la mancha" (U, p. 112)[41] (Alfonso approached me especially on those days to bathe in impurity, to extract vigor from that which repelled him most: the stain). Given medieval superstitions about menstruating women, Urraca had to pay for her husband's desire with imprisonment (though this is of course not reported as the reason for her imprisonment in "la crónica, la que escriban los demás," (U, p. 110)) (the chronicle, that which others may write). Urraca reveals what others have left or will leave unsaid or unwritten. In this compensatory text, the Queen's confinement points to the magnitude of her powers, her status as a source of

---

[41] In medieval writings fear and suspicion of the menstruating woman are common. Shulamith Shahar writes: "One of the pupils of Albertus Magnus writes that woman's menstrual blood is injurious to the penis and to any plant she touches. Thomas Aquinas writes that the gaze of a menstruating woman can dim and crack a mirror." *The Fourth Estate*, trans. Chaya Galai (London: Methuen, 1983), p. 73. Barbara G. Walker, in *The Woman's Encyclopedia of Myths and Secrets* (San Francisco: Harper & Row, 1983), p. 643, adds to our knowledge of these Christian beliefs and superstitions about menstruating women: "St. Jerome wrote: 'Nothing is so unclean as a woman in her periods; what she touches she causes to become unclean.' From the 8th to the llth centuries, many church laws denied menstruating women any access to church buildings. In 1298 the Synod of Wurzburg commanded men not to approach a menstruating woman." See also Robert Briffault, *The Mothers*, 3 vols. (New York: MacMillan, 1927), 2, p. 396.

fearful magical potency, perhaps because, as Jane Gallop has remarked, "menstrual blood ... marks woman as woman with no need of man's tools."[42] So, though imprisoned as the hapless victim of her husband's projection and rejection of his fear and desire, the Queen's subsequent chronicling of such desperate moves to insulate male power serves to expose them and displace them in a subtle maneuver against phallic sexual/textual authority.

The Queen's resistant or independent voice can perhaps be traced to two mentors whose initiation of the adolescent princess conferred upon her the signs and letters of an alternate maternal, androgynous, and self-affirming text. Poncia, a wise old woman and mother figure, initiates the pubescent Urraca as "única sucesora en la tierra de la gran reina madre" (U, p. 60) (sole successor on earth of the great queen mother). From Poncia, Urraca acquires maternal wisdom: a knowledge of the use of herbs and of the languages of sea and moon. Cidellus, the Jewish physician of Urraca's father, teaches the young future monarch alchemy, through which she discovers a link between the body and the text and the importance of recombining letters — or a theory of writing as rewriting: "delante del papel vacío juega con las letras, mézclalas, permútalas, trastócalas, hasta que tu corazón se exalte y, cuando te des cuenta de que de esa combinación surgen cosas nunca antes dichas ni sabidas, cosas que jamás hubieras podido conocer gracias a la tradición, concentra tu mente y permite que fluya la imaginación" (U, pp. 162-63) (before the blank page play with the letters, mix them up, interchange them, reverse them, until your heart leaps up and, when you realize that from that combination things never before said nor known emerge, things that you never would have been able to know thanks to tradition, concentrate your mind and let your imagination flow). Most importantly and most significantly, through Cidellus she discovers her determination to acquire the elixir of androgyny and relish its effects: "Yo seré ese Andrógino, ya que no de cuerpo, sí en espíritu y voluntad" (U, p. 171) (I shall be that androgyne, if not in body, then in spirit and will). The elixir of androgyny becomes a symbolic force, not unlike the philosopher's stone, which empowers the Queen to become "la unión de los contrarios, mujer y hombre" (U, p. 171) (the union of opposites, man and woman): soldier, lover, mover

---

[42] Gallop, p. 83. Walker confirms this view by citing examples of how "menstrual blood occupied a central position in matriarchal theologies ..." She also provides historical evidence that "medieval peasants thought it could heal, nourish, and fertilize." *The Woman's Encyclopedia*, pp. 641 and 644. See also Ernest Crawley, *The Mystic Rose*, 2 vols. (NY: Meridian Books, Inc., 1960), p. 241.

of men, moved by men. Through that boon from Cidellus's workshop, Urraca also acquires a discourse of her own, words incorporating the teachings of the old physician, the myth of the androgyne. So, though she seems to fall victim to her manchild, Urraca never stops straining for the herbs of wholeness and psychic integration. And in her abandoned and solitary state, she also feels closer to her own mother, Constanza, who was similarly abandoned, alone, yet unlike Urraca, condemned to virtual silence. Thus through a weave of memory — of her mother's songs and sudden fits of tenderness, Poncia's matriarchal ritual and Cidellus's alchemical initiation — Urraca forges a text which at once strains for androgyny and the energizing mythos of her matrilineal roots.

Through the linking of her text with the desires of her female body, Urraca, as narrator, succeeds in creating the kind of text envisioned by recent French feminist theory, or as Helene Cixous has proclaimed: "women must write through their bodies, they must invent the impregnable language that will wreck partitions, classes, and rhetorics, regulations and codes."[43] The very words Urraca employs to describe her sexual games with don Pedro are analogous to the theory and practice of this kind of text: "el deseo ... requiere la construcción, el invento ... sólo se desea aquello que sorprende, lo que se arranca al tiempo, lo que provoca" (U, pp. 122-23) (desire ... requires construction, invention ... one only desires that which surprises, that which is wrenched out of time, that which provokes). Through these moves, this inventive game of words and bodies, "la historia se recompone" (U, p. 176) (history is recreated). Thus by combining history with novelistic fabulation, Ortiz, through her narrator, Urraca, succeeds in fashioning a text which blends into one that Hayden White would call a "discourse of the real" (history) with a "discourse of desire" (fiction).[44] This alchemical melding of genres — which enhances both the authority and desirability of woman's discourse — emerges as final testimony that the Queen and her woman-writer descendant have successfully incorporated into their writing the boon of androgyny and the boldness of their self-articulated desire.

Any consideration of recent narrative texts by Spanish women would hardly be complete without a few concluding remarks on the relationship between text and context. Because literature never exists in a vacuum, the tex-

---

[43] Helene Cixous,, "The Laugh of the Medusa," in *New French Feminisms: An Anthology*, edited by Elaine Marks & Isabelle de Courtivron (Amherst: The Univ. of Massachusetts Press, 1980), p. 256.

[44] Hayden White, "The Value of Narrativity in the Representation of Reality," *Critical Inquiry*, 7, no. 1 (Autumn 1980), p. 23.

tual transformations we have been charting also point to a revised roadmap of cultural terrain. The quest for a self-defined sexual/textual voice may be seen to correspond to woman's struggle for greater political voice. The two go hand in hand, for as Cixous maintains: "a woman without a body, dumb, blind, can't possibly be a good fighter."[45] Urraca applauds her own deeds as a warrior; the words of Fabia's grandmother are impelled by her warrior spirit; Señora Efe would go to the ends of the earth with an Urraca "sin pelos en la lengua para decir lo que pensaba del injusto trato" (OM, p. 78) (outspoken enough to say what she thought about unjust treatment): Clara decides, on her own, to forego abortion for the transformative powers of childbirth. Perhaps these characters — straight talkers, fighters, women in full possession of their bodies — are fictional analogues of real Spanish women. Perhaps these fictional protagonists encode the projects of their real-life counterparts in Spanish society, currently engaged in ongoing struggle for complete and legal control over their bodies, for a voice in a government which, though democratic, is still dominated by men. If one speaks only of cultural politics, then these voices can be heard to cry out, too, for recognition in a literary marketplace which, though now officially uncensored and open, still bestows more generously of its support and promotion upon "los consagrados" (the "hallowed" ones). Though the threads binding text to context are often implied and subtle, the quest for voice, autonomy, self-definition, and the promise of pathways beckoning toward a better tomorrow is seldom confined to the inscription of black marks upon a white page. The "other voice" of today's literature by women is committed to nothing short of complete recuperation of all that which, as Evelyn García has noted, "el poder en todo tiempo y lugar ha usurpado o coartado"[46] (those in power at all times and in all places have usurped or restricted).

---

[45] Cixous, "The Laugh," p. 250.
[46] García, "Lectura,' p. 57.

Historical Novel from a Feminine Perspective: *Urraca*

Birutė Ciplijauskaitė

The last 10-15 years have witnessed an increase in the number of historical novels authored by women. It is as if there were an effort being made to inject new vigor into a declining genre by supplying a new perspective. The causes of this phenomenon are multiple and at times overlap: the desire, on the part of women writers, to attain excellence in a discipline heretofore predominantly — especially if one thinks of historiography and philosophy of history — pursued by men; the determination to explore and uncover the motivations of a determined focus or total silence regarding certain historical figures; an intent to recreate the pleasure of the word which was and still is intimately linked with interior psychic movements, thereby dictating a language and attitudes different from those traditionally traced by men.

The historical circumstance today seems favorable to the historical novel which usually flourishes, according to Gyorgi Lukacs, in times of stress, transformations and upheavals.[1] As far as Spain is concerned, the latter two are quite evident since Franco's death. The historical novel studied by Lukacs was concerned with changes in social class structures. Today it comes forth as an important aspect of the independization of women. Galdós used to say that he had started to work on his *Episodios Nacionales* in order to search for an explanation of the situation in which he was involved. In a similar manner, women today are investigating the causes of scant visibility and of unilateral focus on the feminine personalities of earlier centuries. In order to achieve

---

[1] *Le Roman historique*, Paris: Payot, 1972.

this, they seek a style which would reveal the authentic "I" and show the inner springs of some of the actions of those remote figures.

The writing of historical novels has changed considerably since the days of Walter Scott. In Spain, the writers of the so-called generation of 1898 approached history from a remarkably new and different perspective: instead of battles and great heroes, they spoke of "la intrahistoria.," instead of lineal progression, they dealt with cyclic time; instead of a single accepted view of things, they emphasized relativity. In their work they stressed demythification, inviting the reader to restructure on his own the pieces of the puzzle presented to him.[2] In recent novels we note further advancements in the use of discourse. In this respect, the work of Lourdes Ortiz is of particular interest. Her first novel, *Luz de la memoria* (1976), has a concrete moment of Spain's history (political resistence in the form of terrorism under Franco's rule) as its backdrop. Her intention, however, is not to create a historical novel; the interval separating narrated and narrating time is insufficient, and no historical figure is brought in, fictionalized, as a main character. Instead, she offers what could very well be considered one of the first really successful psychoanalytical novels in Spain. History enters as a determining factor in the interior psychic processes of the protagonist, resembling more closely what we find in Galdós's "novelas contemporáneas" than in his *Episodios Nacionales*. Ortiz's technical presentation is truly innovative, reproducing some psychiatric procedures and developing the argument on various spatial and temporal levels simultaneously. It is to be noted that in the novel, the main character, who speaks in autobiographical form, is a man. With *Urraca* (1982), to be discussed in greater detail in this paper, Ortiz decidedly enters the realm of the historical novel.

One novel which marks a dramatic change in historical writing is Margarite Yourcenar's *Mémoires d'Hadrien* (1951). Narrated in the first person from the Emperor's deathbed, the novel is an interiorization of the protagonist's concerns: his attempt to justify his own personal ideas regarding what an empire should be, his glorification of his love for Antinoo, and his defense of his right to a private life, all filtered through his conscious mind like an almost existential examination of the whole.

What is really important here is the man, not the Emperor. In this novel Yourcenar meets what Kate Hamburger describes as the most prominent

---

[2] For a more detailed explanation of the differences between the historical novel of the 19th century and that of the early part of the 20th century see my *Los noventayochistas y la historia* (Madrid: Porrúa Turanzas, 1981).

criteria in differentiating a fictional historical character from a character presented in a historical text: Hadrien is endowed with the power to subjectively perceive the world around him (e.g., to taste a fruit, p. 8).[3] The author insists that it is not actions alone that justify man's existence.[4] Autobiographical writing serves, "pour me définir, me juger peut-être, ou tout au moins pour me mieux connaitre avant de mourir" (p. 21) (to define myself, perhaps to judge myself, at least to get to know myself better before I die).

In Yourcenar's novel, Hadrien, the soldier, pales by comparison with Hadrien, the dreamer, with artistic inclinations, who, among other things, changes the rules that govern certain situations, often going so far as to defend the rights and privileges of women.

A subsequent work which deserves mention is Bertolt Brecht's *Die Geschafte des Herrn Julius Caesar* (1957). The novel is of particular interest because of the use of multiple perspectives in defining its structure. Julius Caesar is viewed through the eyes of several characters, each representing a different level of society: the liberated slave who was his constant companion, the young man who is preparing to write the emperor's biography, and one of his former legionaries. From each of their descriptions emerges a different Julius Caesar. If in *Mémoires d'Hadrien*, Yourcenar made good use of self-irony on the part of the novel's protagonist, here the more pronounced ironic effects are achieved by fragmenting and juxtaposing temporal elements (the famous *Verfremdungseffekt*).

In the 1970s and 80s the historical novel continues to be popular, especially in France where it merges with the feminine novel. It is surprising that nearly all of the contemporary women writers of this country have looked for historical subjects, as did their predecessors in this genre, the early romanticists. The lack of precise historical documentation and the countless myths that have spread throughout the centuries concerning these historical characters leave open the field to "supplementation," and, at the same time, seem to call for more rigorous investigation.[5] The characters of these novels

---

[3] *Die Logik der Dichtung* (Stuttgart: Ernst Klett, 1957).

[4] "Les trois-quarts de ma vie échappent d'ailleurs à cette définition par les actes: la masse de mes velléités, de mes désirs, de mes projets même, demeure aussi nébuleuse et aussi fuyante qu'un fantôme" (*Mémoires d'Hadrien*, Paris: Plon, 1951, p. 27). (Three quarters of my life cannot be defined by my actions: most of my whims, my desires, even my own projects remain as nebulous and evasive as a ghost.)

[5] One need only take a look at the number of sources cited in *Mémoires d'Hadrien* or the relation between the documents consulted in *L'Allée du Roi* by Fran-

have been carefully selected, which appears to suggest an attempt to reaffirm the presence of exceptional women throughout history.

The first person narration, so skillfully manipulated by Yourcenar, continues to be the preferred form, allowing the reader to discover the more intimate side of the characters and garnishing the long narration with lyrical passages. The act of writing is a subject that recurs throughout these novels, and more than one writer introduces her own views regarding "feminine" discourse. Of particular interest are those works in which the argument is presented through one or more narrative voices, as in *Nefertiti et le rêve d'Akhnaton*, by Andrée Chedid (1974), in which two types of discourse, each with a different focus, can be perceived. The scribe's more objective narrative contrasts sharply with the more lyrical and totally personal invocations of Nefertiti.

Another example we could cite is *Très sage Héloise*, prizewinning novel of Jeanne Bourin (1966), which dares to reconstruct the all too well known fable-myth-history. Through a series of personal letters said to have been written by the protagonist, Bourin reveals a rather different Heloise than the *official* image presented by the chroniclers of history. Bourin emphasizes the feminine aspects of her protagonist. Her Heloise is a woman of extraordinary intellectual abilities and an uncontrollable passion who, despite her many attributes, sees herself doomed from the outset because of the pre-existing social conditions of the times (the Middle Ages).

In Germany Irmtraud Morgner experiments with even more innovative and intricate narrative techniques. In *Leben und Abenteuer der Trobadora Beatriz nach Zeugnissen ihrer Spielfrau Laura* (1974), a novel with a strong implicit political message, history is relegated to the level of pure fantasy as contemporary society is perceived — and simultaneously judged — through the eyes of a 12th century character.

Without necessarily entering the world of fantasy, other German writers utilize this same technique of juxtaposing the accepted image of a historical character with their own more personal, perhaps more realistic image. According to Peter Axthelm, this juxtaposition originates in a dialogue between the protagonist and other characters who act as foils, and ultimately leads to the protagonist's self-discovery.[6] In addition, it supplies a note of irony. The

---

çoise Chandernagor (Paris: Julliard, 1981) to realize that narration is not a product of the imagination.

[6] *The Modern Confessional Novel* (New Haven: Yale University Press, 1967), p. 11.

common denominator of these novels is the desire to show the protagonist as different from the one depicted by historians, and in so doing, reveal the differences, not only in the social roles of men and women, but also in their preconceived ideas of one another. The feminine characters are all exemplary individuals, but ones whose behavior was considered scandalous for their time[7]—scandalous, the very term that has been applied to more than one woman who dared to oppose norms established by society while holding her ground as a writer: George Sand, Sibilla Aleramo.[8]

One of the more innovative historical novels recently published in Spain is Lourdes Ortiz's *Urraca*, which incorporates many of the previously mentioned characteristics and develops them in a unique way, revealing a great technical mastery on the part of the author. The choice of this particular historical character could not have been more appropriate. The lack of reliable documentation and the ambiguity surrounding Urraca allow Ortiz a good deal of freedom in the manner in which she develops her character. Although Urraca had been queen of Castilla and Leon, there are countless history books which fail to mention her name. When she does appear it is usually in a reference to her rather libertine behavior or to her stormy marriage to Alfonso "el Batallador," a marriage which could and should have accomplished what the marriage of Fernando and Isabel finally did achieve three centuries later, the unity of Spain.[9] Moreover, Ortiz exploits the fact that little has been written concerning Urraca's death in order to create an original ending for her novel: "Unos dicen fue al salir de San Isidoro, de León, sacando el tesoro de la iglesia, y que causó muerte de repente. Orderico Vital refiere que solicitó quitar la vida al rey de Aragón por armas y por veneno y que al cabo murió de parto. Algunos añaden que murió reclusa en la iglesia de San Vicente."[10] (Some say it happened as she was leaving San Isidoro in Leon, trying to get away with church treasure, which

---

[7] Some notable examples are *L'Allée du Roi*, which pieces together through conversations, letters and other documents of Madame de Maintenon the court life of Louis XIV, and *Verfolgte des Glücks*, by Karin Reschke (1982), which traces by means of Henriette Vogel's notes, the details of the suicide death of Heinrich von Kleist.

[8] Among the views espoused by early feminists is the idea that professional freedom appears to go hand-in-hand with sexual freedom; a phenomenon that deserves further study.

[9] Modesto Lafuente, *Historia General en España; III* (Barcelona: Montaner y Simón; 1889), p. 223.

[10] P. Eugenio Flórez de Setien, *Memoria de las reinas católicas de España*, I (Madrid: Aguilar, 1945), p. 353.

supposedly caused instantaneous death. Orderico Vital infers that she tried to inflict death upon the King of Aragon by means of arms or by poison, and finally died while giving birth. Others add that she died a recluse in the church of San Vicente.) The technical skills that captured the attention of the readers of her first novel *Luz de la memoria* have not diminished in this work: they appear in what seems to be a less fragmented but is, in actuality, a more complex, narration. The chronicle's implied demands for "objectivity" are met by innovative stratagem. Like *Luz de la memoria*, *Urraca* is open ended. The theme of writing gains more and more importance as the novel develops.

In the very brief first chapter of the novel, the reader is informed of the procedures to be followed: the book will be written (like *Mémoires d'Hadrien*) in the first person and will present a dying queen's retrospective view of her reign. Already in the first paragraph the two narrative voices of the text are juxtaposed: I versus my role as a queen. The separation and the coming together of these two personalities will be effectuated by means of the continuously fluctuating use of first and third person narration. This juxtaposition affects the narrative perspective, revealing a hidden irony: her book will be a confession, but not the public confession that her Abbot demands of her, which might imply some sort of repentance. Her writing will represent, rather, a kind of soul searching in an attempt to justify her actions. The character is assigned three distinct roles: Urraca — queen, Urraca — chronicler, and Urraca — woman. In a similar manner, allusions are made to three rather different ways of transmitting history, dismissing accepted historical documentation with an ironic smirk while stressing the importance of the popular folk tradition as expressed in the songs of the minstrels.[11] Such an affirmation underscores the idea of relativity and announces the very ambiguous nature of her novel: Urraca will tell her story "para que los juglares recojan la verdad" (so that the minstrels may gather the truth).[12] Emphasis is placed on the living history and the living word, subject to de- and re-construction: "Cuando oigo el rezo de los monjes ... me parece percibir aún el ruido de los cascos del caballo" (p. 11) (when I hear the monks praying ... it seems to me that I still perceive the sound of horses' hooves). Details of the present evoke images of the past, changes occurring through words, sounds, and colors. Already in the first chapter the inevitable

---

[11] In *Luz de la memoria* we find an ironic comment regarding how to to write a biography.
[12] *Urraca* (Barcelona: Puntual, 1982), p. 12. Hereafter all quotations from this work will be indicated by the page number following the quote. Translations are my own.

presence of the "interlocutor" is felt. (In *Luz* ..., the role of the "interlocutor," who helped to clarify the real happenings, was assumed by a number of characters on different temporal levels: the psychiatrist, Ignacio, Pilar. In *Urraca*, there is only one, always the same: the monk, who, by a curious inversion of the psychological phenomenon of transference, falls in love with the confessing queen, and, in the end, also assumes two voices and two personalities.) It is insinuated that none of the other men that surround her is able to "understand the magnitude of my undertaking" (p. 12).[13]

The structure of the novel, of each of its three parts, and of some of the chapters themselves (Chapter IX, for example) is circular, suggesting that time itself is cyclical. The idea of eternal return is stressed by the parallels which are drawn among the various generations. Each part of the novel is developed under a predominant leit-motif while those of the previous parts simultaneously continue to develop and intertwine. The work in its entirety is dependent on a dominant leit-motif. If in *Luz de la memoria* one could speak of death and violence as variations on a theme (the initial image of the squashed dog, the obsessive memory of the young suicide victim, the final vision of the dead man described in practically the same terms), in *Urraca*, the principal theme appears to be desire (on various levels). It is accompanied by the image of the chess game, implying of course, that fate has a hand in the matter: "Todo se recompone como una historia donde aparecen en primer término unos protagonistas que creen ser dueños de su actuación, cuando, la mayoría de las veces, son las cosas, las situaciones, las que actúan en nombre de uno" (p. 191). (All is re-structured like a story where some characters appear in the forefront thinking they are masters of the situation, whereas, in most cases, it is the things, the situations, that act in our name).[14] At the same time, the basic idea of the search for and the relevance of truth, insinuated (all along) since the second chapter of the novel continues to manifest itself: "Pero eso yo no podía saberlo ... sólo oía los ecos, aunque todavía no podía entender los sentidos" (p. 14) (But this I could not know as yet ... I only know that I heard echoes, although I could not understand their meaning), and is even present as the narration ends: "trasladarse, sin apenas esfuerzo, a ese lugar donde, según tú, hay una luz que ofusca a todo ... de modo que cada uno de los bien aventurados es todo él ojos y

---

[13] This observation reminds us of Adriano's complaints in Yourcenar's novel.
[14] This idea (with reference to war) can be found in such authors as Tolstoy, Unamuno and Baroja who derived it from Joseph de Maistre. In Schopenhauer we find it used with reference to life.

oídos y entonces se descorren los velos" (p. 206) (to move, with hardly any effort, to that place where, according to you, there is a light which confuses all ... in such a way that each of the blessed ones is all eyes and ears, and then the veils are suddenly removed).

The circular structure of each of the three parts of the novel is noteworthy: the first begins and ends with the importance of the role of the king and queen. In each chapter we find references to Spain's rich oral tradition: the ballads, songs, ancient Arabic recitations, and an occasional variation on the popular theme of "una mujer es sólo mediadora" (p. 28) (a woman is just a go-between) which appears as a refrain. With the death of Alfonso VI, whose presence dominates this first part, the feminine characters who accompany him also disappear. The conviviality of the three races and religions is graphically presented in the next to last paragraph of the final chapter. It will reappear in the third part of the novel, but only as a nostalgic invocation.

The second part begins with the vows in Mexía and ends with the recollection of these. Throughout, there are repeated references to superstitions, witchcraft, black masses, fortune telling and supernatural auguries — as if to imply with a certain irony that a woman could only assume the throne with the aid of such devices. The theme of the collapse of the kingdom is revealed in the structure: short paragraphs, temporal and spatial shifts, fragmented syntax. The multiplicity of points of view as well as tricks to which Urraca resorts presents a polyphonic composition suggested by the author's technique of naming various instruments in the epigraph. In terms of its rhythm, it follows faithfully Urraca's definition of her own life: "y todo lo demás son vaivenes de una misma historia de encuentros y desencuentros; episodios de una larga partida de ajedrez" (p. 116) (and all the rest is nothing but variations of the same story of encounters and partings; episodes of a long chess game).

The third part of the novel — the final circle of the progression (Urraca-child—Urraca-queen—Urraca-lover) — emphasizes the feminine side of the protagonist. It begins with the seduction of Brother Roberto which — as Proust's *madeleine* — evokes the memory of all her other lovers. Faithful to the idea of circularity, on the next to last page we find yet another rather discursive paragraph about her lovers.

It is in this third part of the novel where the author's preoccupation with the question of writing is clearly revealed.[15] The chess game is replaced by

---

[15] Writing as duty and salvation (p. 114); as companionship (p. 149); as final Judgment (p. 169); as revelation and repose (p. 173); its magical qualities (p. 176).

the word game. This entire section is conceived on the basis of a leit-motif introduced earlier: the theme of metamorphosis. The queen is transformed into lover; the attentive monk, into the object of her love; desire into the written word; the polyphonic voices of the second part into just one voice whose inspiration comes from an interior strength born out of loneliness. An even more subtle transformation is detected thanks to the novel's structure: the princess who earlier celebrated the death of Sancho, which left her the undisputed successor, is now the mother who chooses to renounce her struggle for the throne, recalling Zaida's sadness upon losing her son. The inferences are many, but, in customary fashion, Ortiz ultimately leaves the interpretation of any implicit meaning to the discretion of the reader.

The circle within a circle pattern is most evident in the narrated material dealing with Urraca's life: from Urraca-child to Urraca-queen, and finally to Urraca-prisoner in the throes of death. This evolution, even with all of the flashbacks, digressions, premonitions, commentaries after the fact, enriches the narration; a narration which is not merely retrospective but analytical and judgmental as well, revealing, thus, a certain affinity with the structuring principle of *Mémoires d'Hadrien*. This circular progression is apparent also in Urraca's relationship to Brother Roberto, who is transformed from an almost silent interlocutor in the first part of the novel to a listener capable of formulating the questions necessary to unravel the polyphonic narration and finally to lover. These transformations are underscored by the visual presence of the monk: for the most part inactive in the first part of the novel, seen whittling chess pieces in the second, and finally painting with "apocalyptical colors" the storyline of the third. From passive listener he evolves into co-creator (reflecting the need for *multi media* narration in order to tell the complete story). Then there is, of course, the progression in the discourse itself which gradually evolves toward lyricism and musicality, with a more conscious and constant use of rhythmic repetition, alliteration, affected lexicon; at the same time, the use of irony is intensified. If in the first part it is suggested that the minstrels should gather and report the truth in their songs, in the third part a shadow of doubt is cast over the manner in which the Cid is presented in epic poetry. In fact, a sense of ambiguity pervades the entire novel. It suggests more than it states forthright. The skillful use of polyvalent words, the juxtaposition of semantically contrasting parallels which allow us to group events both horizontally as well as vertically (three generations and at least three different reigns), and the repetition of key words and images which make the transitions easier (following the technique introduced earlier in *Luz de la memoria*), all tend to reinforce with a marked parodoxical accent, the maxim that history repeats itself: "La historia se repetía y mostraba un lado irónico. ¿Cómo, quien había dado muerte a su hermano, iba a atreverse a someter a juicio de Dios a otro de quien se afirmaba que había quitado la vida al suyo?" (p. 140) (History was repeating itself, and showing its ironic side. How could one who had murdered his brother dare submit to God's judgment another who, it was said, had done the same to his own brother?).

The technique of juxtaposition is used also to graphically depict the reinforcement of certain psychological processes at work in Urraca the child who not only witnesses her father's lustful pleasures with his concubines, but then hears about them through her mother's conversations with her confessor. These parallel experiences prove to be apocalyptical: "Fue como una revelación ... comprendí que si yo era capaz de aunar el rigor de mi padre con el saber hacer de Constanza, no habría nadie que pudiera interponerse en mi camino hacia el Imperio" (pp. 20-21) (It came as a revelation ... I understood that if I could combine my father's rigor with Constanza's know-how, nobody could come between me and my path to the Empire). This idea is reiterated in Chapter XVI. Using terminology similar to that already employed by Virginia Woolf, Ortiz's protagonist declares: "El mercurio pasivo se une con el azufre que da fuerza gracias a la sal poderosa y nace el andrógino purificado que supone la unión de los contrarios. Yo, Urraca, emperatriz, mujer y hombre" (p. 171) (Passive quick-silver combines with sulphur which adds strength thanks to the powerful salt, and thus is born the purified androgynous substance from this union of opposites. I, Urraca, empress, woman and man). This union of intelligence and beauty, severity and compassion fails to prevent her reputation from being inevitably tarnished. Urraca's insatiable sexual appetite and inconstancy might have been an accepted mode of behavior for a man or even a king, but for a woman, it was considered scandalous.[16] There is, no doubt, a latent and implicit attack here on the existing social structure.

The technique of juxtaposition is used also for revealing two different points of view; for example, the author's use of the words "God" and "god" on the same page of the text. Sometimes the intent is cruel as in the parallel which is drawn between Alfonso VI and his concubines and Alfonso "el Batallador" and his effeminate monks. One of Ortiz's greatest virtues as a writer is her ability to veil her intent. In the case of Alfonso "el Batallador" her

---

[16] All of the French women historical novelists deal with this aspect. In Ortiz's *Luz de la memoria* we find Pilar cohabitating with Enrique and Carlos and jumping from one bed to the other.

tongue-in-cheek comments (pp. 71, 96) correspond to the portrait the historians paint of this king, describing him as "misogynistic" if not "misogynist" (Ramos Loscertales). One of the few reliable pieces of information we have concerning Alfonso's true inclinations comes from the historical Urraca herself: "casándome con el cruento, fantástico y tirano rey de Aragón, juntándome con él para mi desgracia por medio de un matrimonio nefando y execrable."[17] (marrying the cruel, fantastic and tyrannical king of Aragon, joining fortunes with him through an execrable and abominable marriage which proved to be my misfortune).

The contrasting parallels are infinite and form a veritable constellation: Constanza and Zaida as the two companions of Alfonso VI; Constanza, Felicia de Roucy, Zaida and Urraca as mothers; Mafalda and Urraca as widowed princesses; Urraca and Zaida as women (feminine-warlike, obsessed by the words of Alfonso to his daughter: "Ella tiene algo que tú jamás podrás tener" (p. 33) (She has something you will never have), words that become a leit-motif in the final chapters, evoking a long list of ex-future selves); the tame bear, Sancho García, and Urraca as prisoners; the courts of Alfonso VI and Al Mutamid, the court of Aragón, the Christian kingdom in Jerusalem. An infinite number of story-lines randomly criss-cross, at every juncture, shedding new light on the facts not merely for the benefit of the reader, but for the chronicler herself.

Perhaps the most shocking parallels are those involving the literary technique of demythification both on a national (the Cid) and religious (the Crusades) level. An anti-clerical spirit pervades the entire work, but, in reality, it shocks us less than the attacks on the character of Spain's national hero. Ortiz achieves this demythification through her insistence on the idea of relativity, and by focusing on the psychological processes at work in her characters. It stands to reason that the various members of Alfonso's family would have different ideas about the Campeador — just like Brecht's legionary who presents *his* view of Julius Caesar.

The pluralistic viewpoints and the multifaceted nature of each of the characters have their counterpart in the nature of the expression itself. Urraca's own interest in, indeed, her preference for, writing — often at the expense of her desire to talk about her life — has already been confirmed. In her struggle to find new ways of communicating her ideas, she displays an extraordinary awareness of style: "Mientras escribo tengo la impresión de

---

[17] Anónimo de Sahagún cited by Risco in his *Historia de León*, Lafuente's source, p. 216.

que el tiempo desgasta y el relato convierte a los protagonistas en muñecos de feria; les roba la palabra, el gesto, y mi juicio les despoja, les desnuda" (p. 68) (While I write I have the distinct impression that time is whittling away, and that the narration changes the characters into puppets in a fair, robbing them of words and gestures, and my own better judgment undresses them and leaves them naked). In the pages which follow, an entire repertoire of modes of narration is introduced — and not simply a mere mention of these, but examples of each: the fairytale, the horror story, folk tales, periphrastic narration (pp. 69-70). Structurally, these essayistic considerations are presented at the very moment in which the instability of Urraca's life and her multifaceted personality are discussed: "Cuatro reconciliaciones en apenas cuatro años de matrimonio. Urraca, la reina loca, dicen muchos. Urraca títere, Urraca inconsciente, Urraca histérica ..." (p. 73) (Four reconciliations in but four years of marriage. Urraca the crazy queen, some people say. Urraca the puppet, Urraca the unaware, Urraca the hysterical ...). The changes in style prepare us for these character descriptions and tactfully communicate her political "about-faces". It is a device that the author has used before in *Luz de la memoria*: "es sólo un cuadro recompuesto por ti mucho más tarde, con tantos y tantos datos recogidos, con pedazos de novelas, con informes mal digeridos de psicólogos, con estudios sobre el edipismo infantil, los celos ... informes que durante cuatro años devoraste buscando raices."[18] (it is just a picture touched up by you much later, with all the data you have gathered, fragments of novels, poorly digested psychologists' reports, studies of cases of Oedipus complex in children, jealousy ... material you have been devouring for the last four years searching for your identity).

There are in addition numerous allusions to the importance of the reader in a text, including concrete references — invested with a subtle irony

---

[18] *Luz de la memoria* (Madrid: Akal, 1976), p. 41. In this novel Ortiz reverts on several occasions to the use of this technique: "Te revelas ante ese recuerdo trivializador que reduce años enteros de tu vida a una simple elección de nombres: Enrique-Gonzalo-Julián—pero, y eso te lo dices ahora, se debe quizá a que tras cada uno de ellos, tras cada nuevo nombre, había un nuevo papel asumido, una nueva personalidad destacándose, configurándose, o tan sólo, te dices, un mismo Enrique que se recubría de diferentes caretas que protegieran a ese último Enrique, agazapado detrás" (p. 56). (Your character is defined through a trivialized recollection of yourself which reduces years of your life to a simple choice of names: Enrique-Gonzalo-Julian—but, and this you now admit to yourself, perhaps this is due to the fact that behind each new name, you assumed a new role, a new personality was revealed, molded, or was it, you ask yourself, that there was just one Enrique crouched behind all those protective masks).

— to the idea of structuring the narrated material with the reader in mind, emphasizing the arbitrariness of it all:[19] "¿Quién iba a hacer caso de cualquier otra versión, de aquella que presenta a una madre que pretende controlar al hijo, encerrarle, quitarle su posible fuerza? Si te contara esta última, empezarías a intuir que el conde malvado no se diferenciaba demasiado de tu reina, y por eso bajo los ojos con modestia y reinvento para ti aquella jornada ... Estoy fatigada y ya no sé lo que digo. Son ya muchos meses de encierro, demasiados, y tu inocencia introduce un desorden en mi relato; y no es bueno vacilar, porque ¿qué quedaría entonces de mi crónica?" (p. 79) (Who would listen to any other version, like the one of the mother who tries to control her son by locking him away and despoiling him of his power? If I were to present this latter version, you would begin to assume that the wicked count was not much different from your queen. Therefore, I lower my eyes with modesty and recreate for you that day ... I am tired, and I no longer know what I am saying. I have been locked up for many months, too many, and your own innocence makes my story seem fragmented. But I must not dwell on these things; or what would be left of my chronicle?). She foresees — and conveys through words to her interlocutor — the ultimate effect of her controlled narration: "'Un rey déspota, un rey maricón que maltrató a su mujer.' Esa sería, Roberto, la versión que me devolvería tu devoción, la que me interesa fomentar en mi pueblo." (p. 80) ("A tyrant king, a queer who mistreated his wife." This, Roberto, would be the version which would earn me back your devotion; the one that I would like to promote among my people).

The active role of the reader/public is affirmed by modulation in the discourse. The presence or absence of an interlocutor in a given chapter affects the structure of that chapter. On several occasions Urraca unleashes lyrical confessions in which she appears to be speaking to an imaginary interlocutor (pp. 66, 156). Of particular interest in this respect is Chapter XIV, where the absent interlocutor evokes all the femininity in her. Her relations with the monk likewise affect the structure of the narrative. When the monk is not present, the story resembles a chronicle, relating only exterior events. His presence in the same, however, tends also to bring out the feminine side of Urraca. This process can be seen in the first chapter of the second part, where on the same page appear the inner thoughts of the character, the transposition of these thoughts into oral expression for the benefit of the listener, the reaction of the latter, and the attempt to transcribe all of this.

---

[19] Recall, if you will, Carmen Martín Gaite's *El cuarto de atrás*.

Among the literary considerations of the author, we find her continuously turning to the theme of "what is feminine literary style?" With a subtle irony, and using words and expressions that have double meaning, she alludes to the fact that she feels somewhat uncomfortable with the traditional masculine model for historical texts: "Me canso. Cada vez que la historia requiere un orden, una cronología, unos hechos, la pluma pesa y siento la nulidad de mi tarea. No son batallas lo que quiero contar." (p. 75) (I tire. Every time the story requires order, chronology, facts, my pen begins to feel heavy, and I feel the uselessness of my task. It isn't battles I want to speak of). Notwithstanding, what Héloise achieves through the systematic imposition of her will in her letters to Abélard (suppressing her expression of passion, and talking about "more transcendental" matters), Urraca attempts in her chronicle: "Yo, la reina ... ya sé que necesito recuperar la gallardía, el orgullo, para que mi crónica sea tal y no lagrimeo de mujercita angustiada." (p. 99) (I, the queen, know that I must regain my poise and my pride, so that my chronicle may be a real chronicle, not a weeping tale of a little anguished woman). Unlike Héloise, however, Urraca is more prone to lyrical and emotional outpourings.

The most interesting page of the novel from a purely stylistic standpoint is found in Chapter XV of the third part: the recollection of Pierre de Tours's accounts of the feats of Bohemundo and Tancredo in Jerusalem. It is an authentic interweaving of voices, points of view, and reactions which lends an extraordinary sense of dynamism to the narration (p. 155), evoking rather than stating explicitly any expression of condemnation.

There are countless additional stylistic details, psychological concerns, and philosophic and historical questions put forth by this magnificent chronicle. The limits of this paper, however, do not allow us to pursue these aspects. Suffice it to say that Lourdes Ortiz gives proof in *Urraca* of a consummate craftsmanship. None of the elements mentioned in the work is introduced as a component *per se*, simply to keep up with new trends or please certain audiences. The novel's complexity obeys the laws of counterpoint, where all voices are masterfully interrelated. In it, Ortiz achieves what Schopenhauer once defined as the essence of history: a net of constantly moving warp-ends that each reader has to provide with his personal weft patterns which the author leaves floating, barely providing subtle suggestions hidden among the multicolored threads.

Personal and Public History in Laforet's Long Novels

Roberta Johnson

In his book *Novela y semidesarrollo*, Fernando Morán says that Carmen Laforet's first novel *Nada* "es una afirmación de la primera generación que no participó en la guerra y que se proclama ajena a ella y, en cierto modo, a la historia. Al menos a la inmediata." (*Nada* is an affirmation of the first generation that did not participate in the war and that proclaims itself alien to it, and, in a certain way, to history. At least to immediate history.)[1] Morán goes on to deny Miguel Delibes's interpretation of *Nada* as a parable of the Civil War in which the family of Aribau Street is "una miniatura de una España conflictiva y turbia," saying that "su evolución posterior no evidencia una preocupación social e histórica ... (a miniature of a conflictive and turbulent Spain ... her later evolution gives no evidence of social or historical preoccupations).[2] Both Morán and Delibes miss the mark in their assessments of Laforet's approach to history. Morán finds no history in her novels because for him history is an interpretation of political and public events infused with a moral or partisan perspective. And Delibes imposes a symbolic paradigm on *Nada* that endows the novel with the quality of political allegory, perhaps equating it with novels like his own *Parábola del náufrago*. There is history in Laforet's novels, but rather than the suprahistorical stance that Delibes adduces, it is history seen from inside or from

---

[1] Fernando Morán, *Novela y semidesarrollo* (Madrid: Taurus, 1971), p. 230. All translations are mine.
[2] Morán, p. 230.

below, "the underside of history" that Elisa Boulding writes about in her book so entitled.[3]

Carmen Laforet's approach to history is inductive rather than deductive; there is no preconceived moral viewpoint or interpretation of historical events operating in her novels. In this approach she departs radically from the way many contemporaneous male novelists, such as Delibes, Luis Martín Santos and Juan Goytisolo, embody history in their novels. The male novelists couch events of recent historical time in a symbolic framework that strives to demythify la *España sagrada* (Sacred Spain): the Spain of the Visigoths, the Cid, the Catholic Kings, Charles the Fifth and the Empire that was heralded by Franco's Crusade and regime. The moral view in their novels forms an a priori bias against which the events of the novel move in a dialectical fashion toward the ultimate destruction or at least exorcism of an intolerable Spanish reality. Such a use of history in the novel coincides with the traditional view that history is the recounting of the great moments in public life (wars, changes in regime, etc.) that are dominated primarily by male political leaders. Morán clearly understands history in this way.

Laforet, on the other hand, details the day to day minutia of individual lives in a particular time and place that weave the very fabric over which the pattern of public history is laid, much in the same way that recent women's historians are now trying to recapture the past of ordinary citizens, particularly women, whose lives have long remained outside the domains of historical interest.[4] History in Laforet's novels is always embedded in individual circumstance so that personal and public life are united in a seamless whole. One of Laforet's principal concerns in writing her novels is to capture the ambience of the particular era and locale in which her characters live out their daily lives; naturally that ambience is infused with political history, but such history is seen only in its influence on the characters' lives. In *Nada* it is war-ravaged Barcelona in 1940; in *La isla y los demonios*, the War is perceived from the remote Canary Islands; *La mujer nueva* depicts life during the mid-

---

[3] Elisa Boulding, *The Underside of History: A View of Women Through Time* (Boulder, Colorado: Westview Press, 1976).

[4] My focus on a women's approach to history in this paper is informed by Boulding's and other landmark studies on the subject, especially Berenice A. Carroll, Ed., *Liberating Women's History* (Champaign-Urbana, Illinois: University of Illinois Press, 1976); Edited by Renate Bridenthal and Claudia Koonz, *Becoming Visible: Women in European History* (Boston: Houghton Mifflin, 1977); and Gerda Lerner, *The Majority Finds Its Past: Placing Women in History* (New York and Oxford: Oxford University Press, 1979).

dle years (1950s) of the Franco regime., and in the trilogy *Tres pasos fuera del tiempo*, of which only one volume has been published, Laforet plans to chronicle three successive decades of the Franco regime (the 40s, 50s and 60s). She says of the second volume of that trilogy — *Al volver la esquina* "sucede alrededor de los años cincuenta, en Madrid. No me propongo en esta novela, ni en ninguna, dar una secuencia histórica y documentada de los hechos del mundo y de mi país, sino captar, con la veracidad que me sea posible y dentro de las limitaciones argumentales del libro, un momento circunstancial al mismo tiempo que el momento íntimo del personaje que sirve de base a todo lo demás." (it takes place around the 50s, in Madrid. I do not propose in this novel, or in any novel, to give a documented historical account of the events of the world and of my country, but to capture, with the veracity of which I am capable and within the limitations of the plot of the book, simultaneously a circumstantial moment and the intimate moment of the character which serves as a basis for all the rest of it.)[5] Laforet's novels begin with the individual in a particular situation — a particular moment in time that is intimately related to the place in which it evolves, and only latently does the larger historical panorama appear.

Let us then consider these personal and undersided aspects of history as they unfold in Laforet's four long novels.[6] In *Nada*, the action takes place immediately after the Spanish Civil War, and the novel refers to this significant historical situation, not by presenting a metaphor of the ideological conflict as Delibes supposes, but by indicating how individual civilian lives are affected by the War. The conflict is seen entirely through the eyes of female characters, whose war experiences are indirect, but whose lives are nonetheless molded by it. Andrea's contact with public events is the most remote, as she was interned in a convent during the War, arriving in

---

[5] Carmen Laforet, "Por qué de esta trilogía," prologue to *La insolacion* (Barcelona: Planeta, 1963), pp. 8-9. All references to *La insolación* are from the same edition; henceforth page numbers will be noted in the text.

[6] The present study approaches Carmen Laforet's four long works of fiction as a body, evaluating one aspect of the Laforet criticism as being rather lopsided with numerous analyses of *Nada*, the first novel, and very little on the other three novels. There are only two articles to my knowledge that address Laforet's work as a whole (aside from sections on Laforet in manuals and histories of the Contemporary Spanish novel). Cyrus C. DeCoster published "Carmen Laforet: A Tentative Evaluation," in *Hispania* (XL, 1957, pp. 187-91) before the last novel *La insolación* appeared. Margaret E. W. Jones's "Dialectical Movement as a Feminist Technique in the Works of Carmen Laforet." *Studies in Honor of Gerald E. Wade* (Madrid: Porrúa y Turanzas, 1979), pp. 109-120, is a pioneering study as the first article to encompass all Laforet's long and short fiction and the first to do so from a feminist perspective.

Barcelona after the hostilities have ended. (I use past tense to indicate actions that occurred at some time prior to the principal time of the novel and that are recounted to Andrea by other characters; much of the historical content is supplied in this oblique way.) Andrea learns of the War primarily from Gloria, wife of her uncle Juan, who fought on the Republican side. Like many women, she followed Juan about on his assignments on the battle-front, and when she became pregnant, they submitted to a civilian marriage, legal under the Republic but considered null during Franco's regime. Juan's wartime activities are never made very clear as we see his involvement only through Gloria's eyes, and Gloria's knowledge consists primarily of information gleaned through a keyhole as she secretly listened to Juan and Román's nightly discussions. But even though her participation in the War was reduced to such a miniscule role, Gloria is not without knowledge of the ideologies at stake in the conflict, and she has her own firm convictions as to the right and wrong sides. Gloria declares that she would have despised Juan for defecting to the winning Nationalists, if he had yielded to Román's arguments that he do so.

Gloria and Juan were separated during the last stages of the fighting when Gloria went to Barcelona to have their child. Juan returned to Barcelona after the Nationalists entered the city with his nerves shattered by his recent experiences, and Gloria's life becomes a nightmare of domestic brutality and survival-level existence. Juan is incapable of financially supporting his wife and child, so Gloria assumes that responsibility, earning money by gambling in her sister's establishment in the barrio chino. Most of the references to Gloria's, Juan's and Román's lives during the War are contained in a dialogued section set up like a formal drama between the grandmother and Gloria at Andrea's bedside as she lies delirious with fever. Andrea seems a mere passive observer of the public aspect of life occurring around her, but in fact she is recording those events as the narrator, intertwining them into her own personal history.

She likewise hears Angustias's story in bits and pieces from several members of the family. As with Gloria, the War signified a liberating experience for this outwardly conservative, traditional Spanish woman, but the solution for her post-War existence will take an opposite trajectory from that of Gloria's independent, family-sustaining role. The War gave Angustias the opportunity to form a relationship with her boss Don Jerónimo, who took refuge with Angustias's family during the early days of the Barcelona revolution when it was dangerous for bourgeois capitalists to remain in the city. In pre-War Spain, Angustias's family had prevented her marriage to Don

Jerónimo because he was not of sufficient social category. In post-War Francoist Spain, Angustias, finding herself once more caught in a web of traditional social constraints, takes vows as a nun. Even though Angustias departs for the convent at the end of the first part of the novel, Andrea has grown and matured from the contact with her as she will from her life with the remaining relatives, whose lives have been permanently altered by their historical circumstances. At the end of her year in Barcelona, Andrea thinks nothing has happened to her during that year, but in fact her more mature view of life, reflected in the greater wisdom of the narrator's perspective, has been achieved in part through these indirect encounters with recent political events.[7]

La isla y los demonios, Laforet's second novel, also incorporates a personal, oblique and distanced view of political events through which the protagonist matures and decides the future direction of her life. Marta grows up in the Canary Islands in the time just prior to and during the Civil War, as did the author herself. The principal temporal frame of the novel is the year before the end of the Civil War when some of Marta's mainland relatives take refuge on the Island to escape the growing intensity of the conflict. These relatives bring the recent events of Spanish history into sharper focus for Marta, who at the beginning of the novel is an egotistical schoolgirl, preoccupied with her juvenile writings. She has constructed an elaborate illusion about the arrival of her "artistic" relatives — Aunt Matilde, a poetess; Uncle Daniel, a composer; and their friend Pablo, a painter. Gradually her *a priori* notions of the relatives tarnish as their failings are revealed. Each of these adults has been diminished in some way by the experience of the War. Daniel, a pitiful hypochondriac who no longer composes music, makes a ridiculous clucking noise at regular intervals — a nervous tic that began at the onset of the conflict. Pablo fritters away the war years in a liaison with Marta's frivolous Aunt Honesta, while his wife remains in the Peninsula to continue her activities in the war effort. Of the four guests, Aunt Matilde has been the most directly involved in the War, having served in women's organizations that support the Nationalists. Through her sobering contact with the War, Matilde has become stern and disagreeable, and her brusque, serious manner opposes Marta's childish innocence, forcing her to confront the harsher realities of the political

---

[7] See Ruth El Saffar, "Structural and Thematic Tactics of Suppression in Carmen Laforet's *Nada*," *Symposium*, 28 (1974), pp. 119-29, for a fine analysis of the dual narrative perspective in the novel and its significance for the work's meaning.

world: "Mira," Matilde says to Marta when the young girl hounds her aunt to read her stories:

> ... te voy a decir por qué no quiero leer tus cosas. No sé si tienes talento o no. Lo más probable será que no lo tengas, pero, al fin y al cabo, es lo mismo ... Me repugna verte todo el día sin hacer nada más que pensar en en ti misma. De la mañana a la noche estás pensando en ti. No te das cuenta de que hay jóvenes que valen infinitamente más que tú, que mueren cada día ... Muchos de mis mejores amigos han muerto, otros están pasando hambre, otros abocados al destierro. ¿Quieres que me extasie delante de una adolescencia, llena de problemas falsos y literarios? Me repugna. Nunca piensas en la guerra, ¿verdad?
> (...Look, I'm going to tell you why I don't want to read your things. I don't know if you have talent or not. It's most likely that you don't, but in any case, it makes no difference ... It repels me to see you do nothing all day but think of yourself. You have no idea that young people worth infinitely more than you are dying every day ... Many of my best friends have died, others are hungry, others forced into exile. And you want me to be enthusiastic about an adolescence full of false and literary problems? I'm disgusted. You never think about the War, do you?)[8]

Marta's rite of passage into adulthood and maturity includes leaving the sheltered island behind and along with it her youthful fancies and writings. At the end of the novel she embarks for the mainland, scene of the recent conflict, and on the eve of her departure she symbolically burns her journals. Her mature vision of herself includes the insertion of political history into her individual life, but in a complex, subtle and very personal way. She is to live in Madrid with the politically aware Matilde who will be her guardian and perhaps her tutor. The effect of history on the development of the protagonist in this *Bildungsroman* has filtered in from below, gradually shaping the direction her life takes and her awareness of herself in relation to others.

Carmen Laforet's historical consciousness and that of her characters becomes increasingly acute in each succeeding novel. The salient elements

---

[8] Carmen Laforet, *La isla y los demonios,* in *Novelas,* I (Barcelona: Planeta, 1972), p. 407. All references to Laforet's novels, except *La insolación,* which was not included in this volume of complete works, are from this edition; henceforth page numbers will be indicated in the text.

of plot design in the third novel, *La mujer nueva* are intricately intertwined with the progress of the Spanish Civil War and the first fifteen years of the Franco regime. The central event of the novel, Paulina's mystic experience and her subsequent dedication to religious activities reflects the emphasis placed on the role of the Catholic Church as an official and all-pervasive force in Spain during the 1950s. In a recent book, Laforet's son says of *La mujer nueva* that it was difficult to escape fanaticism in "la atmósfera de plúmbea beatería que reinaba entonces en España" (in the atmosphere of heavy religiosity that reigned at that time in Spain).[9]

Paulina attends the University during the Republic (1931-36), when there was much more freedom for women in Spain. Nineteen thirty-six, the year the Civil War began, is a turning point in twentieth century Spanish history, and a pivotal year in the protagonist's life: she turns twenty and receives her university degree in Physical Sciences. That summer she begins a relationship with Eulogio in her home town in Leon — a relationship that will remain inextricably bound up with the political events of the next few years. Paulina, a devotee of freedom and sincerity, prefers Eulogio's socialist father to her own, a hypocritical Catholic and political conservative. When the Civil War breaks out and Paulina's father is executed by the mine workers, she is free to accompany Eulogio, now a Republican militiaman, to Barcelona. As in the cases of Gloria and Angustias in *Nada*, the social chaos of the Civil War affords Paulina a large measure of personal freedom that will be effaced in the conservative backlash of the post-War period: "A Paulina le pareció que era demasiado aquello: ser jóvenes., quererse, poder ser el uno del otro sin ningún obstáculo .. Algo así pensó, debieron de experimentar Adán y Eva en el Paraíso Terrenal" (p. 1100). (All that seemed too much to Paulina: to be young, to love each other, to belong to one another without any obstacle ... Adam and Eve in Paradise must have experienced something like that.) Paulina and Eulogio live as man and wife without benefit of matrimony in the spirit of exhilaration and freedom that pervaded Barcelona during the first stages of the revolution in that city. Having experienced the personal and political equality possible for women during the workers' revolution, Paulina never finds a comfortable niche for herself in post-War Franco Spain.

When Paulina becomes pregnant, she and Eulogio submit to a civil marriage, an option afforded them in Republican Spain, which will ultimately set

---

[9] Agustín Cerezales, *Carmen Laforet* (Madrid: Ministerio de Cultura, 1982), p. 22.

the stage for the array of personal choices that Paulina faces at the end of the novel. Since her marriage is not recognized under Franco's regime, she is legally free to choose between her newly-found religious vocation, marrying her lover or returning to her husband. (One cannot help but note the irony of the repressive regime's affording Paulina the opportunity to make such choices.) The Nationalists take Barcelona, and Eulogio leaves his pregnant wife behind to seek political asylum abroad. When his promise of an early return remains unfulfilled, Paulina lives as an independent woman in Madrid, teaching school to support herself and her child, and forming friendships with some intellectual, free-thinking people.

Eulogio finally returns to Spain after having spent some years in Latin America, and Paulina's life changes radically. Her once revolutionary husband has been so transformed by the experience of war and exile that he now insists on a traditional family life in their Leonese village. But village life amongst her husband's relatives proves to be suffocating for Paulina, especially since she and Eulogio no longer share the intimacy they did during the war years in Barcelona, and she ultimately gives in to an adulterous relationship. The sense of enclosure and entrapment arising from this complex situation drives Paulina to return to Madrid where she can be alone and recover her sense of self. On the train to Madrid, however, she undergoes a mystical experience which compels her to re-orient her life toward devotional activities.

Even during the most intensely personal part of the novel, Laforet does not lose sight of the larger socio-political context and its relationship to Paulina's personal situation. In Madrid Paulina reestablishes contact with friends from her days as a single woman when Eulogio was in America. These once bohemian friends have succumbed to the prevailing materialism and superficial Catholicism of the 1950s. One male friend tells her: "Yo ahora soy también un hombre de negocios, aquí donde me ves, Paulina" (p. 1186). (I too am now a business man, right here as I stand, Paulina.) The new Paulina is a woman who has lived the freedom of Republican Spain before and during the Civil War and who, through religious regeneration, has found a way of coping with the personal changes brought about by the War and the stifling atmosphere of life during the Franco regime. Hers is a profoundly personal religious experience rather than the superficial and socially promoted interest in the Church that her friends embrace. But she eventually gives up this mode of escaping the prevailing political ambience of the Franco era, and accepts the traditional role of wife and mother that the regime was so anxious to promote.

La insolación, Laforet's last published novel, most directly reflects contemporary history, as its very structure juxtaposes Spain and the rest of Europe in the 1940s. To adequately portray this historical period, Laforet spent many hours in Madrid's *hemerotecas* reading newspapers from the early post-Civil War days. The announced title of the trilogy—*Tres pasos fuera del tiempo*—of which this novel is the first volume, suggests the work's attitude toward historical time. Spain during the Second World War was in many ways "out of time" — isolated from the events of Europe and still preoccupied with the aftermath of her own recent war. Says Laforet of that projected trilogy: "Estos tres libros ... marcan tres momentos de la vida de un hombre y apuntan también tres momentos de la vida de estos últimos veinte años en España." (These three books ... mark three moments in the life of a man and point to three moments in Spain's last twenty years.)[10]

It is interesting to note that Carmen Laforet's most overtly historical novel has a male protagonist. Martín grows from adolescence to early manhood during the summers of 1940, 1941 and 1942, years that coincide with the early part of the Franco regime and World War II in Europe. The passage of time between the three summers that form the three main parts of the novel is marked by two interludes — brief descriptions of the progress of the War in Europe and the important changes that have occurred in Martín's development during the school year:

> Conversaciones sobre la estrategia de la guerra. La escuelita de arte sigue funcionando. Martín empieza a pintar al oleo bajo la dirección de su maestro. Se habla de arte abstracto en la escuela y el maestro se enfada. 1942 trae dentro de él muchas matanzas. Los alemanes se extienden por todo el mundo. En Alicante también hay alemanes. Aunque existe la División Azul, existe una paz en España. Es una paz débil, quizás, como un cascarón. Pero del cascarón uno se siente protegido y puede hablar de estrategia con los amigos. (p. 267)
> (Conversations on war strategy. The little art school continues to function. Martín begins to paint in oils under the direction of his teacher. They talk of abstract art at school and the teacher gets angry. 1942 brings many killings. The Germans are everywhere. There are Germans in Alicante too. Although there is a Blue Division, there is peace in Spain. It is a weak peace, perhaps, like an eggshell. But from the shell one feels protected and can talk of strategy with friends.)

---

[10] "Por qué de esta trilogía," p. 8.

Martín's life is suffused with the prevailing socio-political ambience at the most personal level; these are the lean years of privation and hunger in Spain, and his health and growth are threatened by insufficient protein in the diet.

Martín's summertime endeavors focus on his relationship with the two Corsi children who live near his father's beach-side home. The Corsis are motherless like Martín, and the two fathers represent opposite poles of the political spectrum: Martín's father is a military officer in Franco's army and stands for all the repressive aspects of the early post-war period in Spanish history, while the Corsi's father is a blackmarketeer, loyal to no regime or ideology. The Corsi children enjoy a large measure of personal freedom, a reflection of their father's ambiguous socio-political situation, while Martín's father is a rigid disciplinarian. The three children unwittingly become entangled in the survival efforts of a Spanish Civil War refugee — an ex-Republican militiaman hiding in the Corsi's summer home. Their discovery of the existence of the refugee, after a series of mysterious occurrences, coincides with Martín's attainment of a certain type of maturity — a maturity hastened by his military father's severity.

Martín's achievement of his own identity and independence as a person and a painter includes rejecting his own personal past and that of his country:

> —Ayer me di cuenta de lo que es una vocación de artista, Carlos ... Ayer, en aquellas horas que estuve pensando, sentí lo que es la verdadera liberación. No sé como explicártelo. No sé si alguna vez tú te has planteado problemas de ataduras religiosas, políticas o familiares, no lo sé .. Ayer supe que nada podrá detener esta fuerza cuando yo la ponga en marcha. No me podrá atar nada. Necesito una libertad absoluta. Ningún lazo familiar. ¿Oyes bien? Ninguno. Ni ataduras ni patria tampoco. Esa idea de la patria es forzada, es utópica. Ni ataduras de religión ni mucho menos sociales ... (p. 322) (—Yesterday I realized what the artist's vocation is, Carlos, ... Yesterday, in those hours that I was thinking, I felt true liberation. I don't know how to explain it to you. I don't know if you have ever confronted problems of religious, political or familial ties, I don't know ... Yesterday I found out that nothing can stop this force once I put it in motion. Nothing can tie me. I need absolute liberty. No familial tie. Do you hear me? None. Neither ties nor country either. That idea of country is forced, it's utopian. Neither religious ties nor, much less, social ones ...)

After a violent confrontation with his father, Martín returns to Alicante to live with his grandmother and to complete his education for his career as an artist. He never sees his father again.

All of Laforet's protagonists encounter history in a personal and indirect way. However, the female protagonists achieve maturity when their lives come into the proximity of political history, and they incorporate it into their personal lives, while the male protagonist achieves maturity and independence by means of precisely the opposite process. Martín enters adulthood upon understanding that he must liberate himself from personal and political history. And it is interesting to note that many male and female novelists of the post-Civil War period approach history in ways similar to Laforet's male and female protagonists. The male novelists seem to feel the need to unburden themselves of their historical baggage, to deconstruct and demythify personal and socio-political history, while the women, especially Carmen Laforet, seek a personal engagement with history in their work which denotes a growth of historical consciousness.

The new women's and social historians are finally unearthing from diaries, journals and yes, even novels the kinds of information we find hidden in Laforet's works. Laforet's novelistic canon, though perhaps less consciously so, coincides with the efforts of the new women's historians to chronicle the lives of ordinary citizens, particularly women. History has informed her novels: she lived through the Civil War years — though in the remote Canary Islands — and from closer range the Franco regime. She has even done formal research on the latter. But rather than making public history the primary object in her novels, she has chosen to record its influence on private lives. Surely such fictional accounts will be useful in the enormous task presently confronting social historians of Spain, namely to rewrite the history of the Civil War and the Franco era.

Portraits of the *Femme Seule* by Laforet, Matute, Soriano, Martín Gaite, Galvarriato, Quiroga, and Medio

Janet Pérez

Portrayals of the single "liberated" woman (simply a woman who is economically independent and content with her unmarried state) are singularly rare in the fiction written by women in the Franco era. Whether the independently wealthy, the professional, the working woman or peasant, women who are self-sufficient and neither seeking matrimony nor frustrated with their not having achieved it appear only infrequently. The woman whose attitudes are "liberated" — who dares to defy convention by her visible behavior, dress, sexual autonomy or occupational non-conformity — is an even more unusual occurrence, even though it would seem logical that on the level of fiction, as fantasy or ideal, it should exist. Curiously, however, the few instances of such economically independent and non-conforming or self-directed females that do appear in post-war Spanish fiction come primarily from works written by men. A number of Torrente Ballester's female characters, for example, display liberated attitudes and behavior, from the heroine of *El golpe de estado de Guadalupe Limón* (1946), to Doña Mariana in *El señor llega* (1957) and *Donde da la vuelta el aire* (1960), and Clara Aldán in three volumes of "Los gozos y las sombras" (1957-62). Cela's fiction also has its share of sexually liberated females, such as Guillermo Zabalegui's Aunt Mimi in *San Camilo, '36* (1969). Even more extreme examples are to be found among the strong, lusty women of *Mazurca para dos muertos* (1983), including Adega, Benicia Segade, Catuxa Bainte, Rosicler and Georgina. It must be noted, however, that in the post-Franco era, the incidence of portrayals of feminine independence and autonomy increases markedly, especially in the works of the Catalan women writers. Few if any counterparts to such portrayals appear in the fiction of several leading postwar women writers (Laforet, Quiroga, Matute, Martín Gaite and others, including Eulalia Galvarriato and Elena Soriano). This becomes especially evident upon examination of their characterization of single women, whether *solteras, solteronas,* divorceés, or abandoned wives and lovers. A possible exception to this norm is Dolores Medio, who has works in which the elusive "liberated" type appears.

Most heroines of Laforet and Matute are adolescents or children, so that no matter how non-conformist or alienated their attitudes, they cannot be called women, liberated or otherwise. Adolescent rebellion may sometimes lead to liberation, but it often ends in conventional adjustment to bourgeois society and accommodation to patriarchal norms. Therefore, only females who have definitely reached adulthood and whose single state — voluntary or otherwise — can be considered definitive will be examined. Through analysis of a series of portraits of single women, it should be possible to derive some common denominator or nucleus of reiterated traits susceptible of serving as a basis for generalization.

Tía Angustias in Laforet's *Nada* (1945) is single apparently by choice, for Juan affirms that she spurned her former suitor and current employer, Jerónimo, "porque a tu padre se le ocurrió decir que era poco el hijo de un tendero para ti" (your father happened to say a storekeeper's son was not good enough for you).[1] Although she may be termed a career woman with her years as a secretary and thus might be assumed to be less traditional, she is totally conservative in her outlook on educating Andrea, equivalent to inculcating in her an unthinking observance of society's norms, a duty which Angustias summarizes as "moldearte en la obediencia" (p. 25) (mold you in obedience). The aunt appears hypocritical in light of the contrast between her severely moralistic expectations for Andrea ("La ciudad, hija mía, es un infierno ... Toda prudencia en la conducta es poca") (The city, my child, is an inferno. All prudence in one's conduct is less than sufficient) and her own long-standing emotional involvement with her married employer. While not unattractive, Angustias is in no way idealized either physically or

---

[1] Carmen Laforet, *Nada* (Barcelona: Destino, 1945), p. 111. All quotations are from this edition. The page number follows the quote. Translations are my own.

psychologically, and the delineation of her character contains elements of the negative stereotypes of *solterona* and *beata*. Searching for imperfections in her aunt, Andrea quickly locates one repugnant detail, "dientes de un color sucio" (p. 27) (dirty-colored teeth). Angustias' dress verges on the ludicrous (an aspect repeated in another of Laforet's spinsters) with her hat "de fieltro marrón adornado por una pluma de gallo, que daba a su dura fisonomía un aire guerrero" (p. 32) (of brown felt adorned with a rooster feather, which gave her hard features a warlike air). After a typical mealtime family brawl, "Tía Angustias sollozaba a mi lado, mordiendo su pañuelo, porque no sólo se veía a sí misma fuerte y capaz de conducir multitudes, sino también dulce, desdichada y perseguida" (p. 33) (Aunt Angustias sobbed beside me, biting her handkerchief, because not only did she see herself as strong and able to lead multitides, but also sweet, unfortunate and persecuted). In fact, Angustias has a well-developed martyr complex, as Juan correctly intimates upon her departure for the convent: "—¡No te hagas la mártir, Angustias ...! ¡Que a mí no me la pegas con esa comedia de tu santidad!" (p. 111) (Don't play the martyr, Angustias. You don't fool me with that comedy of your sainthood!). Román terms her diary masochistic (p. 109), and openly alludes to her twenty-year relationship with don Jerónimo (which may never have been physically consummated), blaming her for the madness of Jerónimo's wife (pp. 65-66). Undoubtedly it is Angustias' fear of public opinion, as Juan indicates (p. 111) which prevents her living openly with Sanz. She is neither liberated nor accepting of the norms under which she has chosen to live — or appear to live.

Alicia in *Un noviazgo* is an unwilling career woman who was forced to work following her father's death.[2] After thirty years in the same office, she is rigid, inhibited, formal, embittered and frustrated, yet also sentimental and incurably romantic, living in a fantasy world where she combines the myths of Cinderella, Sleeping Beauty and Snow White, although this secret aspect of her life is invisible to the world around her. Alicia is compulsively neat from the "peinado perfecto de sus cabellos a la limpieza impecable de sus trajes. Ni una mancha, ni una arruga ... Era su lema" (p. 7) (perfectly combed hair to impeccably clean dresses. Not a spot, not a wrinkle. That was her motto). This intolerance for a wrinkle or a spot visibly exteriorizes her inhibitions, and her fear of men, who are envisioned as predatory and dangerous. Alicia's

---

[2] Carmen Laforet, *Un noviazgo* (Madrid: La novela del sábado, 1953). Quotations are from the original edition. The page number follows the quote. Translations are my own.

cold, correct features, discreetly aging, are in perfect harmony with her character and behavior. Laforet's delineation seems calculated to emphasize Alicia's exaggerated sense of honor and unwavering morality, thereby implicitly combatting the notion that secretaries are expected to be sexually attentive to their superiors: "En aquellos tiempos era raro, o por lo menos más extraño que ahora, encontrar a una muchacha de buena familia en una oficina" (p. 16) (In those days it was strange, or at least more so than now, to find a girl of good family working in an office). Thus, Alicia indignantly rejects her employer's suggestion that after thirty years, she cease addressing him formally as "usted". "No sé qué pretende, De Arco. Jamás he sido para usted otra cosa que una secretaria ... Y que yo sepa, no le he dado permiso nunca para tutearme" (p. 9) (I don't know what you think you're doing, De Arco. I've never been anything but a secretary for you. And if I remember correctly I've never given you permission to address me in the familiar form).

Long before her age clearly branded her as a spinster, Alicia's manners, dress and outlook combined to counteract her pretty face and forestall the approach of suitors: "iba resultando un poco anacrónica para la vida corriente" (p. 19) (she was becoming a bit too anachronistic for everyday life).[3] This anachronistic trait is further evidence of conservative or even reactionary attitudes, not merely a consequence of limited economic straits, for Alicia seems deliberately to wear outdated clothes: "solía parecer un figurín de la moda más acusada, con varios años de retraso siempre" (p. 7) (She seemed a mannequin of the most extreme fashion, always several years behind). Furthermore, she appears to indulge in conscious bad taste and unflattering styles: "Era amiga de volantes, plisados y toda clase de adornos en los vestidos" (p. 7) (She was fond of hoops, pleats and all kinds of ornaments on her dresses). Taken as a whole, Alicia's dress is part of her defense against the masculine world: clothing is a protective barrier behind which she withdraws or conceals herself. Such exaggerated caution in her relationships with men is not merely the result of fear or discretion, however, for Alicia has been totally brainwashed by the fairy-tale image of Prince Charming and life "happily ever after," with herself as a princess. Nothing less than a titled aristocrat will do (p. 26), and her fantasy re-enactment of the *petición de*

---

[3] This attitude is shared by De Arco, who upon contemplating Alicia during their brief engagement, "tuvo un sentimiento mezquino al considerar el mal gusto y el poco garbo que para vestirse tenía Alicia ... Y aquella manera de andar a saltitos debajo de una pamela negra ..." (p. 56). (had a low opinion of her, considering the bad taste and little style with which Alicia dressed ... And that strange way she had of bouncing around under that black hat.)

mano draws upon fairy-tale archetypes as well (p. 29). Her antiquated concept of honor is more appropriate for the Eighteenth Century than for the Twentieth, and quite incomprehensible to her mother: "Doña Ana ... estaba harta de oír hablar a Alicia de orgullo y de delicadeza" (p. 43) (Doña Ana was fed up with Alicia's talk of pride and refinement). Alicia's fantasy world is a selfish one, however, and the novelist neither idealizes her nor sympathizes much, judging by the description of her relationship with her mother. Despite reminding Doña Ana continually of the sacrifices she has made in her behalf, Alicia "no pensaba nunca en ella, esto era la verdad, aunque todo el mundo la admirase por haberle sacrificado la vida" (p. 41) (the truth is she never even thought about her mother though everyone admired her for sacrificing her life for her).

Romantically, Alicia becomes enamored of her employer before their first encounter, and "Estaba bien segura de que De Arco no ignoraba el amor que durante años y años gastó inútil, silenciosa y abnegadamente en él" (p. 13) (She was quite sure De Arco was not unaware of the love which for years and years she had devoted to him in abnegation and silence). Her silent adoration is so intense that she feels a guilty joy at the death of his wife, but there is no reciprocal attraction. Despite appreciating her clerical skills, De Arco considers Alicia "durante mucho, muchísimo tiempo, un mueble más de su oficina" (p. 25) (for a long, long time, just another piece of office furniture). When her aging, infirm and lonely employer finally proposes in order to have a live-in maid, Alicia is torn between fulfilling her years of fantasizing about marriage to a titled aristocrat, the desire for a story-book engagement, and her decades of accumulated rancor and resentment against De Arco for ignoring her. Hate wins out among the conflicting emotions (both Alicia and De Arco experience epiphanies, realizing that her real feeling was hate, cf. pp. 44 and 61-62). The novelist's ironic distance is clear in the metaliterary language chosen to describe the climactic luncheon scene in which Alicia rejects De Arco's proposal: "Los tres personajes tenían un extraño aire de conspiradores, mirándose" (p. 63) (The three characters had a strange, conspiratorial air, looking at one another). "Alicia estaba teatral, magnífica" (p. 63) (Alicia was theatrical, magnificent). "Un asombrado camarero veía la escena desde una prudente distancia ... Le parecía que representaban una comedia aquellos tres personajes ... Era divertidísimo" (p. 63) (An amazed waiter watched the scene from a prudent distance. It seemed those three characters were putting on a play. It was most amusing). Laforet also displays a decided lack of sympathy for Alicia in the concluding paragraph which reveals that De Arco's marriage two months later to a widow "fue un matrimonio verdaderamente acertado" (p. 64) (a truly wise marriage). While treating Alicia's stunned reactions to the unexpected proposal with considerable psychological penetration, Laforet at no point idealizes her nor presents her as a model to be imitated. A victim of her own fantasies, social prejudices and snobbishness, Alicia is as far as is Angustias from anything resembling liberation in her attitudes.

If these single women in Laforet's work occasionally resemble caricatures and are obsessively servile in their compliance with middle-class morality and prevailing conventions, this novelist is by no means alone in a predominantly negative portraiture of the unmarried female. Some of the spinsters in Matute's works are further still from autonomy, and equally distant from being attractive characters or human beings. In the novelette, *El tiempo*,[4] two elderly, unmarried sisters who run the telegraph office exhibit uniformly unpleasant traits: "en el pueblo no se las quería mucho, por ser maldicientes y avaras. Tenían un gran brasero de cobre junto al que se sentaban, con las manos en los sobacos, bajo sus amplias y sucias toquillas, o tejiendo con largas agujas de acero interminables prendas de lana. Murmuraban, bostezaban y, a veces, sacaban una de las largas agujas y se rascaban la cabeza" (p. 28) (they weren't well-liked in the village, because they were gossipy and avaricious. They had a huge copper charcoal-burner by which they sat, with their hands tucked under their arm-pits, with their ample, dirty nun-like head-coverings, or else they would knit interminable garments of wool with long steel needles. They gossiped, yawned, and sometimes would take out one of the long needles and scratch their heads). This scene, with its emphasis on knitting and the disagreeable attributes of the two old crones, inevitably evokes the furies or harpies. Given Matute's tendency to expressionistic characterization, their vulgarity and lack of pulchritude are intended to reveal psychologic smallness and dirtiness.

Eskarne Antia and her younger sister Mirentxu are the old maid aunts of the protagonist in *Pequeño teatro*.[5] Matute's description of Eskarne is caricaturesque: "alta, huesuda, dueña de una imponente nariz sobre la que se envalentonaban unos ojos duros y brillantes" (p. 69) (tall, bony, with an imposing nose above which hard, brilliant eyes challenged one). Elsewhere

---

[4] Ana María Matute, *El tiempo* (Barcelona: Editorial Mateu, 1963). This is a short-story and novelette collection, of which the title narrative was originally published separately. References are to this edition.

[5] Ana María Matute, *Pequeño teatro* (Barcelona: Editorial Planeta, 1949). All quotations are from this edition. These and other references are indicated by the page number. Translations are my own.

her nose is termed impressive, and Eskarne is envisioned as a tall, bony, domineering shadow. According to her sister, she is a hypocrite, with some negative trait which, although unnamed, is perceived as "cruel y reseco, algo dañino y limpio, como el filo de un cuchillo," (cruel and dried-up, something harmful and yet clean, like the edge of a knife) while her typical manner of speech or self-expression is "lengua acusadora de vieja señorita" (p. 69) (an old maid's accusing tongue). It seems fairly evident that a portion of Eskarne's unpleasant attributes are intimately related to her spinsterhood: "reseco," "dañino y limpio" (dried up, harmful, yet clean). Her dry, authoritarian voice cuts like a knife, and she is hated, feared, yet also respected by the village women. Like Laforet's spinsters, she dresses in a manner which verges upon the ludicrous, and once again the hat epitomizes eccentricity, for Eskarne characteristically wears a "sombrero de tres pisos" (three-story hat). The two sisters seem to have been conceived as positive and negative poles of a single whole, for the younger Mirentxu is the opposite of her tall, wiry, frigid and dictatorial elder: "bajita, de párpados anchos y labios rizaditos en los extremos, los ojos mansos, como un perro fiel, y se llenaba la frente de bucles foscos, con cierta gracia pasada de moda" (p. 67) (short and dumpy, with droopy eyelids and lips curled at the corners, tame and gentle eyes like those of a faithful hound, and a forehead covered with limp ringlets, with an amusing outmoded air). Contrasting pairs are frequent in Matute's work, as may be seen, for example, in Jacqueline and Valba(nera) of *Los Abel*, or Isabel and Verónica of *Los hijos muertos*, so this conception is not peculiar to her portrait of the spinster. Clearly, however, the sisters were conceptualized as opposites: while Eskarne is tall, bony and authoritarian, Miren is short, pudgy and submissive. Their niece, Zazu, reflects that Miren "es una gran muñeca muerta" (p. 68) (a huge dead doll), like the dolls of her own childhood shut away in a chest, much as she herself is kept apart from life, "una enorme muñeca, monstruosa, guardada en una enorme caja. Los ojos de Miren tenían una insistencia untuosa, una fijeza de vidrio" (pp. 68-69) (an enormous, monstrous doll, kept in an enormous box. Miren's eyes had an unctuous insistence, a glassy fixation). In further contrast to her sister, Miren seldom speaks, and is limited in her capacities for self-expression, having always kept quiet in "un continuo reprimir" (a continual repression) of heart and feelings. The novelist refers to Miren's virgin breast, "pecho de muchacha envejecida," (the breast of an aged adolescent) her pale cheeks and dimly innocent eyes. Eskarne, too, is pale, with "labios pálidos de cólera contenida" (lips pale from holding back her anger), but without any of the redeeming pathos of the younger sister. It is worth observing that the note of outmoded dress or fashion, not merely poor taste, seen in Alicia (*Un noviazgo*) is also utilized by Matute, in her description of Miren's hairdo: "bucles foscos, con cierta gracia pasada de moda," (limp ringlets, with an amusing outmoded air) a note which is emphasized or underscored by the "labios rizaditos" (curled lips). Such touches belong to the general cultural stereotype of the old maid.

Another typical small-town spinster is Emelina of *Los Abel*, repeatedly termed an amateur nurse and undertaker's assistant, who appears time and time again dressing the deceased for burial, or caring for the sick, "jeringuilla en ristre" (hypodermic at the ready).[6] She seeks to approach the widower Abel through his children, but to no avail. A similar figure is that of Beatriz, a fortyish spinster with typical village background in *Los hijos muertos*.[7] A bland, easily manipulated woman with a small inheritance, she is far from being liberated, despite a measure of economic independence, and easily falls prey to the machinations of Isabel, who plans a marriage between her widowed father and Beatriz in order to appropriate her money to help save the Corvo estate. Beatriz is eclipsed by the marriage, of interest to no one once her money is used, and dies soon afterward in childbirth. The other single woman in *Los hijos muertos*, Isabel (eldest daughter of Gerardo Corvo) is more interesting and lacks the stereotypical traits of Emelina and Beatriz. Strong, decisive, vigorous, hard-working and authoritarian, Isabel dominates her weak and sickly father and the entire family. Religious, demanding, rigid and strict, she is well on her way to becoming a *beata* (another stereotypical attribute of the spinster). Isabel gains in breadth and interest, however, thanks to her concealed, potentially sinful love for her young cousin (whom she has raised almost as a son or younger brother), a boy who loves and is loved by Isabel's younger sister, Verónica. Isabel's sublimated erotic urges are expressed in intolerance, without this sufficing to make her thoroughly unlikeable, for she is clearly victimized by her education and internalization of the values of the society in which she has been raised. Attractive without being beautiful, she grows harder as she ages, but perhaps because she is more fully developed as a character, she does not acquire the stereotypical traits of the spinsters examined heretofore. On the contrary, she is portrayed with considerable sympathy as a woman vitally and emotionally frustrated, to whom happiness has been denied in the name of family and

---

[6] Ana María Matute, *Los Abel* (Barcelona: Destino, 1948).
[7] Ana María Matute, *Los hijos muertos* (Barcelona: Planeta, 1958).

convention, and who is consequently embarked on a route of increasing bitterness.

Susana, an old maid wno cares for the orphaned Paulina in Matute's novel for adolescent girls, *Paulina, el mundo y las estrellas*, is described by her young charge as "muy limpia, muy madrugadora, muy trabajadora, muy alta, muy fuerte. Todo de todo. Pero Susana era para mí como una pared ... no tenía ni oídos ni ojos, nada más que para oír y ver lo malo" (very clean, very early-rising, very tall, very strong, very everything. But Susana was like a wall for me ... she had neither ears nor eyes, except for hearing and seeing what was bad).[8] Not only is Susana inflexible and perhaps overly virtuous, with an excessive, demanding intolerance, she lacks warmth in personal relationships, has a voice "like a file," a hard shoulder, and is almost always dressed in hard, scratchy wool (an expressionistic touch which further externalizes her personality). She grumbles frequently, and although she seemed like a different person when she smiled, according to the child's description, smiling was something she seldom did. She gave the impression of being continually angry, but was very conscientious in fulfilling her duties to the Church. Clearly then, Susana also has a number of traits drawn from the nucleus of stereotypical attributes associated with the spinster: extreme religiosity, hardness, frigidity, frustration expressed in authoritarian or unpleasant behavior, a cutting voice, unattractive clothing, and an inability to communicate with or relate to those younger than herself.

From this small sample of the spinsters portrayed by Matute, it is evident that no given one of them is happy with her situation in life, none is considered (or considers herself) successful, and none emerges as especially attractive, interesting or deserving. With the possible exception of Isabel Corvo (who has devoted her energies to saving and managing the family estate), none appears to be an old maid by choice. None of them has a viable alternative to matrimony: the idea of a career of any vocation whatever excepting wife and mother is nowhere to be found. Not only does Matute not idealize the single women, but most exhibit caricaturesque or pathetic traits — or a combination of both. The range of possibilities seems to be nearly exhausted by two basic types of old maid, of which Eskarne and Mirentxu are extreme examples: either the excessively strong, intolerant, domineering and not especially "feminine" type, who sublimates her frustration in activity (Susana, Isabel Corvo, and to a lesser extent, Emelina), or the submissive, patient,

---

[8] Ana María Matute, *Paulina, el mundo y las estrellas* (Barcelona: Gardo, 1960), p. 9. References are to this edition.

timid, resigned, dreamy and passive type (Mirentxu, Beatriz). To a certain extent, such portraits of the stereotypical spinster reflect the deprecation of a society dominated by masculine values, in which failure to ensnare a husband must reflect defects in the woman's appearance and/or personality. Much the same can be said of Tía Angustias and Alicia in Laforet's portrayals, although the caricaturesque aspects are somewhat offset by the more extensive psychological presentation and development. Insofar as neither novelist makes an overt protest against society's view or treatment of the single woman or her limited range of choices for life, it may be said that there is no feminist statement made by either. However, it must also be observed that by reflecting faithfully the male-dominated society's negative evaluation of the spinster, both novelists subtly call attention to the feminine plight. Clearly, it would not improve the situation of women in Spain to suggest that the village spinster had a range of career options, or that her lot was a pleasant one. The only single woman with ability, energy and intelligence, Isabel Corvo, is thoroughly traditional and conservative in her moral and social attitudes, so bound by convention and the usual prejudices of her class that she lacks autonomy, and her managerial and administrative capacities not only are offset by a narrow environment and spendthrift father, but can be said to lead to her downfall in a relative sense, since her possibilities of personal fulfillment are sacrificed for the sake of the family estate.

Elena Soriano's trilogy, "Mujer y hombre," has single women as protagonists of the first and last volumes, both of them strongly characterized individuals whose lives have been unorthodox, who have defied convention to affirm their own desires. Upon examination, however, neither qualifies psychologically as "liberated," although each has the economic capacity to be self-sustaining. The nameless narrative conscience ("yo") of *La playa de los locos* has returned to the wild and solitary Galician beach which was the setting for a decisive love idyll twenty years before.[9] Initially, she was much closer to liberation than the average woman of her time in Spain. Having completed her university training and won a *cátedra* of secondary education shortly before the Civil War, she took a vacation by herself and met a young man. Although he identified himself as a doctor, she suspected he was only a student. Considering herself his superior, she repeatedly rejected physical

---

[9] *La playa de los locos*, *Espejismos*, and *Medea 55* were first published in Madrid in 1955. The first volume, banned from circulation by the censors, was unavailable for many years, finally appearing in a new edition in 1984. Quotations are from the first edition. The page number follows the quote. Translations are my own.

consummation of their passionate, sensual relationship. Her intellectual snobbery and social prejudices stood in place of the familial or economic restraints from which she had gained a measure of independence, and because he fell short of her image of the ideal man, she flirted without permitting sexual involvement. After a few brief, tempestuous weeks, mysterious strangers took him away and, incredulous, she heard of his involvement in politics. With the outbreak of hostilities, her efforts to trace him proved fruitless. Refusing to believe that he could be more than a simple, provincial student (i.e., that she could be mistaken), or that he might have voluntarily left her, she refused to forget, beginning each day with the pretense of his impending return. For twenty years, during which she never married, her whole life centered on the obsession of this frustrated romance, as she became progressively more abnormal and eccentric. Like Laforet's spinsters, her dress is outmoded, fanciful or romantic, for she continued to wear the styles of her twenties and to behave like a young coquette: "anhelo amorosas aventuras, busco ocasión de conocer personas y lugares nuevos, deseo cantar y bailar ... y me pongo a coquetear con los hombres" (p. 15) (I long for amorous adventures, I seek ways to meet new people and go to new places, I want to sing and dance ... and I begin to flirt with the men). In a manic-depressive cycle, she would proceed from this phase to hysteria, taking to her bed for extended periods, refusing to admit the passage of time: "nadie puede atreverse a retraerme hacia el presente, ni a enfrentarme espejos que reflejen mi imagen real y lamentable" (p. 15) (no one dares draw me back to the present, nor place me in front of mirrors which reflect my lamentable true image). Various empty parentheses in her memories suggest that she may have spent time as a patient in a mental hospital.

Despite external signs of independence (i.e., economic self-sufficiency, a measure of autonomy, daring to flirt), her internal subjective life has been near-slavery to a man who, if not dead, abandoned her two decades earlier. The approach of menopause precipitates an existential crisis, with its reminder of aging, ultimate death and extinction: "¿Puedes tú, hombre, comprender lo que significa para una mujer saberse a punto de dejar de serlo? Voy a convertirme en un ser híbrido, asexuado, sin objeto ni fin entre mis semejantes ... condenada a morir del todo, sin posible retoño" (p. 16) (Can you, a man, understand what it means for a woman to know she is at the verge of ceasing to be one? I'm going to become a hybrid, sexless being, without any object or reason for being among my kind ... condemned to die totally, without any possible descendant). The narrator-protagonist's evaluation of her existential situation — unmarried, without children, on the verge of menopause and thus without further possibilities of becoming a wife and mother — reflects the values of a male-dominated society, which attributes to the female no function other than reproduction: "un ser híbrido, asexuado, sin objeto ni fin" (a hybrid, sexless being, without object or reason for being). Her anguish inspires a desperate attempt to return to the scene of her lost love in an effort to recapture the past; its inevitable failure leads to a moment of self-discovery and confrontation with the evidence of her self-deception, madness (or at best, inauthenticity) and wasted life. The habit of avoiding reality is so ingrained that she considers suicide, but rejects it out of pride, finally recognizing her age and solitude. Although this epiphany does not in itself constitute a liberation, she may finally achieve a degree of "liberation," by symbolically breaking with the man who has dominated her life for two decades. Her closing words express a resolve to forget the past and live differently in her remaining years: "Ahora mismo, me iré de aquí para siempre" (p. 200) (This very minute, I shall go away from here forever).

The third novel of the trilogy, *Medea 55*, an updating of the Greek myth, suffers from the obvious restrictions on plot and characterization imposed by the mythic structure. Despite behavior which might be termed liberated in its defiance of convention, the protagonist lives in essential servitude to one man. Daniela (Medea) and Miguel (Jason) met during the Spanish Civil War, she of wealthy, conservative family, he a mysterious foreigner of leftist ideology. Daniela's uncontrolled, passionate ardor, and the fact that her wealth and beauty made her a useful tool led Miguel to make her his mistress. Appropriating as much of the family fortune as she could, she ran away with him to a life of wandering and intrigue. Her acting talents kept them from starvation during difficult years, while Miguel shamelessly exploited her attractions to influence men in power, thus advancing his own political career. Daniela cooperated willingly, determined to do anything necessary to keep him. Their one nearly idyllic period during early years in Latin America brought the birth of an adored daughter, who died in infancy. Because she wishes to hold Miguel with "pure" love, Daniela resolves to have no more children, secretly aborting several pregnancies. She becomes a famous movie star, continuing to aid Miguel's unscrupulous political maneuvering, and he succeeds in being appointed Minister of State. Driven by a desire for respectability and his frustrated paternal instincts, Miguel decides to marry a young aristocrat. Not even Daniela's revelation that she is at long last expecting a child suffices to dissuade him, and filled with hate, she determines to destroy all possible happiness for Miguel and his bride. Her wedding present includes a complete picture of her life with Miguel, documented by photos, clippings, old love letters — all the intimate and sordid details, crowned by her aborted fetus.

Daniela's morally and sexually deviant behavior challenges a myriad of ethical norms and social conventions, as well as abusing existential freedom without ever being autonomous or authentic. Not only is she a slave to her own passions and to Miguel's ambition, she is not single by choice, and in fact devotes her life to Miguel far more completely than would have been the norm in a conventional marriage. Despite circumstances more favorable to liberation than those of Laforet's spinsters or of Matute's, Soriano's women cannot transcend the emphasis on marriage fostered by their socialization, and even though they are less traditional in behavior, their lives are totally male-oriented, and are frustrated and unhappy as a result of the failure to achieve the goal of matrimony. Both may be considered completely monogamous, notwithstanding the absence of a wedding ceremony, and devote their lives to one man with a singlemindedness which totally contradicts their otherwise unconventional actions.

Carmen Martín Gaite presents a number of single women — widowed, divorced, unmarried — three belonging to the family of Natalia, central consciousness of several sections of *Entre visillos*.[10] Included are Natalia's older sisters, Julia and Mercedes, and tía Concha, who has raised the girls since the death of their mother. Concha is a stereotypical small-town spinster whose life is limited to home, occasional visits from middle-aged or elderly ladies, and attendance at Mass. Mercedes, well past thirty, without a suitor, and unwillingly destined for spinsterhood, has a budding martyr complex and frequent attacks of tears. Both she and Julia — whose life hinges upon obtaining paternal permission to live with a relative in Madrid in order to be near her *novio* — are thoroughly conventional, inhibited and unliberated. Less conventional at first glance is Rosa, the thirty-five-year-old *animadora* of the Casino, who supports herself as a songstress and therefore is ostracized by provincial society. Notwithstanding a measure of economic independence, smoking and drinking and inviting Pablo to her room, Rosa is also maternal, sentimental and quite conventional in what she wants from life: "Si tú ganaras cuatro mil pesetas y te casaras conmigo, verías como echaba raíces para toda la vida, y de cantar mambos, ni esto" (p. 106) (If you were earning 4,000 pesetas and would marry me, you'd see how I'd put down roots for life, and no more singing). An unusual note in Spain during the

---

[10] Barcelona: Destino, 1958. All quotations are from the first edition. The page number follows the quote. Translations are my own.

1950s was the woman separated from her husband, living alone, as is Yoni's sister, Teresa, who is described as frivolous, with "un escote exageradísimo y los ojos pintados con abéñula" (p. 155) (really exaggerated, low-cut dresses, and her eyes painted with kohl). Despite enjoying the provincial equivalent of *La dolce vita*, Teresa is economically dependent on her wealthy family, associates with only the upper class, and shows no independence or originality of thought. Martín Gaite's next treatment of this figure — the woman separated from her husband — is both more lengthy and more interesting, if ultimately still conventional.

The closest thing to a divorcee possible in Franco Spain, the legally separated woman, reappears in the person of Eulalia, one of the two narrative consciousnesses of *Retahílas*.[11] Although she is university-educated and was an adolescent rebel who studied abroad, lived in Paris and traveled widely, she has difficulty in learning to live alone after the break with her husband. She finds it almost impossible to go to a restaurant by herself: "me horrorizaba cenar sola" (p. 67) (it horrified me to dine alone). After a prolonged period of depression, scarcely sleeping, smoking and drinking heavily, disoriented and indecisive, she has reached a point where her doctor advises "que tenía que buscar un aliciente distinto de los habituales, que estaba como muerta y que la curación dependía nada más que de mí" (p. 68) (that I had to find some stimulus apart from the habitual ones, I was the same as dead, and the cure depended on me). Even though she had not been completely happy in her marriage (finding her husband a bit of a bore and taking trips alone), she clearly finds it difficult to be alone. Although their marriage had been mutually unsatisfactory, Eulalia is at a loss without an interlocutor: "me daba miedo estar callada, me ocurre ahora con frecuencia" (p. 75) (it frightened me not to talk, that happens to me frequently now). She impulsively makes dates with an old friend, then is worried at her own audacity, wondering what he will think of her: "todo el día intranquila, sin poder conciliar el sueño ni quitarme aquella desazón tonta, hasta que a mediodía tomé los tranquilizantes para no estar nerviosa cuando le viera" (p. 77) (restless all day, unable to sleep or free myself from that stupid worry, until noon when I took tranquilizers in order not to be nervous when I saw him). Like Soriano's protagonist in *La playa de los locos*, she is anguished by the vision of aging (cf. pp. 102, 107), by solitude, and by her inability to accept having been abandoned: "a Andrés le doy vueltas y aunque me desespere y me duela, no

---

[11] Barcelona: Destino, 1974. All quotations are from this edition. The page number follows the quote. Translations are my own.

me aburre, no me resigno a darlo por perdido ... claro que pienso, 'está perdido', pero me gustaría recobrarlo" (p. 133) (I keep thinking about Andres, and although he drives me up the wall and hurts me, he doesn't bore me, and I can't resign myself to losing him ... of course I think, 'he's gone,' but I'd like to get him back). As she herself realizes, her liberty is illusory while her trajectory is so influenced by the past: "Decidir romper amarras y ser libre vale de poco" (p. 135) (Just deciding to throw off your moorings and be free isn't worth too much). Liberty, she recognizes, is more than words, an attitude of proprietorship with respect to time. Somewhat like the anonymous yo of *La playa de los locos*, she may yet achieve a measure of liberation, as she is a woman of independent means. With the apparent benefit of psychiatric counseling (cf. pp. 186-87), but more because of coming to terms with life and with herself—"llevo más de un año haciendo revision de mis errores y aguantando a pie quieto la soledad ... me duele como los hijos que me negué a tener y que ahora desearía," (pp. 189-90) (for more than a year I've been going over my mistakes and putting up with solitude ... it hurts me like the children I refused to have and which now I'd like)—, Eulalia seems close to achieving existential authenticity. Whether this will include liberation in the feminist sense is less clear; to date, she has been unconventional, spoiled, and self-indulgent, or lonely, neurotic and self-pitying by turns, always with plenty of money and a minimum of responsibilities, having a good deal of what is often called freedom with no need either to confront the establishment openly or take a stand with respect to her own life. Although Martín Gaite portrays her with a sympathy which may reflect a portion of her own experience as a legally separated woman in Spain, she is far from idealizing or accepting Eulalia as she is. Eulalia has had everything and thrown it away, coming to appreciate it only when it is too late: husband, youth, love, potential motherhood, happiness, carefree existence. With a lonely old age before her, she is more vulnerable than before, and also more vulnerable to the judgements and values of male-dominated society. The reader conjectures that while still a youthful rebel, Eulalia would not have suffered while eating alone in a restaurant, and that her attitudes were less male-oriented in earlier years when she refused to have the children which now she misses. Unless she manages to transcend her futile longings for what she has lost, she will probably become even less liberated psychologically, as she is in the process of accepting a number of male-oriented norms which she previously rejected. This should not be construed as an anti-feminist statement by Martín Gaite, however, so much as a thoroughly realistic awareness that possessing youth and beauty and the possibility of choice with respect to husband and potential motherhood endowed Eulalia with defenses which time has taken away.

By contrast with the realism and relative objectivity of Martín Gaite's portrait of the "abandoned wife," *Cinco sombras en torno a un costurero* presents an idealized vision of five single women.[12] Three of them die without marrying, while a fourth, who marries at paternal behest, dies on her wedding day. In this lyrical, retrospective reconstruction, Eulalia Galvarriato traces the lives of the five daughters of a reclusive, tyrannical widower, who becomes more despotic and unreasonable with passing time. Alienated and solitary after his wife's death, he gives little attention or affection to the girls, showing interest only in his bird collection, and that but briefly. He opposes the daughters' going out, having friends, or marrying: "No quería que sus hijas se casaran. No daba razones; no quería, y bastaba" (p. 78) (he didn't want his daughters to marry. He didn't give reasons; he didn't want it, and that was enough). Even more unusual than this arbitrary exercise of patriarchal authority is the daughters' meek acceptance of it. Although virtually prisoners in their own home, none of the five ever questions the father's absolute right to control their lives. The eldest, María, dutifully breaks off the romance he opposes, although she continues to adore the man silently for the rest of her life and leaves all she has to his children. Although none dares oppose the father's autocratic power, with María's frustrated life as a precedent, the daughters unanimously unite to aid and abet the elopment and marriage of Isabel, the youngest and only one of the five who ever experiences life "on the outside." The remaining four quietly submit to the months of solitary confinement imposed by the father as punishment for their complicity in Isabel's escape, daring only to write each other occasional notes, delivered by the maid. Gabriela, Isabel's fragile twin, dies young, and the young wife does not long survive. The remaining three are well en route to spinsterhood when the father capriciously and quite unexpectedly decides to arrange a marriage for Rosario, his second daughter, who reacts with anguish because of her secret love for Diego (the novel's asexual narrator, and the family's only regular visitor). With the help of Laura, the younger sister who adores her and offers herself in her stead as bride, Rosario escapes the unwanted match, but never confesses her love for Diego: it is revealed by her diary following her death. Laura dies in a boating accident on her wedding day, leaving Rosario to wonder perpetually if Laura had married for

---

[12] Barcelona: Destino, 1947. Quotations are from the first edition. The page number follows the quote. Translations are my own.

love, or merely to save her sister. Self-torture because of her sense of guilt over Laura's untimely end precipitates Rosario's own death.

It would be difficult to imagine a less liberated family, and given the extreme circumstances, a skeletal summary, abstracted from the novel's lyrical language, nostalgic and melancholy atmosphere, its tender romantic sentiment, might suggest some attempted satire by Galvarriato of women's lack of freedom in Spanish society. In context, however, it is clear that this was not the novelist's intention. The fact that the narrative is retrospective (with most of the action between 1880 and 1920) helps to make slightly less incredible the girls' uncomplaining submission to patriarchal tyranny, as well as the extremely cloistered environment in which they are confined, polar opposites of "liberated" women. There is nothing of an unconventional or potentially "revolutionary" nature in the novel which would explain its being set several generations earlier as a means of avoiding possible censorship via the suggestion that any criticisms therein did not apply to the present. Although the novel is limited almost exclusively to the presentation of feminine characters, it presents — uncritically — a totally male-dominated world. In retrospect, it might be said that the most astounding thing about *Cinco sombras* is that there were no suggestions at the time of its appearance that it portrayed an exaggerated or unrealistic situation, and although it achieved a measure of popularity, no one criticized its portrayal of unquestioned patriarchal absolutism. Estelle Irizarry has correctly observed several similarities between *Cinco sombras* and the sentimental novel.[13] It is not sentimentalism alone — nor even the occasional, attenuated touches of melodrama — which most differentiates this portrait of single women from the others studied: it is the dulcification and idealization of the feminine figures, gentle, ethereal wraiths of almost angelic beauty, who acquire none of the caricaturesque traits of the old maid as they age, but fade instead as flowers. Indeed, they are drawn not from the spinster archetype, but from that of the virgin and martyr.

Portrayal of stereotypical spinsters usually presumes that the object of the portrait "failed" to snare a husband, for reasons related to her own defects or deficiencies, thereby reflecting the male-oriented value system and (perhaps unconsciously) the regime's emphasis upon marriage and the family as woman's whole reason for living. The difference in presentation of the girls in *Cinco sombras* may be due in part to the fact that they did not fail to

---

[13] "*Cinco sombras*, de Eulalia Galvarriato: Una novela singular de la postguerra," in *Novelistas femeninas de la postguerra española*, ed. Janet W. Pérez (Madrid: Porrua,. 1983), pp. 47-56.

attract men (María had received a proposal of marriage), but obediently sacrificed themselves to masculine will, thereby avoiding the stigma of stereotypical or caricaturesque spinsterhood. The five girls are all beautiful, and none have anything unpleasant about their personalities (even though their passive submissiveness may suggest to the present-day mentality that they were lacking in normal quantities of autonomy, maturity and healthy ego development). Neither the ludicrous dress of Laforet's old maids nor the extreme neuroses of Soriano's protagonists are suggested in any way, and in fact, positive idealization and stylization of Galvarriato's five "shadows" is so thorough and so extreme that no negative elements remain to form the basis of the balanced realism which characterizes most of that writer's short stories.

Two novels of Elena Quiroga provide three instances in which significant roles are played by single women, one a spinster, one an "abandoned wife," and the third the "other woman." In *Algo paso en la calle*, the novelist has essentially inverted the stereotypes of the long-suffering wife and the "other woman" with the former taking on a cluster of negative character traits and the latter becoming an extreme case of positive idealization."[14] Esperanza, the legal wife, is frigid, domineering, petty, vain, frivolous, hypocritical, shallow, and totally selfish. She is a female Don Juan who goes to the extreme of becoming her own daughter's rival, not only competing for the affections of the husband/father, but in carrying on a flirtation with Agata's fiance. Beautiful, wealthy, with attributes of the femme fatale, she apparently marries less out of love than to acquire an additional ornament. Abandonment by her husband, while a blow to her vanity, gives her greater freedom and allows her to surround herself with an aura of martyrdom much admired by her conventional women friends. By contrast, Presencia — who occupies what society designates as the place of the "other woman" usually a temptress of doubtful or no virtue — is modest, plain, quiet, self-effacing, patient, charitable, altruistic, honorable, self-sacrificing, prudent — a model of wifely and maternal values, despite the fact that her common-law marriage is viewed by society and the Church as concubinage. Physically, too, Presencia represents an inversion of the stereotypical temptress or adulteress, for she is almost childlike, lacking in all suggestion of sensuality, adornment and vanity. Her only attractions are intellectual and spiritual. Neither Esperanza nor Presencia qualify as "liberated" women, even though the former is economically independent and indulges in unrestricted flirtation, and the latter has defied convention as well as the legal establishment to live with the

---

[14] Barcelona: Destino, 1954.

man she loves. Both, however, are quite traditional in their attitudes and values. Esperanza is both inhibited by and a slave to public opinion, so that her flirtations do not exceed certain limits, and Presencia lacks only the blessing of the Church to render her marriage normal, conservative and even somewhat old-fashioned.

La enferma has as its protagonist an unmarried woman, past forty, ironically named Liberata, although she is in fact a prisoner of her own passions and possible madness, victim of a frustrated love and of the conventions of the village society in which she was raised.[15] While Liberata must be considered the protagonist, her role is comparable to that of the dead protagonist, Ventura, in *Algo pasa en la calle*, in that she neither moves nor speaks, and her motivations and personality must be reconstructed by other characters and the reader on the basis of sometimes contradictory evidence from the past. Liberata, who is clearly unbalanced emotionally, became enamored at an early age of Telmo, whose family considered her an unhealthy influence and sent him away (even the priest, a sympathizer of Liberata's, advised him to leave). Although they were engaged, Telmo subsequently married someone else; the news provoked an attack in Liberata, who first had to be tied to the bed and later confined for a time to a sanatorium. She never again spoke, and remained in bed for life, with her face turned to the wall. By this symbolic suicide, a death-in-life, Liberata avoided the unpleasant role of the jilted bride, irrevocably condemned to spinsterhood by conventions which made of the previously engaged female an unsuitable candidate for a wife. Liberata's only "freedom" consisted in turning her rage and frustration against herself, refusing to play the gently aging spinster and *beata* roles to which she would otherwise have been condemned. Although Liberata was reportedly beautiful (a deviation from the stereotypical old maid), this positive attribute was counter-balanced by her negative psychological make-up, which both provoked her abandonment and dictated her peculiar manner of dealing with it.

By contrast with the portraits of single women examined heretofore, none of whom could be said to be happy with the unmarried state (with the possible exception of Teresa in *Entre visillos*, a minor character whose presentation is too sketchy to permit a judgment), Lena Rivero in Dolores Medio's *El pez sigue flotando* is quite well-adjusted to her slightly bohemian existence with her attic room in Madrid.[16] Lena occupies a somewhat

---

[15] Barcelona: Destino, 1955.
[16] Barcelona: Destino, 1959. Quotations are from the first edition. These and

marginal position in society, taking full advantage of the freedom which her existence as a budding writer affords her. She comes and goes as she pleases, accountable to no one, and although most of her activities are quite innocent, her enjoyment of them is uninhibited. She works, reads, sleeps, or goes out in response to her mood of the moment: "Una alegría infantil, como un retozo, le recorre el cuerpo al pisar la nieve. La pisa con deleite, sintiéndola crujir bajo sus botas" (p. 79) (A childish glee runs through her body like a thrill upon treading the snow. She stomps it with delight, feeling it crunch beneath her boots). Her independence and determination are evident in her having arrived in Madrid without a cent, with nothing but her dreams and an old suitcase filled with family keepsakes (pp. 136-37). She also defies convention by smoking, at a moment in Spanish history when this was not acceptable behavior for women. She harbors some unconventional ideas about social reform (cf. pp. 142-43), as well as occasionally permitting herself to behave in manners which social norms define as inappropriate for her age: she slides down the banister, and sticks out her tongue at the neighbors (p. 144); she walks in the rain, "metiéndose en los charcos, chapoteando, jugando con el agua" (p. 243) (getting into puddles, splashing around, playing with the water); "persigue con el pie la tapa de una botella de cerveza y se entretiene viéndola rodar" (p. 245) (she kicks a beerbottle top and enjoys watching it roll around). Her spontaneous transgressions of the norms of propriety are affirmations of her freedom, symptoms of an independent attitude toward convention which is evidenced in her initiation of a love affair with the sculptor she meets at a Christmas party, a decision in which no considerations of morality or of marriage are introduced. Lena may fall short of total "liberation," but she is economically and psychologically independent, autonomous, unconventional, and quite happy with her existence.

Two other unmarried women in this novel are worthy of mention, for their situations show that Medio does not idealize the unmarried state per se; their struggle to support themselves is unrewarding, and their emotions are frequently in conflict. Marta Ribe, a poor typist who works long hours to support herself and her old servant Tata, is obliged to work at home and care for the invalid maid. She longs for independence, torn between her affection for the old woman and guilt at her awareness that Tata's death would mean release. Annoyance alternates with repentance, her sense of duty conflicting with her need for self-fulfillment and her desire to be more self-indulgent. Guilt prevents Marta's enjoyment of her independence when it does come at

---

other references are indicated by the page number. Translations are my own.

last, with Tata's death. The other single woman, Veva Martínez, a dime-a-dance girl, is repulsed by the sordidness of her job and the offers from men who wish to make her their mistress. Gratuitously, she gives herself to a young student because she senses in him a purity and innocence which help to restore her own tarnished sense of merit. Because Veva is driven by emotions which she does not understand and hence does not control, this is not a "liberated" act, and nothing indicates how she will be affected by it in the future. It is clear, however, that Veva's values are male-dominated, and she needs the symbolic act of giving herself to a pure male (and thereby sharing in that purity) to cleanse herself of the sense of unworthiness which other males' treatment of her has caused.

Irene Gal, the protagonist of *Diario de una maestra*, shares a number of traits with the nameless *yo* of *La playa de los locos*.[17] Both are university-trained educators who begin their professional careers shortly before the outbreak of the Civil War, and the love affairs of both are interrupted by the conflict. But Irene is a much stronger, more straightforward, healthy and progressive character. Her independence and unconventional attitude are evidenced by her innovative teaching methods, introduced in the village school in La Estrada, even though departures from traditional methodology meet with distrust. Irene ascribes philosophically to a doctrine of love and good will, put into operation on an individual level with her students and later, in her work in a Nationalist hospital during the war. She faithfully lives up to this philosophy, also, in her commitment to her teacher and lover, Máximo Sáenz. Unable to find work after the war because of her liberal affiliations, Irene shows her determination to survive and her lack of prejudices by going into domestic service until it becomes possible for her to return to the village, where she divides her life between helping children, the poor and needy, and waiting for Max's release from jail. But while Irene has been strenghthened by adversity and her basic attitudes reaffirmed, Max is broken and disillusioned by his imprisonment. He abruptly terminates their affair, proclaiming his right to live only for himself (p. 223). On the verge of suicide after this abandonment, Irene is stopped at the edge of the abyss by the voice of a paralytic child she has been helping. Her idealism prevails, and she returns to devote herself to the villagers. This is a significant change, because although she was independent and progressive, economically self-sufficient and able to overcome certain prejudices and conventions, Irene to this point

---

[17] Barcelona: Destino, 1961. References are to this edition and are indicated by the page number.

had nonetheless been completely male-oriented, living for Max's return. Her decision to continue living, living for her work and for others, is based upon a recognition of a certain self-worth, the knowledge that the villagers need her and that she can help them. Although her dedication of her life to this altruistic endeavor may in fact be the modern lay equivalent of becoming a nun, neither she nor the society in which she lives makes that connection. In finding another meaning for her life and rejecting the conventional melodramatic solution, Irene shows not only commitment to her ideals, but demonstrates that she is strong, mature and disciplined.

In analyzing Irene and Lena, who are the most original, autonomous and unconventional of the single women whose portraits have been examined, it is impossible to overlook their resemblance to their creator. They share a number of similarities with the novelist, similarities of age, family and geographical background, education and profession (Medio was a teacher before becoming a writer). While definitely not all details of their respective histories are autobiographical, some additional elements are drawn from Medio's own experience.[18] Whether or not Lena and Irene are viewed as masks or alter egos of the novelist, it is important that Medio knows from personal experience that women can be self-supporting, autonomous, and wholly devoted to a profession (she is the only one of the women writers studied here who has never married, although others have experienced "single" life via separation from their husbands). Perhaps it is not surprising, then, that Medio's protagonists are able to succeed on their own, alone, in a male-dominated world. At the same time, however, she is not tempted to generalize or to exaggerate, for she does not portray the independent, successful woman as something other than an exception in Spain during the Franco years, nor does she present extremes of "liberated" behavior. Her protagonists believe in love and commitment, and although they accept a premarital sexual relationship, only one relationship is shown for each. This may be seen either as a vestige of the values (fidelity, chastity) imposed on women by their male-oriented upbringing, or a reflection of their own idealism, which has to some extent been formed by the same upbringing. Although Medio's protagonists are exceptional in being the only single women who accept the unmarried state and do not consider matrimony or

---

[18] Margaret E.W.. Jones, *Dolores Medio* (New York: Twayne Publishers, 1974), observes for example that "Miss Medio has answered the charge of inconsistency of character by stating that Max comes directly from an important episode in her own life" (p. 101).

motherhood necessary to their personal contentment and fulfillment, they are unconventional only to a mild degree, especially when compared with those portrayed in works written in the post-Franco era.

A completely balanced view of each novelist's concept of woman's situation in Spain at the time of writing is not obtainable from their portraits of single women only, without reference to depiction of the married (or widowed) counterparts. Although such comparison is beyond the limits of this essay, it is worth noting that happy marriages are almost as rare as the happy single woman. Laforet and Matute usually concentrate upon adolescent protagonists, so that when married women appear, they are secondary characters, often little more than shadows. In a majority of Matute's novels, the child or adolescent is an orphan, with the mother having died before or shortly after the beginning of the action. Soriano's other novel presents a frustrated marriage, without communication or real love, held together by convention and inertia as well as the stigma attached to divorce.[19] Martín Gaite in *El balneario* presents a Kafkaesque view of the marital relationship, where the husband's arbitrariness and the absence of any real communication compound the wife's existential solitude to a pathological extreme. Other examples of negative depiction of marriage might be adduced, but the point to be made is that women's lot is not presented as a happy one by most of them, quite independently of the issue of marriage or spinsterhood.

Since Medio happens to be the only one of the novelists examined here who nas never married, the critic cannot avoid the question as to how decisive marriage and related experiences may be in forming the writer's image of the single woman. It should be noted, however, that personal experience or autobiographical input, however significant, are not the only factors involved, for Medio has produced very convincing portraits of married women in *Funcionario público* and Bibiana, to cite only two instances. Medio's single women are the best-rounded and most individualized, not only the best adjusted or most successful. Excepting Galvarriato, whose idealized portraits stand apart, the remainder of these novelists — Laforet, Matute, Soriano, Martín Gaite, Quiroga — render portraits wherein the single woman is flawed in one or more significant ways, most often exhibiting traits of the stereotypical old maid, and at the negative extreme, is little more than a caricature: ludicrous, frustrated, benighted. The margination and

---

[19] The novelist stated privately in an interview many years ago with the present author that the resumption of marriage at the end of *Espejismos* was "monstruoso," inasmuch as it results not from love or commitment but cowardice and self-deception.

ridicule to which the unmarried woman has historically been subjected in any number of societies is thus reproduced, perhaps unconsciously, on the literary level.

Self-Discovery in Quiroga's *Presente Profundo*

Carolyn Galerstein

Elena Quiroga's most recent novel, *Presente profundo* (1973) has been highly praised for its complex structure and manipulation of time[1] and the evocation of the loneliness and alienation of the two main female characters. While Phyllis Zatlin views these women as responding "to their isolation by embarking on a path of self-destruction,"[2] I believe that their recent pasts may be interpreted as a path toward self-discovery and that their suicides represent the culmination, not of existential anguish, but of fulfillment of existential awareness. Moreover, this self-discovery is attained within a specifically feminine context because of the strictures which traditional Spanish society has placed upon women.

The suicide of Daría occurs at the beginning of the novel and sets the stage for the probing of the two women's psyches, as reflected through the attitudes of the male doctor-narrator, Rubén. Although the village priest is convinced that Daría was temporarily insane and thus entitled to burial within the Church, her death may be interpreted as the one deliberate rational act of her life.

Daría's first act in the novel is to wave away the sound of her son's voice, as if to resist any distraction on this last-minute voyage of self-discovery. This ride in Eugenio's truck is symbolically the trip to an awareness of the nothingness that her life has been and an understanding of her own being. As

---

[1] See: Martha Alford Marks, "Time in the Novels of Elena Quiroga," *Hispania*, 64, No. 3 (September 1981), pp. 376-81.
[2] Phyllis Zatlin Boring, *Elena Quiroga* (Boston: Twayne, 1977), p. 113.

if a sticky film were being removed from her eyes, Daría sees her own hands, and for the first time those hands have meaning for her. They are the hands of a woman who has worked hard all her life, rearing children and serving as the mainstay of the family bakery business. Daría's hands give the impression that she is shedding her skin, and now she can view what goes on beneath the surface. Within this introduction of Daría there is a reference to a "pozo profundo"[3], a deep well that is herself, until now unfathomed. Only now, in late middle age, her children grown, her husband's affections detoured to a younger woman, can she discover herself and "se descorta," — cuts herself away from the woman she has appeared to be to herself and others. (9)

Daría has lately felt detached; her body weighs nothing; everything happening to her is taking place outside her. But now, in this moment of self-recognition, "nada es si no es ella" (nothing exists if it is not she) (11). For the first time she is aware of herself. After a life of menial household tasks performed routinely, she for one moment "vive la unidad suya" (lives her own unity) (11). She has unified body and spirit, and in a flash of self-understanding, she possesses herself. Thus she is able to stride, deliberately, with firm steps, toward the precise spot on the shore where she takes off her jacket, and walks into the sea. By intentionally placing her jacket on a rock for all to see and realize what she has done, Daría has made her statement. Although aware of the willful nature of Daría's act, the reader never has the opportunity to know Daría directly. There is only the one brief direct glimpse of her as she walks along the shore and then carefully folds her jacket. Relieved of the jacket, it is as if she is free of all the constraints of society., "como si el cuerpo no pesara nada" (as if her body weighed nothing) (15). Free of corporeal weight, she is at liberty to walk into the water., weightless, bodyless, for a brief fraction of a second, "se posee" (she possesses herself) (15). In possession of herself, she has discovered her being.

The examination of her life and analysis of her psyche provided to the reader is filtered twice. An understanding of Daría is transmitted through Rubén, the doctor, who comments upon her death. But Rubén never knew Daría, and thus can only surmise certain things about her character and her life by filtering what he learns about her through her husband, her children, her daughter-in-law, and a woman friend, Soledad. We learn that Daría was self-sacrificing, yet from the age of 14 when her father sold her sexual ser-

---

[3] Elena Quiroga, *Presente Profundo* (Barcelona: Destino, 1973), p. 9. All subsequent references to this work will be indicated by the page number in parentheses in the text. All English translations of quotations are mine.

vices to an older married man, Daría felt used by the male-dominated society. Although Daría behaved in a way that was accepted by her provincial Galician society, she was isolated from that society by her unspoken longing to understand herself and bring some enrichment to her life. Within her society there was no life for her other than her husband and children, and she was a tireless worker. Husband, work and children form the parameters of Daría's life. According to Soledad, Daría wanted to continue living "entera" (a full life) (72), but it seems that the only way she could have a full life was to work. Work represents the friend's traditional view of what life consists for a woman. Even Daría's work is maternal; she bakes bread to feed the town as a mother nurtures her children. The warm oven of the bakery symbolizes a womb, issuing forth the staff of life as the woman issues forth life itself.

Daría had been ill and growing thin before her suicide. This loss of weight may be interpreted as symbolic of her loss of being. Or it may be that she is discovering a being within herself, an existence which will first displace, then destroy, then replace the body, the substance by which she is known in the community. Soledad has her own diagnosis: "... parecía que se le iba el alma" (p. 73) (it seemed as if she were losing her soul). Soledad does not intend the word "soul" in the religious sense, but means metaphorically that Daría was dying, thus "losing" her body. On the contrary, she may have been finding her soul, discovering a substance different from the sort her family and community view her as possessing.

It would not occur to Soledad, nor to the doctor who listens to her, that a woman could have an interior life, that she could transcend the work and the family and discover meaning within her own self. The doctor must also filter the analysis of Daría's existence contained in the comments made by her husband, Serafín. Serafín is ashamed over her suicide, seeing the act as something she did *to him*; he misses her labor much more than he misses her. He claims he did not leave her bed for another woman but that he was forced out, that she had been the first to draw away. It is evident that Daría drew away from him because there was nothing there for her to respond to, not because she was "dry," as he claims.

Daría leaves an unintended legacy; her daughter-in-law Amelia has begun to emulate Daría after her death. The more learned, refined Amelia now wants to work in the bakery like Daria, and she wants to have children so that the cycle of women and children will not be broken. With these desires she accepts the standard expectations of her society, and reinforces what Zatlin calls "Amelia's existence as a repetition of Daría's."[4] However, Amelia has also taken on a whole new existence as the incarnation of Daría's new self. The reader may assume that if Daría learned anything in life it was that meaning can be found only in one's existence, not in that of one's children. Amelia does not yet consciously understand this. Society — and most emphatically her husband, who may be sterile — expects that she will have children, that is her role in the society. It will take another conscious act of self-discovery for her to utilize Daría's legacy to go beyond those societal limitations.

At the end of the novel Amelia sees a shadow in the doorway, and this shadow can only be Daría, whose seemingly pointless life will be repeated in Amelia, unless the next deliberate step is taken. However, if Daría's life was pointless, her death is not, even though her family and the town cannot understand her action. It is only in death that she is able to exercise her will purposefully; it is only by destroying her physical life that she can give her life form and substance.

Blanca, the other suicide of the novel, is the other side of the same coin. She and Daría represent two different milieus, but one common problem: detachment from their society.

As Rubén reflects on his affair with Blanca, he refers repeatedly to her lassitude, her "agotamiento de la vida," (p. 16) (exhaustion with life), her horror of *la nada*. While the text may imply that nothingness is within Blanca, it seems more likely that the emptiness is within Spanish society itself. Rubén comments on her instability and emotionalism and her lack of adaptation, but it is her inability to adapt to what society expects of her as a woman that causes her withdrawal into a world of drugs.

Languid Blanca spends most of her time in bed, or languishing on a couch. She rarely goes out, except to a discoteque or some other place which symbolizes her superficial life, with its constant seeking of sensation. But since she claims this life is very boring, she opts for inactivity most of the time. She escapes into alcohol, which she maintains liberates her, although she does not say from what. She evidently wants to be free of society and the expectations society has of her as a wife and mother, responsibilities she has decided to abandon. Rubén claims that she is seeking "libertad *de sí* misma" (italics mine) (p. 52). This idea of freedom *from* herself would imply that she does not like herself, that she does not like the life of "libertad sin cortapisas"

---

[4] Zatlin, p. 112.

(p. 48) (freedom without conditions) which she has chosen. But if she does not like rebellion, she likes traditional attitudes even less.

The often-solitary Blanca must be contrasted with Daría, who was constantly surrounded by family. But neither solitude nor family can give these women identity. If Blanca seeks an existential silence, as if wanting to lose herself in a desert, this is equal to the irritation Daría feels on hearing her son's voice shortly before she leaves his truck to walk into the sea.

Although Blanca carries a picture of her abandoned son, he forms no part of her life, and he rejects her efforts to bring him back to her world. She exchanges lovers with easy abandon, and her alienation is emphasized by the fact that she even dances best alone. Since other people barely exist for her, she seems narcissistic; but it is the kind of narcissism which forces one to look inside oneself. How can Rubén, although he is smitten with her, have any idea what goes on inside her? How can traditional society, which Rubén represents, understand how a woman wishes to have more in her life than the society's norms have to offer? Quiroga's depiction of a seemingly vacuous woman may be interpreted not as a condemnation of the woman, but of the society which represents that emptiness which Blanca fears. If Blanca fears that she will "desintegrarse en la nada" (p. 52) (disintegrate into nothingness), then the only way to avoid such disintegration is suicide, an escape from a life of intrinsically unimportant conventions, whether they are those of traditional Spanish society or of its opposite, the cosmopolitan, affluent, free-spending, alcohol and drug-imbibing society to which Blanca belongs.

Rubén considers the maid-companion Sabina to be Blanca's only link with reality. But, for Rubén, reality is only external. He does not comprehend that Blanca has the right to a reality of her own. He considers her alienated from society, but believes she has wanted to get out of herself (the self imposed by society), and escape her own bonds, rather than escape society's bonds and find reality within herself. Rubén often refers to her as "huyendo de sí misma" (p. 78) (fleeing from herself), unaware that she may be fleeing to the refuge of her inner self.

Psychoanalysis was horrible for Blanca, evidently because she did not want to find out what was hidden in her psyche. Given the standard attitudes of psychoanalysis at the time toward non-conformist women, it is understandable that a woman would not want to discover those feelings and desires of which society — and the psychoanalyst — disapproved.

Blanca conceives of her own being in plastic terms. When she rejects the bust of her made by a sculptor friend, she says, "Te quedas tú con él, un poco de mí misma" (p. 113) (You keep it, a little piece of me). Once again, this is because that is how society has taught women to view themselves, as things, as possessions. Quiroga refers to Daría as "un ser cosificado" (p. 18) (a thingified being) because that is what her husband and children have made of her. The same term could apply to Blanca as she, in some ways, parodies the "thingification" of women by society by surrounding herself with objects and lounging listlessly, uselessly on her divan.

Pondering their lives and their deaths, Rubén cannot "concretize" the two women, because for him they have no real meaning. He speaks of their self-destruction and their denial of life, but it would seem that the only way these women can become real and develop an identity is by destroying the one they have, the one society has created for them and forced upon them. By denying social conventions, Blanca is affirming herself. Refusing to comform to the norms of the Spanish society in which she is living, Blanca has adopted another set of conventions, those of her "Hippie" set, but they do not bring her satisfaction either. Her death is not a result but a rejection of that culture.

Rubén wonders more than once whether Blanca's death could not have been an accident, although he realizes that "su muerte era la vida" (p. 146) (her death was life). Death was growing in her; however, this growth of death could be interpreted as a retreat into the self. As that self-understanding developed, it had to carry itself forward to its ultimate end. One might say that Blanca died of death.

In counterpoint, Quiroga claims that Daría "se murió de la vida" (p. 132) (died of life). Neither woman could tolerate the life into which she was thrust — Daría, the demanding life of Galician country people, Blanca, the conventional society of her husbands and parents and the new clichés of the drug culture of the 1960s.

Quiroga's development of the women characters only hints at this process. Rubén recounts no act of self-discovery on the part of Blanca. He refers to her as "un ser aparte" (p. 22) (a being apart), segregated from authentic humanity because of her money. Blanca's body is not real either; he first sees her in the hospital where she has been brought after her first suicide attempt, and the memory of "el bulto de su cuerpo exánime bajo la sábana" (p. 22) (the bulk of her lifeless body under the sheet) remains with him. The lifeless body is also a spiritless one. Rubén also says that Blanca "no tenía morada" (p. 81) (she had no home), implying not only that she had no physical home, but that she had no body as well, no home for her spirit.

Blanca's legacy is a curious one. She is remembered by the men who loved her. But one has already married a conventional woman; Rubén has removed himself to a remote corner of Galicia, where he is more attentive to lab samples than people; her last lover has travelled to seek out an Indian guru. In what appears to be a perversion of Blanca's own personal ideals, Sabina wants to marry and have children.

Marriage and childbearing still represent women's fate and only recourse. Yet, Blanca suffered for having a child; Daría's children brought her no joy. Rubén sees Blanca's nonconformity as a threat to his manhood, and the predominant view the reader has of Blanca is only through his conventional eyes. Only when Sabina speaks of Blanca and Soledad speaks of Daría do we see these women through the eyes of another woman. Even though she is unconventional in the sense that she has never married, Soledad's attitudes represent the restrictive society which conceives of women only in terms of husband and children, not in terms of what women can be as individuals.

Throughout the novel both Daría and Blanca are presented as bodiless, weightless, floating through life. They must create a person out of the spirit, and in so doing, deny the body by drowning it. For just as surely as Daría walks into the water, Blanca also drowns herself by sinking into the deep pool of alcohol and drugs, submerging herself in "la nada" (p. 78).[5]

Daría wanted to live "la vida entera", but her notion of a full life would undoubtedly be the antithesis of Blanca's quest for sensation. With all their seeming contradictions, their contrasting environments and lifestyles, Daría and Blanca are one and the same. Both are only on the margins of their worlds, and this remoteness leads to self-understanding.

Why then does Quiroga put them at a distance from the reader? Why are they viewed through Rubén's conventional eyes; and in the case of Daría, observed second-hand because he never knew her? Perhaps Quiroga dared not get too close. The rural Galicia she knows so well and treats so effectively in other novels is also filtered through the eyes of a foreigner. The drug culture of the cosmopolitan set is not presented convincingly, as the

---

[5] To accent the metaphor of drowning, water images abound in the novel. Daría sees that her hands are made of flesh, blood and water. As she walks to her watery grave, her hair is wet, her lips salted with sea spray. The people of Daría's town live by the water; they search for her in the sea and examine the damage done by the water to the body. Serafín returns immediately to his mistress after Daría's death because "la primera noche la cama estaba como mojada" (the first night the bed seemed wet) (p. 108). Everything is humid in this town, where it rains a great deal.

outsider Rubén, never comfortable while dragged through that milieu by Blanca, interprets it for the reader.

Perhaps Quiroga selected this method of distancing her characters in order to conceal the true horror of examining the psychic tortures these women must have experienced. However, Quiroga does make it clear that by abandoning life, they affirm their selves. Because of their determination to escape the imposed world, their deaths may be viewed, not as a denial of life but as the discovery of an identity which makes the rejection of social formulas possible.

The Challenge of Martín Gaite's Woman Hero

Joan Lipman Brown

A glance at almost any compendium of analyses of so-called "major works of modern Spanish literature" reveals that those novels deemed "most significant" in the eyes of literary critics and historians have been those which chronicle men's, rather than women's, lives.[1] Literary testimony of Spanish life has concentrated overwhelmingly on the experience of Spanish males. Yet despite having been relegated to the sidelines, or (at best) included as exceptions among the male elite, there exists a cadre of female writers writing about the lives of women. Among this group are those who may now, in view of their recently expanding younger ranks, be considered the "old

---

* Portions of this essay were included in a paper entitled "Woman and Social Change in the Fiction of Carmen Martín Gaite," presented at the 1981 Modern Language Association in the Division of Twentieth Century Spanish Literature's session entitled "Women Critics Consider Contemporary Women Novelists in Spain," December 29, 1981, New York, New York.

[1] Statistics compiled by Janet Peréz confirm the neglect of Spanish women writers, and by extension their frequently female subjects, which is suggested by the perusal of indices of authors included in virtually any of the major "histories of modern Spanish literature." She notes that "a ... review of five major periodicals for Hispanists ... over a ten-year period turned up only twenty-six articles on Spanish women writers. Of 215 Twentieth Century Spaniards covered in the second edition of the *Columbia Dictionary of Modern Europeran Writers* (1980), only nine are women, while the Revista de Occidente *Diccionario de Literatura Española* (4th ed., 1972) included only thirty women among more than 550 Twentieth Century authors, or 1.8%." See Janet Peréz, "Some Desiderata in Studies of Twentieth Century Spanish Fiction," *Siglo Veinte/Twentieth Century*, 1, no. 2 (Spring 1984), pp. 4-6.

guard" of Spanish women writers. These authors, including Matute, Laforet, Quiroga, Martín Gaite, Medio and Moix, are the subject of increasing attention, both for the qualities of their texts and for the information they offer regarding the situation of women in postwar Spain. The claim that critic Patricia Spacks has made for eighteenth-century English women writers is equally valid for postwar twentieth-century Spanish women writers: they "help to define what it means to perceive works of imaginative literature partly as social documents."[2] Through the lives of these writers' women characters, the situation of all similar women in a particular historical context is revealed and recorded.

With regard to women writers in modern Spain, one in particular — Carmen Martín Gaite — offers an unparalleled source for learning about the changing lives of women. Carmen Martín Gaite is the only woman author from among the "old guard" who has continued to chronicle the changing realities of Spanish women from the Civil War to the present day. Because of Martín Gaite's longitudinal perspective, an overview of representative female heroes in her novels yields a rich understanding of the changing lives and self-perceptions of women in postwar Spain. Although the female main characters that populate Martín Gaite's novels *Entre visillos* (1958), *Retahílas* (1974), *Fragmentos de interior* (1976) and *El cuarto de atrás* (1978) have been studied individually, their evolutionary depiction of women's lives has not yet been traced.[3] The goal of this study is to examine the lives of women characters in these novels, in order to more fully understand the changing circumstances of women in Spain, as perceived by this premiere writer. As shall become apparent, each of Martín Gaite's woman heroes carries out a personal challenge to achieve success as a creative, intelligent individual. Society, as much as or even more than the woman herself, determines whether or not her goal may be achieved, and also dictates the measure of personal cost exacted for her achievement. In this way the degree of success achieved by the woman hero reveals the changing social climate for women which has been felt in Spain over the past three decades.

Martín Gaite's first full-length novel, *Entre visillos*(1958; Premio Nadal of the same year) has been noted since its appearance for its immersion in the details of women's lives, and especially the lives they lead inside their

---

[2] Patricia Meyer Spacks, *Imagining a Self: Autobiography and Novel in Eighteenth-Century England* (Cambridge, Mass. and London: Harvard University Press, 1976), p. 90.

[3] Joan Lipman Brown, *Secrets From the Back Room: The Fiction of Carmen Martín Gaite* (University, MS: Romance Monographs, 1985).

homes.[4] The novel offers a detailed portrait of a provincial town, the unnamed but recognizable Salamanca of the author's youth, during the course of a six-month visit by a young male schoolteacher. The novel is structured with alternating omniscient chapters and first-person chapters by the teacher Pablo Klein, interrupted by two inserted diary entries by the other main character, the schoolgirl Natalia Ruiz Guilarte. Together, these distinct but objective observers report on the society of the town, focusing on the circumstances of its female protagonists.

Enormous courage was shown by the author, writing near the inception of her career in the late 1950s, in choosing a predominantly feminine focus for her first full-length novel. To do so was to take a very real risk of being dismissed by the critical elite. In *Entre visillos*, Martín Gaite provides the backdrop against which the challenges of all of her future women heroes may be understood. With this novel Martín Gaite shed light on what Virginia Woolf termed "the feelings of women in drawing rooms," in this case the feelings of the majority of women in Spanish drawing rooms in the 1950s. She showed how these feelings could indeed be significant, when observed in aggregate as one inexorably standardized pattern. The overwhelming majority of the women in *Entre visillos* accede to the traditional role definitions which lock them into inevitable self-abnegation; the role that Sandra Gilbert and Susan Gubar see as the sole option of a patriarchal society, in which "women exist only to be acted on by men."[5] The young hero Natalia's older sisters and their friends personify this status. Lacking any means of self-actualization, they seem indistinguishable from one another. Nowhere is this more apparent than in their superficial conversations, which are so trivial that they seem to bore even the participants, leading them to skip from one shallow thought to another.

Of all the characters in the novel, only Natalia shows promise of formulating and expressing her own ambitions: among the many women who populate *Entre visillos*, only she aspires to what Carolyn Heilbrun has termed a "quest" plot in her life.[6] Natalia's challenge takes the form of rebellion

---

[4] Carmen Martín Gaite, *Entre visillos* (Barcelona: Destino, 7th ed., 1978). All quotations are from this edition and the page number follows the quote. All translations from the author's novels are my own, unless otherwise noted.

[5] Sandra M. Gilbert and Susan Gubar, *The Madwoman in the Attic: The Woman Writer and the Nineteenth-Century Literary Imagination* (New Haven and London: Yale University Press, 1979), p. 8.

[6] Carolyn G. Heilbrun, "Discovering the Lost Lives of Women," *The New York Times Book Review*, June 24, 1984, pp. 1, 26 and 27. The term is introduced on page 27.

against the trivialities of the circumscribed lives of her sisters. She resists the restrictions which she senses both psychologically and even, through metaphors of asphyxiation, physically. "Si tengo que ser una mujer resignada y razonable," she informs her father, "prefiero no vivir" (p. 233) (If I have to be a selfless and sensible woman, I'd rather not live at all). Her nonconformity is such that academic studies engross and exhilarate her, while inane social intercourse baffles and bores her. However, at the novel's close, it is not clear what form her challenge will take. Success remains uncertain in the rigidly ordered society of the provinces of Spain in the 1950s.

Martín Gaite's next full-length novel to include a female main character is *Retahílas* (1974).[7] The novel records a night-long conversation between a woman and a man. *Retahílas* chronicles the interlocking monologues of Eulalia, a cultivated and successful woman in her forties, and Germán, her nephew, a young man in his twenties. They have come together on impulse, to spend the long night keeping a death vigil for Eulalia's grandmother. Alone except for the grandmother's caretaker, in the decaying old house in Galicia where Eulalia and the young man's father, her brother, grew up, the two conversational partners speak in long torrents throughout the night. Their conversation ends with the grandmother's death at dawn.

The central focus of this extended discourse is the figure of Eulalia; she is the novel's hero, the axis around which *Retahílas* revolves. She is unquestionably the most intimately-known of any of Martín Gaite's fictional women characters. In Eulalia, the author creates a protagonist whose resolution of her challenge to society might well be what young Natalia of *Entre visillos* would have dreamed for herself: Eulalia is an independent woman, successful, well educated, strong and free. However, through both choice and circumstance, she has been kept apart from emotional commitments which she now feels would bring happiness.

The "quest" or personal adventure plot was elected and fulfilled by Eulalia, in spite of keenly-perceived social obstacles to success. From a young age, she possessed a sharp sense of her own uniqueness. In adolescence she came up against the notion of comformity, and the social definitions of a woman's traditional role, which she resisted. Any social contracts, including marriage, were rejected, since she felt they compromised her goals (p. 108). As Eulalia matured, her resistance increased:

---

[7] Carmen Martín Gaite, *Retahílas* (Barcelona: Destino, 1974). All references are to this edition. The page number follows the quote.

Pasaba entonces por una etapa de feminismo furibundo y estaba orgullosa de mi excepcionalidad y mi rebeldía frente a la postura acomodaticia de las otras chicas de aquel tiempo que solo pensaban en ser como sus madres y no tenían interés por nada. (p. 145)
(In those days I was going through a phase of vehement feminism. I was proud of being an exception, of being a rebel com-pared to the rest of the girls in my day, who were very eager to please. Their one goal was to be like their mothers; they had no outside interests.)

Eulalia found a man who valued her as a person, and they built a marriage based on mutual respect. Now, however, she is separated from him, and mourns her loss deeply. Regret over the failure of her marriage is accompanied by regret over never having had a child. Eulalia's most serious commitment to feminism was her view that motherhood and self-expression were mutually exclusive: in Spain, she recalls having told Germán's mother Lucía, a woman can be either a mother or a person (p. 145). Now, however, after decades have elapsed, Eulalia regrets the absence of commitments which she feels might bring her happiness.

Counterposed against Eulalia is the figure of her nephew's dead mother, Lucía, who selected the opposite route from Eulalia. Bright and talented, she chose to be a traditional wife and mother, rather than pursue a career. Now Lucía assumes near-mythic proportions in Eulalia's memory, abetted by Germán's voracious curiosity about his mother. Lucía's apparent happiness may or may not have been a result of the path she chose in life, and the same is true of Eulalia. What reappears in the depiction of women's lives in *Retahílas* is Martín Gaite's unflinching honesty: "living happily ever after" does not necessarily follow liberation. For a Spanish woman of Eulalia's generation, the choices implicit in following one's own ambition clearly demand some measure of personal discipline; in the case of Eulalia, however, the sacrifices she thought necessary may have been overestimated in her youthful commitment to feminism.

At forty-five, Eulalia's age is now becoming a source of increasing bitterness. She is acutely aware of her physical deterioration, despite the fact that she looks much younger than her true age, thanks to the "cuidados, ... gimnasia y dinero" (p. 107) (treatments, workouts and money), available to privileged women. Eulalia asserts that any physical decay begins to matter only when it is defined as important: "Son como las arrugas de la cara las grietas de una casa, que existen cuando empiezan a importar" (p. 45)

(Cracks in a house are like wrinkles in a face: they exist only when they begin to matter). And yet, the novel's Epilogue ends with the bright light of a lamp calling Eulalia's bluff, revealing her true age, and breaking the magical spell of the evening.

In Martín Gaite's first depiction of the predicament of female aging, she joins with women writers across centuries and cultures who share what Patricia Spacks calls a "fundamental unity of perception" with regard to a woman's loss of youth.[8] In England and the United States, no less than in Spain, women writers "in their denials and affirmations, reveal the crucial importance of physical attractiveness in feminine psychology. They suggest the necessity for finding defenses against the loss of attractiveness which means a loss of a woman's most obvious power."[9] While this theme surfaces in *Retahílas*, it is developed even more fully in the author's subsequent novel, which contains the oldest fictional protagonist as well as the most avant-garde social milieu of any of Martín Gaite's novels.

Martín Gaite's fourth novel, *Fragmentos de interior*, offers a panoramic view of the actions (rather than the mental deliberations) of a diverse cast of characters.[10] In sixteen objectively-narrated episodes, the novel traces three days in the life of a fragmented, well-to-do family in Madrid. The members of the Alvar family include Diego, the middle-aged husband who is a failed novelist; Isabel, his estranged wife, a poet; Gloria, Diego's thirty-year-old live-in mistress; and Isabel and Jaime, the Alvar's two nearly-grown children. Just a review of this disjointed family situation indicates the enormous social changes that have occurred since the decade of *Entre visillos*. In the Madrid of the late 70s, custom has given way to casualness as the reigning mode of social behavior, influencing both the "older generation" and its adult children.

The women who populate this fast-paced adventure novel come from two social classes: the privileged Alvar family, and the servants who maintain their lifestyle. Among both groups, the age of the women determines their reactions to the social changes that have occurred or are imminent. The two servant women in the novel, Luisa and Pura, typify this dichotomy. For the younger girl, Luisa, service represents a temporary delay of her personal challenge to find a fulfilling occupation, which she will obtain by means of fur-

---

[8] Patricia Meyer Spacks, *The Female Imagination* (New York: Alfred A. Knopf, 1975), p. 292.
[9] Spacks, *The Female Imagination*, p. 292.
[10] Carmen Martín Gaite, *Fragmentos de interior* (Barcelona: Destino, 1976). All references are to this edition. The page number follows the quote.

ther schooling. In contrast, the older woman accepts her role as a lifelong servant, and compensates by cultivating family interests instead of occupational ones.

Among the upper-class women in *Fragmentos de interior*, the younger women again fare differently than their older counterparts. All are personally ambitious. Isabel Alvar is competent and extremely successful; cynical and brittle at twenty, she is unable to make an emotional attachment to another person, though she does not perceive this as a problem. She has a strong sense of social justice, as when she informs Luisa that she would do well to leave her employ: "El servicio doméstico está llamado a desaparecer," she observes, "es un trabajo anticuado y sobre todo injusto" (p. 160) (Domestic service is on its way out. It's old fashioned and, above all, unfair). Although the highly intelligent Isabel benefits from the gains made by the previous generation in securing acceptance for thinking women, her emotional life is empty. Love to her is "mentira, literatura, veneno que esclaviza a las mujeres incapaces ... de reaccionar a tiempo" (p. 186) (lies, literature, poison that enslaves women who can't manage ... to react in time).

Isabel's chronological contemporary, her father's girlfriend Gloria, thinks she is seeking success in a modern way, though in fact she is unwittingly a victim of the new freedom: valued for her looks and willingness to pose nude in front of a film camera, she does not realize that her usefulness as a feminine commodity is limited. While she defines herself as liberated, the men around her consider her "easy." Her meager role in the novel has to do with her cheating on the man with whom she lives. Even he has no illusions about Gloria's behavior. Imagining that he might confront her with evidence of her "infidelity," a concept he knows she will dismiss as irrelevant, he muses that surely she would confess everything, in accordance with the vacuous, cliché-ridden philosophy of a well-endowed girl who wants to be in the movies (p. 67).

Of all the women characters in *Fragmentos de interior*, the most poignant is the poet Agustina Sousa, who remains in love with her husband despite his new liaison. Although in her youth she had been more beautiful than almost any other woman, now at fifty she cannot compete against women half her age. Her ambition as an artist was compromised when she married, and she never achieved recognition for her talent. Depressed and isolated, Agustina drinks gin and re-reads her husband's old letters. At the end of the novel, she commits suicide. Agustina represents Martín Gaite's most clear-cut example of society's devaluation of the older woman, no matter how triumphant a youth she may have enjoyed. The author criticizes the cult of youth and the influence of externally-imposed standards on women, ideas also discussed in her nonfiction essay "La influencia de la publicidad en las mujeres."[11]

In *Fragmentos de interior*, the much-wished-for freedoms of women such as Natalia of *Entre visillos* are shown to have only partially arrived. Freedom to plot one's life independently has become less of a struggle to attain, as Isabel, Luisa and even Gloria illustrate. But a vicious double standard still exists, by which young women are exploited sexually and older women are discarded as less desirable than easily-available younger ones, regardless of inner worth. As usual, Martín Gaite depicts her characters' lives without judgmental pronouncements or sentimental implausibilities. Regardless of her putative loyalty to her sex, the author does not refrain from ridiculing women: Gloria, for instance, is every bit as vain and shallow as her male consort, Diego. But in this novel, as in its predecessors, social forces are seen as having as much or even more impact than personal choices on characters' lives.

Nowhere is the theme of the power of social forces more pervasive than in Martín Gaite's 1978 novel-memoir *El cuarto de atrás*, (Premio Nacional de Literatura of 1979) in which she discusses her own life and works over the course of a night-long interview with a mysterious "man in black."[12] The final woman hero to be discussed represents a unique case among those who populate Martín Gaite's novels, for the woman's life it highlights is indistinguishable from her own.[13] After creating fictional women heroes over the course of three decades, subject to the rules of censorship and the autonomy taken on by fictional characters, Martín Gaite used her creative freedom to produce a work that resembles no other. Within the context of a

---

[11] Carmen Martín Gaite, "La influencia de la publicidad en las mujeres," in *La búsqueda de interlocutor y otras búsquedas* (Madrid: Nostromo, 1973), pp. 113-121.

[12] Carmen Martín Gaite, *El cuarto de atrás* (Barcelona: Destino, 1978). All references are to this edition. The page number follows the quote. English translations are from Helen R. Lane, translator, *The Back Room* (New York: Columbia University Press, 1983).

[13] The woman hero/narrator in the novel is unanimously recognized as representing the author herself. Published affirmation of this relationship exists in documents such as a newspaper interview in which Martín Gaite refers to the narrator as "yo." (J. Bigorda, "*El cuarto de atrás* o el desvelo de unos recuerdos," *El Correo Catalán*, 25 de junio 1978, p. 9). However, since the character is the protagonist of a novel, it seems appropriate to this critic and also to the author to consider the narrator as a character. On this point see Joan Lipman Brown, "A Fantastic Memoir: Technique and History in *El cuarto de atrás*," *Anales de la Literatura Española Contemporánea*, VI (1981), pp. 13-20.

Fantastic (as defined by Todorov) conversation with a mysterious interviewer, the text of which comprises the novel, Martín Gaite constructs a memoir of growing up as a young woman in Franco's Spain.

The most significant detail about the woman hero in *El cuarto de atrás* — the fact that she coincides in every discernible respect with Carmen Martín Gaite herself — has a number of ramifications. The most wide-reaching is the incontrovertible success of this hero's challenge. Autobiography implies stature for the writer; that people should want to know the details of the author's life, and that she should be aware of this, is recognition of thirty years of literary achievement. Through her own success, Martín Gaite insures importance not only for "the feelings of women in a drawing-room," but also for the feelings of one particular iconoclast in her own "back room."

The events and circumstances in *El cuarto de atrás* include elements of all of the author's previous novels, but most especially *Entre visillos*. The woman narrator of *El cuarto de atrás* focuses on her youth in Salamanca, including specifics regarding the Civil War and postwar era which would not have been admitted in fiction before the demise of Franco. But the underlying plot of the novel is the story of Martín Gaite's evolution as an artist. Not only is this the story of a successful "quest" plot, tracing the inception of a brilliant literary career, but it also addresses the question of the origins of literary creativity in her personal experience.

The hero of *El cuarto de atrás* recollects the rigidly enforced role definitions for women of the postwar era, typified and reinforced by the mandatory Social Service obligation expected of each adolescent woman. The specter of spinsterhood was held up as the ultimate threat to female well-being, as the ideal of the self-sacrificing wife and mother was elevated to saintly status. Young women were taught to aspire to be valiant in their role as complement and mirror to a man (p. 94). However, in her own case, compliance with such external dictates was minimal: significantly, these expectations were not shared by her family. The young girl was forced to endure her Social Service stint, just as the family suffered the Franco regime, but neither set of values was internalized. Martín Gaite learned, as did Eulalia in *Retahílas*, to distance herself from external norms. And unlike her fictional woman heroes, she was supported by a strong mother in her search for self-fulfillment, which in her case took the form of a literary career.

The narrator of *El cuarto de atrás* traces the beginning of her long involvement with literature to the end of the innocence of her youth. Symbolic of lost freedom, the back room of her home — which ceased being a playroom when space was needed for hoarding household supplies —

represented her first loss. Her immersion in fantasy was a response to loss, as she tells her interviewer: "...Siempre se idealiza lo que se pierde," she muses, "pero puede que ahora me defraudasen [las memorias]. Por otra parte, si no se perdiera nada, la literatura no tendría razón de ser" (p. 195) (One always idealizes what one has lost, though perhaps I might find [the memories] disappointing now. Moreover, if one never lost anything, literature would have no reason for being).

A girlhood friend is described as another extremely influential factor with regard to her choice of career. This young woman introduced Martín Gaite to the pleasures of keeping a diary, and stood as a model of courage. Despite the fact that the girl's parents were both in prison, accused of being Reds, she maintained her equanimity and dignity. She granted scant importance to trivial concerns or material possessions, and she showed the narrator how to invent a fantasy escape — to a magical island — in order to flee the oppression of the real world. Even her handwriting was bold and admirable, unlike that of any other girl.

The writing of this courageous young woman, Sofía Bermejo, fulfilled for Martín Gaite the liberating function that other literature by women failed to offer. In contrast with the sentimental novels which comprised virtually all of the author's reading of contemporary literature by women, her friend's writing helped her to find her own literary path. "Frequently," Gilbert and Gubar observe, "[The female artist] can begin such a struggle [for self-definition] only by actively seeking a *female* precursor who, far from representing a threatening force to be denied or killed [as in Harold Bloom's theory of male warfare with forefathers], proves by example that a revolt against patriarchal literary authority is possible."[14] Although Martín Gaite was not in the least concerned with partriarchal literary authority, her forays into fiction and fantasy were unquestionably a rebellion against the dreary restrictions of the real world — an escape which she continued to cultivate, her interviewer informs her, throughout her career. (p. 58)

Concentrating as she does on the origins of her literary vocation, the narrator's present circumstances — her life as it has evolved in maturity — can only be glimpsed between the lines. She lives with her daughter in an apartment with a large terrace; she struggles against disorder; she is aware of her fame but, except for the tedium of repeated interview requests, is able to live more or less as she wishes. The question of loneliness, raised in Martín Gaite's earlier novels, is not introduced. The reader does not have as com-

---

[14] Gilbert and Gubar, p. 49.

plete an understanding of the narrator's current life as of her past. If it is true that, as feminist critics suggest, "the woman writer uses her text, particularly one centering on a female hero, as part of a continuing process involving her own self-definition," then *El cuarto de atrás* symbolizes the frankest and most personal exploration of the writer's origins.[15] However, the intimate feelings of the narrator in the present are not divulged to the mysterious man in black. In a sense, they are irrelevant: what matters is that a mysterious man is lucky enough to be allowed to listen to the brilliant woman throughout the night. The very circumstances of the interview are sufficient to connote the triumph of the woman hero.

In conclusion, the female heroes of Martín Gaite's novels challenge society to permit them to succeed. Spanning three decades in modern Spain, the lives of Martín Gaite's women heroes reveal as much about contemporary Spanish society as they do about the author's depiction of her gender. Over more than three decades, Martín Gaite has depicted women's lives with courage, risking dismissal by the male gatekeepers to literary success, and producing a body of literature that chronicles the changing circumstances of women over time. Throughout her novels *Entre visillos, Retahílas, Fragmentos de interior* and *El cuarto de atrás*, women heroes are situated in, and forcibly influenced by, the mores of their surrounding society. The proscriptions, inhibitions or — in later works — the freedom granted by society are seen in all these novels as being major determinants of women's lives. Over and over again, social circumstances become personal circumstances, with a number of effects.

Two major "eras" of Martín Gaite's women heroes represent distinct sets of social circumstances. And two generations of women cope in different ways with the environments they face. In the 1950s and early 60s, young women such as Natalia of *Entre visillos* were forced to expend great energy if they sought a "quest" plot for their lives. Role models did not exist. To fulfill personal ambition in this period, as did Eulalia of *Retahílas*, was perceived as requiring personal sacrifices such as foregoing motherhood which in later years caused deep regret. In the second era, the later 60s and 70s, vast social changes have had both positive and negative implications for women's lives. For women of the second generation, who are the age of Isabel and Luisa in *Fragmentos de interior* (also the age of the narrator's independent daughter

---

[15] Judith Kegan Gardiner, "On Female Identity and Writing by Women," in Elizabeth Abel, ed., *Writing and Sexual Difference* (Chicago: University of Chicago Press, 1982), pp. 177-191. This assertion appears on page 187.

in *El cuarto de atrás*), individual struggles for autonomy are much less brutal than they were in their mothers' day. However, emotional rapport with another human being is no easier, and possibly more difficult to achieve in the casual, hedonistic society of contemporary Madrid. And the much-touted "new standards" do not vitiate the cruel "double standard" by which women traditionally have been judged. If anything, the cult of youth which dominates modern life has intensified discrimination against older women. Gloria of *Fragmentos de interior* has not yet become aware of this fact at thirty, but — since her career is based upon how she looks — she cannot escape it much longer. In her forties, valued for her intellect as well as her beauty, Eulalia begins to worry about the ravages of time. And in her fifties, the sensitive, still-attractive but once breathtakingly beautiful Augustina of *Fragmentos de interior* concludes that her life has become meaningless, and ends it.

The one woman hero to surmount the prejudice that plagues a woman who has passed her zenith of physical beauty is the narrator of *El cuarto de atrás*: the successful literary artist who represents Carmen Martín Gaite herself. Her triumph is implicit in the absence of worrying references to age, found in the speech and musings of all other women heroes old enough to be aware of its encroaching effects. The narrator is questioned, listened to, catered to and challenged by the mysterious male visitor, with whom the possibility of explicit romantic involvement is always present; the narrator is not in the least concerned with the superficialities of how she looks. It is assumed that she looks her age, and that that is fine. What matters is what she thinks and feels, and the mysterious visitor is honored that the important writer about whom he knows so much has let him come into her home.

The success of the woman artist may be the most intriguing woman's life among Martín Gaite's depictions of women heroes; certainly, it is the most triumphant scenario for the challenge of any artist, male or female. It is also an optimistic conclusion to the trajectory of women heroes that spanned the preceding years. In addition, the successful challenge of the woman artist is the topic to which Martín Gaite will next return, in *El pastel del diablo*.[16] In a sense, the woman's life in *El pastel del diablo* is a fantasy combination of Natalia's life with that of the narrator in *El cuarto de atrás*. It tells the story of a young girl who learns, after many adventures, that she has the power to be both self-sufficient and important, regardless of the obstacles posed by her surrounding society. Martín Gaite's most recent woman hero is a glorious culmination of the challenges of women heroes of the past thirty years, and a

---

[16] Carmen Martín Gaite, *El pastel del diablo* (Barcelona: Lumen, 1985).

beacon to those who follow: her name is Sorpresa, and her gift is the power to create beautiful, magical, enthralling stories.

The Feminist Message: Propaganda and/or Art? A Study of Two Novels by Rosa Montero

Eunice D. Myers

Rosa Montero (born in 1951 in Madrid) is an award-winning journalist and a noted interviewer. She published her first collection of interviews in 1976, followed six years later by a second group *Cinco años de País*.[1] In addition, Montero edited the Sunday literary supplement of *El País* (1981-1982), thus becoming the first Spanish woman to edit a newspaper section other than the society page. This position of power has enabled her to hire and encourage other women journalists.

Montero has also used her literary talent to write novels. Her first two novels were published before her thirtieth birthday.[2] While both feature female protagonists seen from a feminist perspective, the techniques and forms used in each differ greatly.

The first novel, *Crónica del desamor*, is an uneven work; in some places polemics obscure its artistry.[3] It tells the story of Ana Anton, a young, unmarried mother who, like the author herself, is a journalist. Her conflicts as both a single parent and a full-time worker are presented, and her

---

[1] Rosa Montero, *España para ti ... para siempre* (Madrid: A.Q. Ediciones, 1976); *Cinco años de País*, (Madrid: Editorial Debate, 1982).
[2] A third novel, *Te trataré como a una reina,* was published in late 1983 (Barcelona: Seix Barral). Its content and theme are outside the scope and topic of this study.
[3] *Crónica del desamor* (Madrid: Editorial Debate, 1979).

psychological needs are explored. In the novel, Rosa Montero touches on most of the major passages in a woman's life: menstruation, sexual education, loss of virginity, marriage or the choice not to marry, bearing children, and the fear of growing old. Only menopause is not mentioned. In addition, she introduces many women's issues, which will be addressed later in this study. This variety of topics is at least partially justified by the protagonist's expressed wish to be able to write a book someday about everyday life. She says:

> Piensa Ana que estaría bien escribir un día algo. Sobre la vida de cada día, claro está. Sobre Juan y ella. Sobre Curro y ella. Sobre La Pulga y Elena. Sobre Ana María, que ha perdido el tren en alguna estación y ahora se consume calladamente en la agonía de saberse vieja e incapaz de hacerlo. Sobre Julita, muñeca rota tras separarse del marido. Sobre manos babosas, platos para lavar, reducciones de plantilla, orgasmos fingidos, llamadas de teléfono que nunca llegan, paternalismos laborales, diafragmas, caricaturas y ansiedades. Sería el libro de las Anas, de todas y ella misma, tan distinta y tan una.[4] (Ana thinks it would be good to write something one day. About everyday life, of course. About Juan and her. About Curro and her. About La Pulga and Elena. About Ana Maria, who has missed the train in some station and now is consumed silently in the agony of finding herself old and incapable of doing it. About Julita, a broken doll after separating from her husband. About slimy hands, dishes to wash, staff reduction, faked orgasms, telephone calls that never come, paternalistic attitudes at work, diaphragms, caricatures, and anxieties. It would be the book of the Anas, of all of them and of herself, so different and so unique.)

The rest of the novel is a combination of the "book of many Anas" and the "chronicle of everyday disaffection" which Ana is planning to write as Montero's novel draws to a close:

> sólo le duele que fuera el propio Soto Amón quien se quitara la corbata en un automático, ... autosuficiente gesto. Un gesto cruel y poderoso que puede ser un buen comienzo para ese libro que ahora está segura de escribir, que ya no será el rencoroso libro de las Anas,

---

[4] *Crónica*, p. 8. Hereafter all quotations from this work will be indicated by C and the page number following the quote. Translations are my own.

sino un apunte, una *crónica del desamor cotidiano*. (C, p. 265; Italics mine.)

(It hurts her that it was Soto Amon himself who took off his tie in an automatic, self-sufficient gesture. A cruel and powerful gesture that would be a good beginning for that book that she is now sure she will write, that now will not be a rancorous book of Anas, but an annotation, a *chronicle of daily disaffection*).

The title of Montero's novel indicates that it is the same "chronicle of daily disaffection." In fact, Montero herself once wrote:

Una novela? No, no considero que mi libro sea una novela. Creo que *Crónica del desamor* es precisamente eso, una crónica sin pretensiones, una mirada rápida al mundo que nos rodea, una aproximación a los problemas y afanes cotidianos de todos nosotros. Y me conformaría con que resultara mínimamente sugerente.[5]

(A novel? No, I don't consider my book to be a novel. I believe that *Crónica del desamor* is precisely that, a chronicle without pretensions, a glance at the world that surrounds us, an attempt to describe the daily problems and dreams of us all. And I will be happy if it comes out minimally inspiring.)

This disclaimer gives Montero the flexibility to emphasize the message more than the creative form, an option she exercises on occasion.

Among the issues raised in this first work are: 1) women in careers, 2) sexuality, sexual passages, and their related problems, 3) stereotypical roles of men and women, 4) relationships between men and women, and 5) motherhood.

The presentation of women in careers is appropriate and natural in this work about a single woman who is trying to support herself and her four-year-old son. For example, she confronts the managing editor of the magazine where she works, pointing out that she has been paid as an extra for more than one year, though she does the work of any other reporter. She needs more job security and higher pay. Her boss assures her that he will do what he can to improve her situation, though all decisions are always made near the end of the year. Since it is only January, Ana feels frustrated and defeated. Near the end of the novel and near the end of the allotted year of

---

[5] Printed on the flap of the paperback edition of the novel.

waiting, Ana learns that her request has been denied. She is furious, accusing the boss of sexual discrimination and exploitation of women workers. She yells:

> esto no se lo habrían hecho a un tío, y si se lo hacen, hubiera montado tal escándalo que la gente se habría asustado ... Llevo dos años trabajando en esta puta empresa, me habéis utilizado de comodín, soy la que más trabaja, ... la que carga con todos los muertos, a la que se le puede llamar un domingo por la noche para decirle que ha fallado tal reportaje y que hay que inventarse uno antes de las doce del día siguiente ... Y todo por dos duros, sin sueldo fijo, sin que me hayáis pagado los reportajes encargados que por cualquier problema vuestro no han salido publicados, vamos, es que me tenéis de esclava y de tonta. (C, p. 254)

(You would not have done this to a guy, and if you had, he would have created such a scene that people would be scared. I have been working two years in this damned job; you have exploited me. I am the one who works the most, the one assigned all the/stories about/ deaths, the one that you can call on Sunday night to tell her that some story hasn't worked out and that she needs to come up with one by twelve the next day. All that for a pittance, without a fixed salary, without paying me for the assigned stories that, because of whatever problem of yours, have not been published. Come on, you take me for a slave and an idiot.)

She has been given all the assignments no one else wants and has sometimes been expected to meet more stringent deadlines than those set for the permanent staff. She also discovers that she has been passed over in favor of a male specialist in national politics for the one new permanent slot available. She points out that women can also write about politics and economics. Her anger makes her recall the time she was fired from the bank teller's position because she was single and pregnant. At that time, the bank manager assured her that the bank would pay her hospital bill and maternity leave, but that he preferred that she seek employment elsewhere after the baby was born. Ana restrained herself then, although she did not thank the banker as he expected. She thought: "él, claro está, tiene siete (o más) hijos, quién sabe la cifra exacta, una manada de niños bendecidos, legales, religiosamente concebidos sin placer." (C, p. 263) (He, of course, has seven (or more) children, who knows the exact number? — a flock of blessed, legal children, conceived religiously without pleasure).

In her book about women, Ana also presents the problem of sexual harassment in the work place, referring specifically to her first job interview. She is propositioned by the government official who has the power to recommend her for a job. He says that she needs more practice so that her spoken French will be up to an acceptable level of competence when she is interviewed by the man's superior. While he leers at her, he suggests that they "practice" after he gets off work. When she continues to refuse his "help," saying that she must go to school and then return home immediately, he angrily informs her that she is obviously not motivated enough to be employed by that government agency. Thus, her refusal to please him results in the loss of an employment opportunity.

Montero's treatment of female sexuality is especially well done, though the justification for the inclusion of some of the material is sometimes questionable. Comments about sexuality are generally included in the thoughts of Ana or other women through free association. It is in dealing with these topics that Montero borders on the propagandizing alluded to in the title of this paper.[6] When speaking of propagandism in *Crónica del desamor*, one must bear in mind that the novel was published only four years after Franco's death, during a time of rapid changes in attitudes. Contraception and sex education were new topics of public discussion while abortion was still illegal under any circumstances.

---

[6] Many preconceived, often negative, ideas are held regarding propaganda and its presence in literature. A.P. Foulkes clarifies some of these misconceptions in the following passage from his book *Literature and Propaganda*:

> First of all, it must be recognized that neither literature nor propaganda can be defined adequately in the terms of any one of the many communicative aspects involved, including authorial intention, message form, textual designata, actual reception, and hypothetical reception. In addition, the point at which literature becomes propaganda or demystification can be described only when we accept that literature functions communicatively within specific historical and cultural systems of discourse ... In recognizing this historicity, and in accepting that our own consciousness as readers is likewise determined by a variety of historical factors, we have the beginning of a dialectical perspective from which literature, and indeed all sign processes, can be observed when they operate in a propagandistic or demystifying way.

A.P. Foulkes, *Literature and Propaganda* (London and New York: Methuen, 1983), pp. 105-106.

In its historical context, Montero's first novel was a bold new approach to some age-old problems. For example, the sexual education of Spanish girls — or rather the lack thereof — is discussed via Ana's memories. She remembers the confusion she felt when a man purposely pressed his body against hers in the subway, or when exhibitionists waited at the entrance to the *metro* for the young school girls. The girls learned to look away or to ask innocent questions such as "Do you know what time it is?" or "How do I get to la Avenida de las Estrellas?" Some of the older girls resorted to more extreme methods of defusing the situation. One girl consistently diminished the man's masculinity by her mocking replies to his indecent proposals while another purposely limped as if she were handicapped in order to "neutralizar con compasión el hambre de sexo de los trabajadores" (C, p. 160) (neutralize with compassion the sexual hunger of the workers). Through the image of the feigned physical handicap of the young girl, Montero is also able to imply that the male attitudes toward young girls cripple them psychologically and socially. Because sex was considered something dirty (especially during the regime of Franco), formal sex education or any passed on from mother to daughter usually consisted of a set of prohibitions. For example, with the onset of menstruation, Ana is given a verbal list of things not to do:

> No puedes tomar cosas frías, ni helados ni nada de eso, no puedes ducharte ni bañarte, no puedes ir a la piscina, no puedes tomar el sol, no puedes lavarte la cabeza, no puedes correr ni hacer gimnasia. Y ten cuidado y mírate la falda a cada rato, no vaya a ser que te la manches.
>
> Prohibiciones, prohibiciones, prohibiciones. Todos esos tabúes inútiles y necios que te obligan a pensar que eso es estar enferma. Y como tantas otras, aun mantiene Ana el viejo hábito y se descubre todavía hoy diciendo "estoy mala", ahora, a sus treinta años. (C, p. 157)
>
> (You can't eat cold things, or ice cream or anything like that, you can't take showers or baths, you can't go to the pool, you can't sunbathe, you can't wash your hair, you can't run or do exercises. And be careful to check your skirt every few minutes so as not to stain it.
>
> Prohibitions, prohibitions, prohibitions. All those useless and stupid taboos that make you think "that" is being sick. And like so many other women, Ana continues the old ways and still finds herself saying, "I'm ill," now, at thirty years of age.)

The author indirectly shows that becoming a woman can limit her activities and possibilities because of prevailing and learned attitudes and "useless taboos." Although Ana has since learned that all of the formerly proscribed activities are permissible, she is still adversely affected approximately sixteen years later in that she considers a natural, normal monthly event as a malady. She has rejected her mother's advice intellectually, but her psychological self-image continues to be negative.

Montero's statements on contraception and abortion are especially polemical and graphic, using the events to press her case for the legalization of both. In the novel, while Ana and her friends are waiting to see the gynecologist, they recall a friend who had an illegal abortion which resulted in a terrible infection. Both the woman and doctor were in danger of being prosecuted for the crimes of allowing or performing the abortion although the woman's condition was serious enough that she had to be hospitalized. It must be emphasized again that abortion under any circumstance was illegal in Spain until October of 1983. Current Spanish law permits abortions in three extreme cases: 1) if the pregnancy results from a reported rape, 2) if the mother's life or health is clearly endangered by the pregnancy, or 3) if three physicians certify that the fetus is seriously deformed. Even today, a Spanish woman cannot freely choose to abort a fetus under any other circumstances, and doing so can result in arrest and prosecution. These are Ana's thoughts on the male attitude toward the legality and availability of abortions:

> Si los hombres parieran el aborto sería ya legal en todo el mundo desde el principio de los siglos. ¿Qué Papa, qué cardenal Benelli osaría ser censor de un derecho que pedirían sus entrañas? Los políticos preñables no malinterpretarían sus propias necesidades, como ahora, cuando mantienen que el aborto es sólo un método anticonceptivo más, exigido sin escrupúlos por las mujeres culpables. (C, p. 21)

(If men gave birth, abortion would have been legal all over the world since the beginning of time. What Pope or what Cardinal Benelli would dare censor the right that his body demanded? Male politicians who could become pregnant would not misinterpret their own needs, like now, when they maintain that abortion is only another method of birth control, demanded without scruples by culpable women.)

Her views on male doctors' attitudes toward contraception are similarly critical. When her new gynecologist sees her friend's diaphragm, it is obvious that it is the first one he has ever seen:

> Está claro que le asquea, relacionanándolo quizá ... con el condón odiado. La píldora, el DIU, son problemas de mujer. Es ella quien las toma, quien lo sufre. El diafragma, sin embargo, es algo mas cercano a la pareja: ¿ha de interrumpir el varón sus acaloramientos previos para que ella pueda colocarse el disco de caucho? ... Son tan cómodas las píldoras o el DIU, esos métodos que el hombre no padece. (C, p. 30).
>
> (It is clear that he is repulsed by it, perhaps because he associates it with the hated condom. The pill, the IUD, are a woman's problem. She is the one who takes them, who bears it. The diaphragm, however, is something closer to both members of the couple. Must the man interrupt his passion so that she can insert the rubber disk? The pill or the IUD are so convenient — those methods the man does not have to put up with.)

In fact, Ana describes her doctor as a typical male gynecologist, a great macho type who suggests methods of birth control that will not diminish the man's pleasure, without giving serious consideration to the woman's health or preferences.

The male professional's attitude toward women is also explored in the context of psychiatry. One of Ana's female friends is a psychiatrist who believes that Freud and his followers were probably completely aware that penis envy did not exist. Instead, they used that theory to camouflage and compensate for the feeling of inadequacy experienced by men because they could not bear children (C, p. 230). The women's discussion of the issue temporarily stops the flow of the narrative, thereby changing an artistic work into a forum for Montero's own ideas.

Related to these views on sexuality, and also incorporated in an important way into sexual and emotional relationships between the sexes, is the whole problem of orgasm and satisfaction during intercourse. Ana shocks a friend with whom she has slept when she points out to him that both sexes have idealized the orgasm. This has led to dishonesty between partners, because a man feels that he has not performed in an acceptably masculine way if his partner does not reach orgasm. Therefore, Ana continues, a woman is afraid to be honest if she has enjoyed intercourse but has not attained the ideal goal of orgasm. She continues to feign the climax so that the masculine image and ego will remain intact. Ana also complains that Spanish men concentrate so intently on the sex act that they never communicate feelings verbally during intercourse. Thus Montero demystifies traditional sexual relationships and the proper roles each gender should assume during the sex act.

Still another feminist aspect of *Crónica del desamor* is the treatment of heterosexual relationships. Montero's novel gives a basically pessimistic view of marriage and cohabitation. In fact, none of the marriages mentioned in the work is successful. One couple has just divorced. The trauma of that breakup is vividly presented. Ana's friend Julita is described as a "broken doll" who can hardly function independently. She consistently bursts into tears when her husband's name is mentioned or when she remembers things they used to do together, and absolutely refuses to date other people. She simply cannot abandon the past in order to continue her life in a new direction. Although cohabitation was practiced during the Franco years, by 1979 this lifestyle was more commonplace and far more acceptable during the years following his death. The narrator, however, does not perceive cohabitation as the perfect alternative to marriage or as a complete solution to one's sexual and social needs. Interestingly, Montero portrays living together as a greater problem for her female protagonists than for the males. For example, Elena, a woman who has been independent for many years and is now living with Javier, is the party who wishes to end the relationship. Although she loves him (or has loved him in the past), she considers the relationship an invasion of her privacy: "Se siente asfixiada desde hace algunos meses por esta relación agonizante" (C, p. 109) (She has felt suffocated for several months by this dying relationship), and again, "Le ha sentido como un intruso que irrumpió en su casa robándole el espacio, espacio en los armarios, en la mesa de trabajo, espacio en su existencia." (C, p. 58) (She has considered him an intruder who burst into her house, robbing her of space, space in the closets, space on the work table, space in her life). On the other hand, Javier believes that he cannot live without her. He was spoiled by his mother and pampered by his estranged wife. He considers solicitousness the normal behavior of women and is baffled by Elena's nontraditional attitude.

In another relationship, Ana lived with Juan for three years. During her pregnancy, she decided that she could not tolerate him any longer and asked him to leave. Now their son is four years old and searches for a father figure everywhere. After a day at the zoo with his grandfather, the child says that he went to the zoo with his father. When his mother corrects him, he says that Tato is his father. No, Tato is his uncle. Apparently afraid to ask any more questions, he busily begins to fiddle with his shoe, "aprendiendo a disimular a los cuatro años, temeroso de saber ya en la niñez" (C, p. 9) (learning to dissemble at the age of four, afraid of finding out [too much] in his childhood). Ana regrets having sent Juan away recognizing the fact that her son desperately needs a male role model. Her struggle is presented in a series of letters she attempts to write to her estranged lover, all of which she ends up throwing away. The problems of both the child and the mother originate, at least in part, in society's insistence upon the nuclear family as the only acceptable family unit. A single mother or a child with no visible father challenges this traditional grouping and is viewed as a threat. Ana's loneliness and fear are captured well in the image of a cold house, cold from winter weather but also from a lack of human warmth and affection. Because of her overwhelming feeling of loneliness, she occasionally spends the night with a male friend, but always regrets it the next day. She, like Elena, feels that her life has been invaded. In addition, she feels that she must for her son's sake maintain the lie that the friend has just arrived to eat breakfast. Despite Ana's precautions, the child understands the true situation, and finally confronts his mother and expresses to her his feelings of resentment. Thus, both mother and child suffer because of Ana's willful attempt to go against society's acceptable norms of behavior.

Perhaps this negative attitude toward any relationship between a man and a woman is best expressed in Ana's thoughts about the gay relationships of one of her friends. As they are waiting for his date, she thinks:

> "Esta torturada espera homosexual, no es más que el último símbolo, el más patente, del desencuentro de todas las relaciones, del hundimiento de la fe en la pareja." (C, p. 133)
> (This tortured homosexual waiting is none other than the ultimate symbol, the most obvious symbol, of the lack of meaningful communication in all relationships, of the collapse of faith in the couple.)

As previously mentioned, many of the issues presented in *Crónica del desamor* are shown in such detail or in such radical terms, that they tend toward demystificiation or propaganda. On the other hand, in *La función Delta*, the work deals with fewer issues, and these are worked carefully into the context of the life and memories of Lucía, a sixty year old woman who is dying, probably of cancer.[7] While in the hospital she begins her memoirs in

---

[7] *La función Delta* (Madrid: Editorial Debate, 1981). Hereafter all quotations

which she narrates one week of particular importance in her life, the week in which her first film premiered. She was thirty years old. It was the 1970s. In a second narrative she describes the present. Most of her friends have abandoned her, and the society of the year 2010 is extremely youth-oriented. She and her one close friend, Ricardo, are considered relics of a past age. During the course of Lucía's illness, Ricardo comforts her and ultimately declares the love he has felt toward her for years. He even makes love to her in the hospital bed when she is feeling especially frightened of death and abandoned by all her other friends. Whereas love scenes in *Crónica del desamor* were almost always described in explicit language, this scene has a romantic, idyllic quality about it. She describes the lovemaking as "una maravilla" in which "dejé deshacer mi miedo entre sus labios ... Me zambullí en su contacto y sentí que eso debía ser algo muy cercano a la felicidad ... Me rodeaba con su cuerpo encerrándome en una burbuja de confortable placidez" (LfD, pp. 269, 279, 281) (a miracle in which I let my fear be dismantled between his lips. I immersed myself in his touch and I believed that feeling must be something very close to happiness. He surrounded me with his body, embracing me in a bubble of comforting peace). Here sexuality is an expression of love and concern for the other rather than a mere temporary gratification of a physical need. They both talk and express honest feelings as well. Although viewed as desirable, true communication between sexes — especially during intercourse — is rare in Montero's novels. The young nurse who cares for Lucía during the day is only interested in enjoying herself — in sex and in all aspects of life. Commitment appears to be rare or nonexistent among the youthful majority of the population in the futuristic society; therefore the expression of one's innermost feelings would be bothersome, even embarrassing.

When she remembers her youth, Lucía must admit that her love life was always extremely complicated. She was usually fond of married men, and she sometimes had two sexual relationships during the same period of time. This led to much self-doubt and self-recrimination:

> Sentía una rara abulia, la angustiosa convicción de no querer a nadie. Yo en aquel entonces aun me consideraba monoándrica ... me educaron monoándrica y tener un solo hombre me parecía lo justo y razonable. Sólo a mí me podía suceder desbarajuste tal como el ser monoándrica de corazón y poliándrica de actuación. (LfD, p. 17)

---

from this work will be indicated by LfD and the page number following the quote.

(I felt a strange indifference, the distressing belief that I loved no one. Back then I considered myself "monoandric" — I was brought up that way and having only one man seemed to be right and reasonable. Only I could suffer from the disorder of being "monoandric" of heart and "polyandric" in actions.)

Only in Miguel did she find someone she could love and from whom she could get love in return. After Miguel's untimely death, she made no commitment of herself and her affections to another person until the incident in the hospital with Ricardo. For her, love is a rare, almost unattainable emotion.

Some of the attitudes expressed in her first novel are also seen in this second novel. The young Lucía delights in stretching or breaking the rules of a relationship. When she is with Hipólito she purposely mentions his wife, and on one occasion she is the one to make the first sexual move. This frightens away the very traditional and insecure Hipólito, who believes that the man should always be in control in a relationship.

Reminiscent also of the views expressed in Montero's first novel is the young Lucía's longing to live with Miguel while fearing that she will lose her territory and independence. She says, "desmayé de miedo y de deseo. Deseo de compartir y convivir, miedo a perder mi identidad, mi territorio, la frágil libertad que encierran estas cuatro paredes de mi casa" (LfD, p. 363) (I fainted from fear and desire. The desire to share and live together, the fear of losing my identity, my territory, the fragile freedom that these four walls of my house enclose). Loneliness is a common theme in her work but here it extends to being alone in old age. The situation is exacerbated by Lucía's terminal illness which causes friends to avoid her. Thus she has time to confront her own mortality and is terrified. *La función Delta* differs from the first novel because of its attention to the process of death and dying. This new emphasis further heightens the protagonist's need to find meaning and purpose in life, to make sense of relationships. Temporary affairs no longer suffice.

Despite these differences between the two novels, clear expressions of feminist ideology appear in Lucía's memoirs and reiterate or augment those expressed earlier. She writes:

> me sentía cercada de ausencias y estrecheces, embargada de urgencias sin motivos razonables. Como aplastada por siglos de educación femenil que hubieran robado mi integridad, mi paz, mi redondez. Era la maldición de la mujer-pareja, la mujer-carente, de la mujer apoyo y

apoyada. Es la maldición de la mujer amputada de sí misma. (LfD, p. 62)
(I felt closed in by absences and intimacies, seized by unfounded obligations. As if crushed by centuries of feminine education that had robbed me of my integrity, my peace, my wholeness. It was the curse of the woman-couple, the woman-lacking, the woman-helper and helped. It is the curse of the woman cut off from herself.)

As she explains, her feelings of suffocation stem both from the limits which society imposes upon her because she is a woman and from her own self-imposed restrictions because of her education.

The only female rite of passage specifically mentioned in this novel is the one which was omitted in the first novel. Menopause is described as both a blessing and a loss and is compared to the beginning of menstruation:

> Casi es una liberación que se termine la embarazable molestia de la regla ... sin embargo, qué duro llega a resultar. Porque la amargura de la menopausia reside en lo irreversible del proceso, en que tu cuerpo cierra una página de vida y tú no puedes detenerlo. Supongo que la primera menstruación sería tan triste como lo son las últimas, por lo que conlleva de pérdida de infancia, de fin de la primera etapa de tu vida, si no fuera porque en esa agitada y temprana adolescencia no has aprendido aún el significado exacto del verbo perder. (LfD, p. 208) (The end of the vexing bother of one's period is almost a liberation; nonetheless, how difficult it becomes! Because the bitterness of menopause resides in its irreversibility, in the fact that your body is closing a chapter of your life and you cannot stop it. I suppose that the first menstruation would be as sad as the last ones — in that it carries with it the loss of childhood and signals the end of the first stage of your life — if it weren't that in that early and agitated state of adolescence you have not yet learned the exact meaning of the verb to lose.)

As has been demonstrated in this study, Rosa Montero's first two fictional works are both written from a feminist perspective, but with varying attitudes about male-female relationships. Love is shown to be nearly impossible in *Crónica del desamor*. In contrast, the second novel includes two relationships which are successful because they are fulfilling and important. In the Miguel-Lucía relationship and, later, in the love between Ricardo and Lucía, both partners benefit from the affection and concern shared. Granted they are exceptional and temporary, but the commitments last until the untimely death of one of the partners.

The two narratives also differ in terms of quality of writing. The initial work sometimes concentrates so much on the message that the artistic qualities are obscured. Despite Montero's disclaimer that the chronicle is not a novel, the work is still considered a fictional narrative and as such should incorporate ideas into the plot without inhibiting the action. Of course the inclusion of the aforementioned feminist issues is perfectly rational in the context of Ana's attitudes as she tries to survive alone in a male-dominated society, and they do not necessarily interrupt the flow of the narration. Overall, however, the writing is superior in the later work, *La funcion Delta*. Because the work is written in a confessional diary format by an older woman living (and in the process of dying) in the year 2010, the perspective can be more personal but also less immediate. Her intimate memories have been reworked over a period of thirty years and have lost their immediacy though not their importance.

As A.P. Foulkes points out, "The propagandistic or demystifying moment of literary communication may be inseparable from its aesthetic function."[8] Often in *Crónica del desamor* and consistently in *La función Delta*, Rosa Montero has succeeded in incorporating a feminist perspective into a work of artistic merit.

---

[8] Foulkes, p. 106.

The Dilemma of the Modern Woman: A Study of the Female Characters in Rosa Montero's Novels

Roberto Manteiga

If there is one thing that recent feminist criticism has taught us it is that it is difficult, if not impossible, to separate the idea of language from the issue of women's rights. Do men and women speak a different language? Should women strive to emphasize their uniqueness and individuality through language, or seek, rather, some type of androgyny by means of an entirely sexless syntax? Has society established such unbreachable barriers that true and open communication between the sexes is no longer possible? These and other similar questions have been examined in recent studies like Elizabeth Abel's, *Writing and Sexual Differences*, Chicago: University of Chicago Press, 1982, Catherine Stimpson's, "Feminism and Feminist Criticism," *Massachusetts Review*, 24 (2) pp. 272-288, and Elizabeth Ordóñez's, "The Decoding and Encoding of Sex Roles in Carmen Martín Gaite's *Retahílas*", *Kentucky Romance Quarterly*, no. 27, pp. 237-244.

The question of language as it relates to women's rights has been a concern of fiction writers as well. The Women's Movement has traditionally found a strong and effective voice in the literary works of caring and committed women authors. This is particularly true in Spain where discrimination against women has been rampant, and where, until Franco's death in 1975, literature was perhaps their only vehicle of expression. But it was a risky proposition when one considers the severe scrutiny to which all literary works were subjected under Franco's strict censorship laws. Still there were women writers, like Carmen Martín Gaite, Elena Quiroga, Ana María Moix, and

Mercè Rodoreda, who dared to address themselves to such sensitive and controversial issues as divorce, suicide and sexual discrimination.

Today, with the advancements made by the various women's movements, the number of concerned women writers has grown. One who has been particularly outspoken on the issue of women's rights is Rosa Montero. Montero is a journalist who reports on the issues in a candid and straightforward manner. Her outspokenness and sensitivity to these issues have earned her the respect of her peers on the staff of *El País* as well as the admiration of her readers, although there are many who take umbrage with her rather liberal views.

Her strong commitment to responsible journalism carries over into her fiction. To this date, she has written three novels that have met with mixed reviews: *Crónica del desamor* (1979), *La función Delta* (1981) and *Te trataré como a una reina* (1983). While we must not downplay the obvious aesthetic sense she displays as an author — which, I might add, is considerably more apparent in her latest novel — her desire to create a work of art, is, at least in this relatively early stage of her career, less important to her than the need to express her ideas, sentiments, and concerns about a number of issues ranging from sex to politics. She considers the work of fiction, like the newspaper article, a viable medium for effecting change. It is not surprising to find that as a woman most of her attention is directed toward what we might define as women's issues: the questions of motherhood and abortion, marriage and divorce, and the struggle for recognition, respect, and understanding in the face of a strong tradition of discrimination at every societal level. Although Rosa Montero has been an avid supporter of equal rights for women, and openly resentful of the subservient role women have traditionally been forced to accept in Spanish society, she cannot be labeled a "feminist" writer in the same sense as some of her more militant contemporaries. Montero's endeavor to earn recognition and respect as a woman in today's world is found wanting when weighed in the balance against her search for love and understanding.

This does not mean that Rosa Montero's novels cannot be studied from a feminist perspective. On the contrary, one could argue that the novelist reveals a markedly feminist attitude with respect to a number of issues of singular importance to women. In *Crónica del desamor*, for example, Montero focuses specifically on the discrimination women encounter every day of their lives, particularly in their careers. She touches upon such timely issues as salary differences between men and women, and the lack of job security and opportunities for advancement for women. Her feelings of anger and frustration are voiced through Ana, the novel's protagonist, a working woman and a single parent trying to raise a child.

In *La función Delta*, the young Lucía is continuously seeking to transcend the limitations of sex role polarities. She cannot understand why men feel a need to dominate in a relationship, why true and open communication between the sexes is impossible. She blames society and its repressive institutions and practices, echoing from time to time ideas similar to those put forth by Charlotte Perkins Gilman in her feminist utopian novel, *Herland*, that, since society is patriarchal, men are, therefore, responsible for all that is negative in this world. Although Montero does not go as far as to propose, as does Gilman, an entirely female society, she does, nevertheless, let her reader know that there are women in this world like Lucía who feel they have every right to be skeptical of men in general.

This message is implicit in the very title of Rosa Montero's third novel, *Te trataré como a una reina*. Women must be wary of those men who promise them the moon or tell them that they will be treated like queens. Bella, whose own experience has taught her to be skeptical of such promises, tries to dissuade the ingenuous Vanessa from making the same mistakes she made when she was young.

But the frustrated Bella, the rebellious young Lucía, and the sincere but confused Ana reveal only one aspect of Rosa Montero's own personality. If Montero is resentful of a society that has relegated women to subservient roles, she is equally critical of the feminist movement itself in so far as it has had a somewhat dehumanizing effect on women.

Originally asserting that sexual differences were the consequence of social conditioning, some feminists proposed deemphasizing or eliminating altogether these differences. Women, they agreed, should no longer consider themselves the weaker, submissive sex, but should, instead, be assertive and self-confident. Traditional values were questioned. Housework and child rearing were no longer considered the exclusive domain of the woman, but responsibilites shared by the husband. Those women who, in the past, had felt compelled to act within society's normative structure, lest they be accused of demonstrating deviant benavior, were now anxious to act in ways that challenged the norm. Yet, Montero believes that in their attempt to achieve equality, women have, in effect, lost their identity, and, in turn, their ability to communicate their true feelings.

More than a struggle for equality and independence, Montero's is a search for understanding. Women, she feels, should not have to lose their identity as women in order to gain acceptance and recognition in today's society. Her stance is not unlike the one taken by Catherine Stimpson in her article, "Feminism and Feminist Criticism." Stimpson argues against the deconstructive side of feminism which stresses androgyny in both language and behavior, and in support of the reconstructive side which stresses heterogeneity. She admits that, while she has always feared the search for a "quasi-permanent, if previously repressed 'female' being" and has been equally apprehensive about the "superficial theory of action that insists that because one is female, one necessarily writes and speaks a female language," she, nonetheless, supports the idea of the female's search for identity, and encourages the quest for "female" writing and language.[1] There are, she believes, female signifiers that flow beneath the various cultures, societies and temperaments, and these must be sought out.[2] Montero would agree that there are inherent differences in the sex roles of men and women. The characters of her novels continually allude to such differences. Even a hardcore feminist like Ana's friend Elena in *Crónica del desamor* comes to view pregnancy as "una opción real y propia," (a very personal choice) and the narrator suggests that, "Quizá es que durante mucho tiempo ha confundido la liberación de la mujer con el desprecio hacia la mujer misma: la liberación pasaba por la mimetización con el sexo del poder, había que adoptar valores masculinos, copiar al hombre, repudiar la identidad de la hembra."[3] (Perhaps it is that, for some time now, she has confused women's liberation with contempt toward women themselves: liberation meant imitating the dominant sex, one had to adopt masculine values, copy the man, reject her own female identity.) For the first time in her life Elena comes to experience "el orgullo de reencontrarse como sexo, como mujer, ... saber que puede parir." (p. 222) (the pride of rediscovering oneself as a sexual being, as a woman, ... to know that one is capable of giving birth.)

The sentiments Rosa Montero wishes to convey to her reader are, in many respects, quite different from the ideas expressed by her protagonists. Yet, in a sense, she shares their dilemma. As women they are caught between two diametrically opposed systems of values. In an attempt to free themselves from their traditional role as the weak and submissive gender in a male-dominated society, they accede to peer pressure and adopt a feminist

---

[1] Catherine Stimpson, "Feminism and Feminist Criticism," Massachusetts Review, 24, no. 2, p. 286.
[2] Stimpson, p. 285.
[3] Rosa Montero, *Crónica del desamor* (Madrid: Editorial Debate, 1979), p. 222. Translations are my own. All subsequent references to this work will be indicated by page number.

posture, only to come to the realization that this assumed and unnatural behavior on their part has discouraged or prevented them from formulating meaningful relationships, especially with men. As a result, these women suffer frustration and loneliness.[4] Ana, the sensitive and caring unwed mother of *Crónica del desamor*, is painfully aware of the fact that she is simply role playing, having assumed the posture of the independent and liberated woman: "sabe que representará con sabio hábito su papel de mujer fuerte y libre, ni exigencias ni lágrimas, que son deleznables y femeninos defectos." (p. 12) (she knows that she will skillfully portray her role of the strongwilled and free woman, no demands or tears, which are fragile and feminine weaknesses.) Although she does not feel comfortable in this capacity, her strong sense of pride and the knowledge that a particular pattern of behavior is expected of her force her to continue the charade, even when it means condemning herself to a life of loneliness and an uncertain future: "e intentó bucear en su futuro, desentrañar qué tipo de agonía le estaba reservada a ella misma." (p. 73) (and she tried to look into her future, and discover what kind of suffering was awaiting her.)

Lucía, the sick and aging protagonist of *La función Delta*, ruefully looks back on her life as a recalcitrant and ambitious young woman, more interested in delighting in life's pleasures than in making any serious commitments which might compromise her independence. Her friend Ricardo, who agrees to read and comment on an autobiographical screenplay she is writing and, thus, functions indirectly as critic of Lucía's lifestyle, tells her the truth she does not want to hear:

> De hecho, tal como tú te obcecas en clasificar las relaciones, en el amor pasión tú adquieres las cualidades que tradicionalmente se llamaban "masculinas," es decir, que te mantienes centrada en ti misma, segura, activa, batalladora, independiente, libre. Y en el amor cómplice asumes el papel tradicionalmente femenino, la mujer necesitada de cobijo, de amparo, de protección. En realidad ese absurdo problema que tú planteas entre esas dos inexistentes categorías amorosas no es más que una sublimación de tu problema de identidad como mujer: entre la mujer independiente que querías y creías ser, y

---

[4] We have to keep in mind, of course, that societal values have changed so dramatically over the past twenty years that what was considered deviant behavior on the part of women in the 50s and 60s is now accepted behavior in many societies.

la mujer "esposa de" que llevas dentro de ti y para lo que fuiste educada.[5]

(In fact, as you yourself insist on defining relationships, in aggressive love you assume characteristics which have traditionally been called "masculine," that is, you remain self-centered, confident, active, rebellious, independent, free. In passive love you take on the traditionally feminine role of the woman in need of shelter, assistance and protection. In reality, that absurd problem that you pose for yourself between those two inexistent categories of love is nothing more than a sublimation of your identity problem as a woman: between the independent woman that you wanted to be and believed that you were, and the wife that you are within, and toward which end you have been educated.)

Bella, the over-the-hill nightclub singer of the seedy Desiré bar from *Te trataré como a una reina*, would rather not dream anymore of love or success, "porque se sufre menos sin deseos."[6] (because one suffers less without aspirations.) While she is quite different from her counterparts in the previously mentioned novels, she shares the same loneliness and disillusionment.[7] The outdated "boleros" that she sings or that her friend "el Poco" sings to her echo Bella's tragic situation:

Es el amor, pregunto yo, una inquietú una ansiedá ... sentir latir el corasón con desesperasión por tiii. (p. 37)
(Is love, I ask, uneasiness, anxiety ... to feel my heart beat in desperation for you.)

---

[5] Rosa Montero, *La función Delta* (Madrid: Editorial Debate, 1981), p. 213. Translations are my own. All subsequent references to this work will be indicated by the page number.

[6] Rosa Montero, *Te trataré como a una reina* (Barcelona: Seix Barral, 1983), p. 115. Translations are my own. All subsequent references to this work will be indicated by the page number.

[7] Coming from a more humble background and lacking the compulsive intellectual drive of either Ana or the young Lucía, Bella's idea of success has always resided in how well she could sing or how attractive she could make herself to a man. This is evident in the advice she gives the awkward and insecure Antonia: "Lo que tú debes de hacer es ceñirte la cintura, así para que resalten las caderas ... y desabróchate el cuello, mujer, que se te vean ese par de tetas tan hermosas" (p. 38) (What you must do is suck in your stomach, to show off your hips ... and unbutton the top button of your blouse, woman, so they can see that beautiful set of jugs.)

Ahora eres alegre y joven pero en lo profundo ya llevas la semilla de tu soledad. (p. 59)
(Now you are young and happy, but deep down inside you bear the seed of your loneliness.)

In the case of all three women — and they themselves are painfully aware of this — their sense of loneliness and frustration is a product of their own making. By shunning traditional values and patterns of behavior, and adopting instead a feminist posture, Ana, Lucía and Bella have camouflaged their true feelings as women, and this, in turn, has made communication with men difficult. As a result, marriage has not worked for any of them.

It is here, with respect to her views on marriage, where Rosa Montero departs significantly from other "feminist" writers. On the one extreme we have the "feminist utopia" novels in which marriage is presented as just another unnecessary societal convention. In many such utopian societies child rearing becomes the responsibility of either a commune or a teacher trained specifically for this purpose. Marge Piercy suggests in her novels that women should disburden themselves of all conventional trappings including marriage. Marriage does not work, it is merely "the patriarchal way, where you lose your name and become property."[8] This idea is expressed in Mercè Rodoreda's 1962 novel, *La Plaça del Diamant*. Natàlia, the protagonist of Rodoreda's novel, upon marriage, is nicknamed Colometa, or (little dove) by her husband, thus symbolizing her subjugation and loss of identity as a human being. Rosa Montero's ideas about marriage are much closer to those of writers like Carmen Martín Gaite. She believes that happiness can only come from a strong and lasting, open and sincere relationship with a man, and like Martín Gaite, criticizes women who out of sheer egotism, refuse to marry, have children, or make any other similar types of commitments. These women neither improve their position in society nor gain any real sense of security, but discover instead isolation and abandonment: "El problema fundamental de las mujeres liberadas del matrimonio ... estriba en su íntima añoranza por las raíces que no han sabido dejar en nadie, en la pesadumbre por no haberse sabido comprometer."[9] (The fundamental problem of those women who choose not to marry ... resides in their intimate

---

[8] Marge Piercy, *Small Changes* (Connecticut: Fawcett Crest Books, 1975), p. 333.

[9] Carmen Martín Gaite, "Las mujeres liberadas," in *La búsqueda de interlocutor y otras búsquedas* (Madrid: Destino, 1982), p. 130.

longing for the ties they have failed to establish with anyone, and in a sense of sorrow over not having known how to commit themselves.) And Montero would shudder at the idea of removing a child from its mother and placing it in the hands of a veritable stranger. She is a firm believer in the idea that motherhood is the true fulfillment of a woman's role. Even a strong supporter of women's rights like Elena in *Crónica del desamor*, alludes several times to "el orgullo de saber que puede parir." (p. 222) (the sense of pride you get from knowing you can have children.)

Still, marriage is a difficult proposition and Montero sadly recognizes this. Ana, of *Crónica del desamor*, talks about having a stable relationship with a sensitive and intelligent man, but between her job and her responsibilities as a single parent, she can't seem to find the time. Besides, past experiences with men have made her somewhat skeptical about marriage. "¿No son todos los amores una simple construcción imaginaria?" (p. 72) (Aren't all loves mere inventions of the mind?) she asks. Her greatest fear is growing old alone, a feeling shared by Lucía in *La función Delta*. Ana takes little comfort in the fact that she has a child who will care for her in her old age or in the suggestion of her homosexual friend, Cecilio, that, "Cuando seamos ancianitos y no podamos valernos por nosotros mismos nos casamos, ¿te parece?" (p. 78) (When we're old fogies and can't take care of ourselves anymore, we'll get married. How about it?) Lucía, on her deathbed, finally discovers in Ricardo the kind of sensitivity and human understanding that she had not been able to find before in any man. She is, however, forced to admit that she could have possibly developed a meaningful and lasting relationship with Miguel when she was younger, but for her own aggressively negative attitude toward all men:

> —Tú me conquistaste aquel día que recordaste que yo tenía la regla.
> —Pero chiquitina, eso es normal.
> —Que va a ser normal. Los hombres jamás se acuerdan de esas cosas, el período es un problema tuyo, ellos lo único que quieren es encontrar amantes siempre dispuestas y sin complicaciones ... En realidad los hombres no son detallistas no se preocupan en conocerte, en saber qué sientes, cómo eres, qué te pasa ...
> —Venga, venga, criatura, los hombres no son así, no generalices de esa manera, tú es que has debido tener muy mala suerte, has debido tropezar con muchos bestias. (pp. 207-208)

(—You really won me over that day when you remembered that I was having my period.

—But sweety, that's only normal.
—Normal? Get serious. Men never remember those things. Our period is our problem, you're only interested in finding lovers who are always willing and who present no complication ... In reality, men care little about such details; they are not concerned with getting to know you or your feelings, what you're like, what's on your mind...
—Oh come now, child, men are not all like that; don't generalize so; you must have had some bad luck in your life; you must have run across a lot of animals.)

In *Te trataré como a una reina* Bella's dreams of any kind of stable relationship with a man were shattered long ago. Her life has since become a series of one night stands as she struggles desperately to combat loneliness and capture fleeting moments of warmth and affection. Only the naive Antonia continues to believe in the idea of marriage in a traditional sense, hoping to find a man to take care of; someone who will make her feel useful and necessary. In the meantime, she enjoys playing the role of housewife and mother to her brother Antonio, slaving over him day in and day out, cooking for him, washing and ironing his clothes, and continually taking his abuse. But, unlike the independent Bella, Antonia comes from a "good" family and feels an obligation to cling stubbornly to an outdated system of values. She still recalls her father's words to her: "Tú eres mi hija y tienes que comportarte como una señorita." (p. 20) (You are my daughter and you must behave like a lady.) So at forty she remains a virgin, masturbating herself each night with her stuffed animal, Lulú.

Montero's message is clear. She finds the idea of the submissive, barefoot and pregnant housewife totally unacceptable. The Antonias of this world are a pathetic anachronism, a frightening reminder of what life was like for women not all that long ago. The fact that women like Antonia do not fit in in today's society speaks well for the feminist movement and for the progress that has been made in recent years in the area of women's rights, progress which Rosa Montero applauds. But there are other aspects of the feminist movement that Montero seems to be questioning. The Anas, Lucías and Bellas of the world who not only have dared to question traditional values, but have purposely acted in a nonconformist manner because the new social codes for women have demanded it, have not found happiness either.

Is Montero's outlook entirely pessimistic? Is she telling us that communication is, in fact, impossible? I think not, and, what is more, I believe that by putting her concerns in writing she is making a genuine attempt to find an "interlocutor," that is, someone to share these concerns with.[10] It is in this "flow of language" that hope resides, or, as Susan Griffin reminds us, "We must trust in words."[11] Society, with its innate prejudices and sex role polarities, has made true communication difficult. Unfortunately, the feminist movement, in its attempt to destroy such barriers, has created others. Many feminist writers and critics have discovered this and are attempting to find other alternatives. Elizabeth Ordóñéz, in her study of Carmen Martín Gaite's *Retahílas*, suggests that Germán and Eulalia seek a "third" code, one that is neither male nor female. Lyman Tower Sargent proposes that women view themselves as "whole human beings with a variety of appropriate roles rather than one sexually defined role.'[12] Rosa Montero, however, appears to share the feelings of Catherine Stimpson that women must search for a "female" heterodoxy at once independent and interdependent.[13] She understands the inherent differences between men and women, and agrees that unless women feel secure and confident in their own uniqueness and individuality, they cannot begin to overcome those societal barriers that make honest and open communication between the sexes possible. Lucía finally comes to recognize this fact, but not until she finds herself in the throes of death. Still she manages to open lines of communication with Ricardo and discovers a brief moment of happiness before she dies. Ana never does, but she is still young, and, although alone, her pride remains undaunted, knowing full well that "en este ajedrez de perdedores, más pierden aquellos como Soto Amón que ni siquiera juegan." (p. 264) (In this chess game of losers, those who lose the most are people like Soto Amón who don't even play the game.) Both Bella and Antonia, victims all along of their respective situations, eventually find the strength to overcome them, Bella, by standing up to Antonio and thus unburdening herself of years of frustration, and Antonia, by finally getting up the courage to board the train that will take her "hacia un destino desconocido y diferente." (p. 244) (toward an unknown and very different destiny.)

---

[10] It is not surprising that two of her protagonists are also seeking to communicate through writing.
[11] This is a message Griffin repeats throughout her work, and is not taken from any one study in particular.
[12] Lyman Tower Sargent, "An Ambiguous Legacy: The Role and Position of Women in the English Eutopia," in *Future Females* (Ohio: Bowling Green Press, 1981), p. 98.
[13] Stimpson, p. 275.

Rosa Montero's characters vividly represent the complexities of what it means to be a woman in today's society. Unlike the writings of some of her more militant feminist contemporaries, Montero offers a sensitive, understanding, and perceptive analysis of the subject that inspires feelings of compassion in all of us.

A Feminist Literary Renaissance in Catalonia

Kathleen McNerney

The recent democratization of Spain and the simultaneous emergence of the feminist movement in that country has resulted in the appearance of many new works by women writers. One group whose political consciousness has been particularly keen because of the suppression of regionalist movements has been Catalan women writers. These authors exhibit a markedly feminist point of view in their treatment of several themes which are prevalent in their work — female adolescence and sexuality, the isolation and solitude of women, their psychological development, and the role and social position of older women. The development of these motifs is often sharpened and enhanced by a strong and constant undercurrent of Catalanism. Several members of this group of writers now in their thirties and forties, whose work began to appear in the 1970s and has flourished since the death of Franco, have gained a good deal of recognition. Montserrat Roig and Carme Riera recently won important literary awards, and the novels and short stories of several others have been reprinted year after year. Although somewhat older, the recently deceased Mercè Rodoreda, whose *La Plaça del Diamant* was made into a film and translated into English, also merits comment in this study of feminist themes in the works of contemporary Catalan women writers.

World literature is replete with novels of male adolescence, Bildungsromans, picaresque tales and the like. But until recently, few books have dealt with the female counterpart, and even fewer can claim the authenticity of having been written by women.[1] Several Catalan writers analyze most effectively the subject of female adolescence. In her delightful novel *L'òpera quotidiana*, structured like an opera, Roig weaves together several interrelated stories. One tells the story of Mari Cruz, a poor and simple Andalusian girl growing up in the Barcelona of the 1970s. She marks time in a convent school, where all the girls, starved for male attention, worship the few fathers who come to visit. Her first sexual encounter takes place at the school with the gardener who takes advantage of the innocence and needs of the girls. Although physically unmarred by this experience, she is nevertheless discovered and ostracized by nuns and companions alike.

Those closest to her in her developing years are influential in shaping her attitudes. Mari Cruz's mother is a woman of weak will who allows her illegitimate daughter to be pushed around by an overbearing and utterly bourgeoise aunt, bent on seeing both mother and daughter married. Her other aunt is a prostitute with a rather unorthodox life style of her own.

Mari Cruz's job is as a maid in the home of "el poeta dels phallus," so dubbed because of his artistic inclinations, manifested in an extraordinary collection of phalli. This bizarre preoccupation has very serious consequences, as he soon tries to take advantage of the unsuspecting Mari Cruz. The man's jealous wife chases her off to her next two jobs, which she holds simultaneously. She cleans house for the elderly Senyora Miralpeix while serving as helper and companion to the even more elderly Senyora Altafulla. Mari Cruz's primary duty as companion is to listen to Senyora Altafulla's idealized memories of her love for Captain Saura. Horaci Duc, a boarder in the Miralpeix house, is also haunted by sad memories. For the first time in her life, Mari Cruz begins to wonder about the significance of memories. She sees them as a sign of adulthood and, rejecting her own seemingly insignificant memories, she invents new ones. Not satisfied with that, she comes to believe that she must create new experiences which will provide her with genuine memories which will accompany her as she enters the adult world. Gender, class, and age limit these choices to love and sex.

Senyor Duc takes the liberty of inviting Mari Cruz to the Cafe de L'Opera for *horxata de xufa*. The first indication of her incipient sexual excitement is that she equates his odors with those of the gardener at the convent school. The nuns, she explains, "m'havien posat la por als homes dins

---

[1] For an analysis of the female adolescent in literature in English, see Patricia Meyer Spacks "The Adolescent as Heroine," in *The Female Imagination* (New York: Avon, 1972), pp. 143-201.

del cos" (had put the fear of men inside my body), but Horaci reawakens the desires the gardener left unfulfilled.[2] Mari Cruz fantasizes, creating words for those she doesn't know, and guessing the meaning of those "naughty" words she has heard. She begins to feel burdened by her virginity, and, thinking that freeing herself of it will make her an adult, finds a man on the street to do her the favor before her inevitable encounter with Senyor Duc. This first hollow and unfeeling experience with a stranger leaves her free to "tastar el cel" (try heaven) with the one she really desires. But Senyor Duc, saddled with his own dreadful memories of a frightful past, is intimidated by the situation and ultimately abandons her, leaving Mari Cruz with her own very real and bitter memories. Emotionally debilitated, she doesn't even have the energy to reject an importunate Dutchman who accosts her in a deserted park.

Muller qui cerca Espill, a TV screenplay by Maria-Antònia Oliver, deals with this theme of female adolescence in a very different way. Mariona, the story's protagonist, is engaged to Martí, and, although she recognizes that he is a good catch, she surprises herself and others with her ill humor towards him. The truth is that Mariona is unsure of her feelings: "no em fa cap il.lusio que vengui ... Però i si no vengués? Què faria, si no vengués? Em posaria trista?" (I'm not at all excited that he's coming ... But what if he didn't come? What would I do? Would I be sad?)[3] She recalls the excitement of only a few years ago when she was the belle of the ball and several men paid court to her, but can't seem to find that excitement in Martí. Her dreams of being an actress or a movie star have all vaporized, and all those beaux, and even a few of her girlfriends, have since gone to the University. Mariona herself was not able to further her education. She reprimands Martí for being so conformist; so much less ambitious than she, a true believer in the double standard. She recognizes, nonetheless, that he is a "bon noi," dependable, and, with scarcely any choice but to marry him, tries to convince herself that she loves him, despite all evidence to the contrary.

The two young women we have discussed, though they come from different classes and have very different lifestyles, share a stifling upbringing and a sense of frustration with the few possibilities open to them. As women they are prisoners in a patriarchal society.[4] Mariona will have a comfortable but

---

[2] Montserrat Roig, *L'òpera quotidiana* (Barcelona: Planeta, 1982), p. 76. Further quotations are from this edition; the translations are mine.

[3] Maria-Antònia Oliver, *Muller qui cerca espill*, in *Vegetal* (Barcelona: Hogar del libro, 1982), p. 80; my translations.

[4] For an exploration of the effects of the patriarchal system on choices and per-

completely unfulfilled life; Mari Cruz will end up "col.locada," pursuing vague fantasies suggested to her by the delirious old Senyora Altafulla, half-mad from her own disillusionments.

Carme Riera's *Epitelis tendríssims*, a collection of erotic short stories with Majorca as a background, features women protagonists of various ages: a teenager who writes very explicit love letters — they represent more an exploration of her own sexuality than a message to anyone — but doesn't send them; a mature woman who falls in love and subsequently has an affair with a voice on the telephone that she hears by accident; and a somewhat older woman who leaves behind a notebook full of very erotic poetry to be found after her suicide. In another eerie tale, depressing for the traditional view of women's status that it presents, an investigative reporter doing research on the Inquisition finds herself in a compromised position with an elderly man who had promised to give her historical facts, but recreates instead his own fantasy of love for a medieval ancestor who was burned at the stake. Parallels between the "witch" and the reporter are inevitable. One of the most curious stories, "Una mica de fred per a Wanda," involves a young man's lust for his father's lover. The sensuous Wanda is willing to satisfy both men, but the young viscount introduces technology into the relationship in an effort to gain the upper hand, and pays the price of eternal frustration.

Several works, including the aforementioned screenplays of Oliver, concentrate on the psychological development of the female characters. A masterpiece of psychological study is Mercè Rodoreda's *La Plaça del Diamant*, which uses a highly subjective first-person narration as a means of revealing to the reader how the central character, Natàlia, comes to grips with herself and her life. What is unusual about Natàlia-Colometa, however, is the established contrast between her seeming passivity and her very real inner strength in the face of great adversity.[5] Set against the background of tne Spanish Civil War, this award-winning Catalan novel traces the development of Natàlia, the young girl whose fingers get raw from tying gold ribbons at the bakery; to Colometa (so dubbed by her husband Quimet), the wife and mother who puts up with a house overrun by doves; to Natàlia the widow with young children who survives the hunger which follows the Civil War; and finally to Senyora Natàlia with the marriage of her daughter. Such a

---

sonal relationships, see Rosalind Coward, *Patriarchal Precedents: Sexuality and Social Relations* (Boston: Routledge and Kegan Paul, 1983).

[5] See Spacks, "Power and Passivity," also in *The Female Imagination*, pp. 43-96, for a discussion of similar situations in English literature.

change of names, initiated by others and resulting from a shift in status, is typical among oppressed peoples: just as North American Indians and Filipinos often bear Spanish names and Blacks the names of ancestral plantation owners, Catalans have seen themselves forced to accept Castilian names, and women, the names of their fathers or husbands. Those nineteenth-century female writers who used male pseudonyms experienced yet a further distancing from their identities as women.[6]

Rodoreda's novel offers a remarkable view of the spiritual growth, or sometimes lack of it, in this solitary and seemingly passive woman. Natàlia stoically confronts abuses at every turn. There are countless occasions in which she would speak, but does not. The contrast between her tumultuous inner being and her serene outward appearance is so marked that when she finally lets out a suppressed primal scream it is not at all surprising. The novel's stream-of-consciousness narration affords us a keen glimpse into the mind of a very withdrawn person, who nevertheless learns to cope with life's problems and survives.

The rhythm of the narration is set by Natàlia's thoughts as she passes through the various changes in her life. There is little dialogue, and no real description which has not been filtered through her own perspective. After having suffered through the war and its hunger, she passively allows herself to be rescued by a kindly grocer, Antoni; the only tenderness she displays, towards the novel's end, is to him, and then only very reluctantly.

Throughout her life, she allows other people to make decisions for her. She goes to the fateful party where she meets Quimet —an experience which changes her life— because her friend Julieta wants her to go. Later she will agree to marry Quimet because of his forcefulness and insistence rather than out of love for him. Quimet schemes to procure Natàlia's earnings, which in the past she had always turned over to her father; she is never consulted. Soon he becomes jealous of Natàlia's boss and pressures her into quitting her bakery job; she tries to resist, but, her spirit broken, she ultimately acquiesces. Later, in a scene of psychological terrorism, Quimet gets her to admit to having seen Pere, her former beau. She is so bullied that in the end she

---

[6]The Cuban poet Nicolás Guillén wrote a splendid poem which speaks to the problem of names and identity, from the point of view of a Black man with a Spanish (Catalan) name. "El apellido" appeared in the collection *La paloma de vuelo popular — Elegías* in 1958, and was reprinted in *Campo Abierto*, edited by Mary Jane Treacy and Nancy Abraham Hall (Boston : Houghton Mifflin, 1984), pp. 77-80.

herself questions whether the event, dreamed up by the jealous Quimet, actually happened:

> Se'n va anar fent unes grans camades. No vaig dormir en tota la nit. L'endemà va tornar i em va dir que li havia de prometre que no sortiria mai més amb en Pere i per acabar d'una vegada i no sentir-li més la veu, que quan estava enrabiat no semblava la seva, li vaig dir que ja el creuria i que no sortiria més amb en Pere. En comptes d'estar content es va posar com un dimoni, em va dir que ja estava tip de mentides, que m'havia posat un parany i jo hi havia caigut com un ratolí, i em va fer demanar perdó per haver sortit a passejar amb en Pere i per haver-li dit que no hi havia sortit i a l'últim em va fer arribar a creure que hi havia sortit i em va dir que m'agenolles.
> —Al mig del carrer?
> —Agenolla't per dintre.
> I em va fer demanar perdó agenollada per dintre per haver sortit a passejar amb en Pere que, pobra de mi, no havia vist d'ençà que haviem renyit.
>
> (He stormed off. I didn't sleep all night. The next day he came back and told me I had to promise not to go out with Pere and to put an end to it and not hear his voice anymore, which didn't sound like his own when he was mad. I told him I'd do as he said and not go out with Pere anymore. Instead of calming down he got madder than a devil. He told me he was fed up with my lies, that he'd set a trap for me and I'd been caught in it like a mouse, and he made me apologize for taking a walk with Pere and then telling him I hadn't and in the end he got me to the point where I believed I *had* gone out with Pere and he told me to kneel down.
> "In the middle of the street?"
> "Then kneel down inwardly."
> And he made me apologize, kneeling down inwardly, for having gone for a walk with Pere who, poor me, I hadn't seen since we'd broken up.)[7]

---

[7] Mercè Rodoreda, *La Plaça del Diamant*, 25th ed. (Barcelona: Club Editor, 1982), p. 40. Hereafter all quotations from this work will be indicated by the page number following the quote. I have used *The Time of the Doves*, trans. David Rosenthal (New York: Taplinger, 1981) for these translations.

Apologizing and capitulating to the demands of others are gestures that Natàlia makes all too often. She only mildly objects when Quimet tells her she must like everything he likes: "I si una cosa no m'agrada de cap de les maneres? — T'ha d'agradar, perquè tu no hi entens. I altra vegada sermó: molt llarg." (p. 27). (What if I just can't bring myself to like something?—You've got to like it, because that means it's something you don't understand. And another sermon, a very long one.)

The first time Colometa rebels is against the doves Quimet keeps in the house, and then in a very underhanded way, typical of the deception practiced by oppressed people in response to their oppressors.[8] At the time Quimet begins to bring excessive numbers of these birds into the house, she is a working mother, exhausted all of the time, and without the strength to resist this incursion. The technique of her rebellion is suggested, unwittingly, by her mother-in-law, who doesn't want to see the doves because she, as an outsider, might disturb them in their nesting and destroy their eggs. Colometa begins to methodically bother the birds so that their eggs will be ruined. She feels guilty and has nightmares about this slaughter; nightmares which serve as a foreshadowing of her awful decision, in a moment of despair, to poison her starving children and then kill herself.[9] Ironically, the grocer, whom she would not have met were it not for the doves, prevents this murder-suicide by offering her a job when she goes in to buy the poison. The job allows her to survive financially. Later he declares his desire to marry her so he can have a ready-made family.

This second marriage to Antoni is a difficult one, but it is the only immediate solution to her problems. With this new relationship and the move to a different place, Natàlia's identity again changes. Her break with the past is underscored by her refusal to bring any of her belongings with her from the old place, not even her clothing, though ironically she notices that the bedspread in her new home is like the one she had before. Her daughter Rita, although more headstrong than her mother, makes a decision to marry that seems to repeat Natàlia's — she marries Vicenç because, like Quimet, he is so persistent. During Rita's wedding, Natàlia's pearl necklace is broken. Afterward she places one of the rescued pearls in the sea shell, one of her

---

[8] See Adrienne Rich, *On Lies, Secrets and Silence* (New York: Norton, 1979), pp. 185-195 for a discussion of the use of deception as a defense by powerless groups.

[9] An interesting explanation of the use of sacrifice as a way of recovering power is found in *Powers of the Weak* by Elizabeth Janeway (New York: Knopf, 1980), pp. 137-156.

most cherished objects. This ritualistic act of putting together of separated things is like a healing for her.[10] It is on this very same night that she goes back to the apartment she shared with Quimet and where her children were born, and carves her name into the wooden door as a reminder that she has passed through there, and through time, and that she finally has come to know who she is. When she returns home, she is able to show affection to Antoni, for the first time. The circle is completed as the novel closes where it began, in *La Plaça del Diamant*.

This theme of solitude also appears in several of the works by the younger generation of Catalan writers. It is, sadly but realistically, much more pervasive than the theme of solidarity among women. Helena Valentí's "L'altre," in *L'amor adult*, much more subtle and less violent than Rodoreda's novel, is somewhat reminiscent of Borges' "La intrusa." It is a story of male bonding among the lover, friend, and son of the female protagonist, a relationship which excludes her. "Desarrelament," in the same collection, adds the experience of exile to the already existing theme of the loneliness of the female character. In Roig's *L'òpera quotidiana*, Mari Cruz needs nothing so much as a friend to talk to. Though she has superficial relationships with several people, she never has an opportunity to speak intimately with anyone. In Oliver's *Vegetal*, Marta speaks occasionally to her dead husband, but shares only insults with her friend Fina and son Carles. Her only real companions are her plants, with which she fills up the house.

Marta's plight is a common one — she is an older woman, a widow, who has never worked outside the home, and feels worthless.[11] She agonizes about having been nothing but a decoration all her life, not unlike her beloved plants. Her final decision, after trying unsuccessfully to make herself useful to society, is to accept her role as a merely decorative object, joining the ranks of the flower pots. Oliver addresses this same theme of the loneliness and feelings of uselessness of older women in an extremely poetic and beautifully written short story whose title echoes that of the screenplay, "Muller qui cerca espill les mans s'hi talla II." Unable to accept her mother's

---

[10] Natàlia's relationship with certain objects is explored by Gene Steven Forrest, "El diálogo circunstancial en *La Plaza del Diamante*," *Revista de Estudios Hispánicos*, 12 (1978), pp. 15-24.

[11] Simone de Beauvoir and Zoe Moss, among others, deal with the problems of older women in society from a feminist perspective. See de Beauvoir's *The Coming of Age* (New York: Warner, 1973) and Moss' "It Hurts To Be Alive and Obsolete: The Ageing Woman" in *Sisterhood is Powerful*, ed. Robin Morgan (New York: Vintage, 1970), pp. 170-175.

death — particularly painful because she had not seen her for years — Marta fills her house with calendars and clocks in an effort to thwart the passing of time. Her husband and son, believing her to be crazy, lock her up in the house, but she escapes to go searching for her mother and for the village of her childhood, across the sea.

Older, lonely women are the protagonists of several of Carme Riera's stories in *Jo pos per testimoni les gavines*. "Es nus, es buit" is a monologue by a woman who upon her husband's death, finds herself free for the first time in her life, only to lose this freedom when her relatives, convinced that she is insane, commit her to a home after she throws away her wedding pictures and the postcards her husband had written to her years before. In the bitterly ironic "Unes flors," a woman loses both husband and child in a divorce resulting from her attempt to attract her husband's attention. She has the local florist send her flowers; her husband feigns jealousy and initiates divorce proceedings — which he has desired all along — on the basis of adultery. She cannot convince the florist to testify on her behalf because her husband is one of his best clients, having sent flowers to all his lovers over the years. In "De jove embellia," a once beautiful woman never marries, choosing instead to live in self-imposed isolation, carrying the stigma of a sexual assault she experienced years before. At first, she is so paranoid that she puts furniture in front of her door, but as the years pass, she comes to wish in vain that someone would enter her lonely room.

There are two interesting older women characters in Roig's *L'òpera quotidiana*. I have mentioned in passing Senyora Altafulla, who hires Mari Cruz to read to her old love letters and passages from romantic stories. In her idealized youth she loved only the gallant soldier Captain Saura who is executed for desertion towards the end of the Civil War. To her, no one else could be as noble, and she spends her life fondly remembering the little contact she had with him. Senyora Miralpeix, Mari Cruz's other employer, enjoys the companionship of Senyor Duc and listens, very nurturingly, to his anguished memories of the past. When he expresses astonishment at the fact that he is able to open up to someone like her, she explains: "Es lògic: amb mi, no li cal dissimular. No em veu com una dona, ja no pot sentir cap mena de desig. Tinc un peu al calaix." (p. 142). (It makes sense. With me, you don't have to pretend. You don't see me as a woman, since you don't feel any desire. I have one foot in the grave.) And she is correct in understanding that Senyor Duc cannot seem to deal with younger women on any basis other than sex.

It is not surprising that, in addition to feminist themes, many of these works also focus on the question of Catalanism. Sometimes the two are linked, both for the writers as well as for the characters in their works. In Roig's short story "Before the Civil War," Catalonia must be defined and explained again and again by a Catalan woman living in England. In Riera's "Helena, Helena," dedicated to "tots els exiliats del meu país" (all my country's exiles), a woman separated from her husband during the war discovers years later that he is alive after she has begun a much happier relationship with another man.[12] Sometimes these themes are in curious opposition, as in *L'òpera quotidiana*, in which Senyor Duc insists on Catalanizing his young Andalusion wife María. He does it so successfully that she becomes radicalized and begins distributing forbidden bulletins, over his desperate protests, and the quarrel ends their relationship. Senyor Duc is tempted by the younger Mari Cruz, who so resembles María that he is driven away from her. And finally, in *La Plaça del Diamant*, The Civil War and its deprivations are almost protagonists in themselves, though the novel is not explicitly political. For example, Natàlia lives in terror that Quimet is not really dead and will one day return to find her with Antoni. The novel is somewhat autobiographical — Rodoreda, who was forced to flee from Barcelona as a young woman, suffered years of hunger during and after the war. She described her reaction to this period in an interview: "I'm sure I've never been as lucid as I was then, possibly because I hardly ate anything."[13]

Literature by women and literature by Catalans both have been neglected throughout history, for varying reasons, but for one in particular — the oppressed status of the writers. With this new wave of post-Franco literature, we now have the opportunity to rectify this situation and gain fresh insights. Many of these novels and short stories have been translated into Castilian, and Rodoreda's classic into English. The topics are relevant, even urgent, and the writing is of the highest literary quality. It is fortunate for us all that at least some of these works are finally finding their way into the mainstream.

---

[12] Carme Riera, "Helena, Helena," in *Jo pos per testimoni les gavines,* 10th ed. (Barcelona: Laia, 1981), p. 27; my translation.
[13] From *Serra d'Or*, quoted and translated by David H. Rosenthal in his introductory note to *The Time of the Doves*, on the second of the unnumbered pages.

The Renewal of the Quest in Esther Tusquets' *El mismo mar de todos los veranos*

Lucy Lee-Bonanno

In her analysis of the female hero in *Archetypal Patterns in Women's Fiction* (1981), Annis Pratt notes a number of striking similarities between the experience of the adolescent protagonist and that of her middle-aged counterpart. Prior to initiation into womanhood, the adolescent girl maintains a degree of independence in her struggle for self-determination amid the pressures of a patriarchal society. Not yet severed from the freedom and protection afforded her by the natural world, she retains her youthful ideals and can still envision future self-realization.[1] The experience of the middle-aged woman parallels that of the adolescent in her intense desire for personal fulfillment. Having for all practical purposes completed the functions of wife and mother required by the domestic enclosure, she is able to renounce the limiting role prescriptions previously imposed upon her and seeks to rediscover the possibility of growth and freedom left behind in the green world of her youth. Middle-age thus provides a second opportunity for self-actualization, for a rebirth of the faculties stifled by a lifelong adherence to patriarchal dictates.[2]

---

[1] Annis Pratt, *Archetypal Patterns in Women's Fiction* (Bloomington: Indiana University Press, 1981), pp. 16-17.

[2] Pratt, p. 135. Elizabeth Abel, Marianne Hirsch and Elizabeth Langland, *The Voyage In: Fictions of Female Development* (Hanover: University Press of New England, 1983), p. 11, refer to this delayed development as "the second prevailing pattern of female growth in fiction: the awakening."

This exploration of adolescent and middle-aged experience has been identified by Phyllis Zatlin as a primary concern of women's fiction of the Spanish post-Civil War period. According to Zatlin, novels of the forties and fifties by authors such as Ana María Matute and Elena Quiroga feature a lonely adolescent protagonist who rebels against a repressive societal and familial milieu. In subsequent decades this alienated youth has been replaced by an equally lonely and disillusioned middle-aged protagonist who seeks release from a lifestyle inimical to personal fulfillment, only to discover in novel after novel that such a release is at best problematic and often impossible.[3]

Though many novels might be cited as representative of either the adolescent or the middle-aged quest for self, Esther Tusquets' *El mismo mar de todos los veranos* (1978) is of particular interest in its presentation of both quests in the life of a single protagonist. Annis Pratt's adaptation of standard archetypal theory proves to be especially helpful in the analysis of these parallel patterns of development.[4]

After studying a broad sample of novels by English and American women writers, Pratt noted a marked divergence of female developmental patterns from the configurations identified by archetypal theorists such as Joseph Campbell.[5] Warning against the forced application of such theories of specifically male development to female experience, she delineated an alternative pattern reflecting the fundamental variations of the heroic quest when applied to woman's developmental process. The "departure" of Campbell's semi-divine hero and his incorporation into a supernatural world is paralleled in the female quest pattern by woman's conscious rejection of societal norms in search of a more authentic existence. His "initiation" stage is substituted for a mental journey into the past in which the female hero must re-establish ties with the green world of youth and confront the repressed images of her past before experiencing a personal transformation or metamorphosis. The final phase of Campbell's quest pattern, the "return" and reincorporation into society, is eliminated in Pratt's schema, for the female hero who has successfully confronted the figures from her past and emerged as a transformed human being cannot reincorporate herself into the society responsible for her initial discontent. Instead, Pratt notes that the creation of a fully-

---

[3] Phyllis Zatlin, "La aparición de nuevas corrientes femeninas en la novela española de posguerra," *Letras femeninas,* IX, no. 1 (1983), pp. 36-37.

[4] Pratt's schema is adopted to great advantage by Elizabeth Ordóñez in "A Quest for Matrilineal Roots and Mythopoesis: Esther Tusquets' *El mismo mar de todos los veranos,*" *Crítica Hispánica,* 6 (1984), pp. 37-46.

[5] Pratt, pp. 138-42.

integrated individual from a socially devalued one frequently results in "denouements punishing the quester for succeeding in her perilous, revolutionary journey." The female's heroic quest is thus as likely to lead to madness or death as to renewal. In his discussion of the modern literary hero's quest in *La estructura mítica del héroe*, Juan Villegas emphasizes the serious nature of the crisis created by the adult's rejection of a life-style previously accepted and for many years maintained. He points out that such a history of accommodation to an unsatisfactory life situation frequently decreases the possibility of liberation from it. The hero's reintegration into the society earlier rejected is thus indicative of a failure to discover new vital options and a consequent conformity to societal norms.[6]

In *El mismo mar de todos los veranos* the return of Tusquets' middle-aged narrator/protagonist to her childhood home after thirty years of marriage gains mythic proportions when viewed as an expression of the female heroic quest pattern. Like the literary hero delineated by Pratt, this nameless protagonist undertakes her quest in response to a profound sense of vital inauthenticity. Experiencing the existence to which she has become accustomed as "un pulido universo de cartón piedra" (a shiny papier-mache universe), she feels that she can no longer continue the farce represented throughout her adult years.[7] A rejection of societal norms offers the only possibility of freedom from a lifestyle no longer consonant with her innermost needs. She thus elects to "depart" from the matrimonial fold in hopes of rediscovering the identity forfeited thirty years earlier with her acceptance of the patriarchal enclosure and its many demands and expectations. It is in search of these fragments of herself that she returns to the home of her youth:

> ... me he encerrado aquí como se refugia una alimaña enferma en su cubil, en un intento quizá desesperado de tender mágicos puentes entre esta niña de aire envejecido, que pende patética y grotesca sobre el vacío de la más espantosa soledad ... y aquella niña triste, que no tuvo otra compañía que la de sus fantasmas, acaso he venido a reencontrar a mí misma en aquella niña, que, aún triste y solitaria, sí existía,

---

[6] Juan Villegas, *La estructura mítica del héroe*. (Barcelona: Editorial Planeta, 1973), pp. 92, 105, 128-29.

[7] Esther Tusquets, *El mismo mar de todos los veranos* (Barcelona: Editorial Lumen, 1978), p. 16. Hereafter references to this work will be indicated by the page number. All translations are my own.

anterior a la falsificación y al fraude de todos los papeles asignados y asumidos. (p. 30)

(... I have enclosed myself here as a sick animal takes refuge in its den, in a perhaps desperate attempt to suspend magical bridges between this aged child, who hangs pathetically and grotesquely over the emptiness of the most frightful solitude ... and that sad child, who had no company other than her own ghosts, perhaps I have come to rediscover myself in that child, who, though sad and solitary, did exist, prior to the falsification and fraud of all the roles assigned and assumed.)

The initiation stage of the protagonist's voyage of self-discovery begins when she crosses the threshold of her former home. The significance of this portal as a passageway separating two distinct worlds or modes of experience is indicated by the contrast established between the external atmosphere and that inside the house. As the narrator enters the cool, shadowy vestibule, she experiences a pleasing change from the noise and suffocating heat of the street. The house's mythic function as a place of refuge and isolation apart from the protagonist's usual environment is underscored by its comparison to the sacred precinct of a church and later to an island, "perdida y escarpada" (lost and steep). Also indicative of its significance as a sacred ground is its air of atemporality. As the narrator surveys the rooms and their dusty furnishings, the thirty years that have passed since her residence in the house seem to disappear and are replaced by a sense of sameness and continuity. The familiarity of this environment serves to revitalize the past, propelling the narrator backward in time to a period when the house and its furnishings were viewed as "aliados, amigos ... cómplices" (p. 27) (allies, friends ... accomplices) in a shared struggle to resist the forces of change and falsification.

A central aspect of the narrator's recuperation of past experience is her re-establishment of ties with the green world of lost youth. As Annis Pratt has noted, nature plays a primary role in the female developmental process by serving as a symbol of growth and fulfillment for the adolescent. Through her relationship with the natural world, she is able to experience herself as one with the cosmos and envision the possibility of future self-realization. Though this wholeness is eventually threatened by the ever-increasing pressures of the social milieu and must ultimately be relinquished, it continues to play an important role throughout the developmental process and is particularly influential during the female's middle years. According to Pratt, "the mature woman hero tends to look back to moments of naturalistic epiphany as touchstones in a quest for her lost selfhood so that when she readies herself for her midlife rebirth journey, images of the green-world remembered once more come to the fore."[8]

The emphasis placed upon the natural world in the return of Tusquets' protagonist to her childhood home supports Pratt's analysis of nature as a symbol of growth and fulfillment for the female. Of particular significance is the correspondence established between springtime as a period of cosmic rebirth and the renewal of vital options signaled by the narrator's rejection of societal norms in favor of greater personal authenticity. The parallel between the growth process of nature and human physical and psychological maturation is continued in the narrator's description of the budding trees visible from the balcony of her youth as "vírgenes yemas asustadas, pezones adolescentes que se encrespan y crecen" (p. 18) (frightened virginal buds, adolescent nipples which stiffen and grow). The protagonist's psychological approximation to the green world of youth is expressed in her sense of having reassumed the identity of the lonely little girl who once inhabited the house. Experiencing herself as a "niñita" or "huerfanita envejecida" (little girl or aged orphan), she returns to reclaim the existence she knew prior to her entrapment and falsification within the patriarchy. Symbolic of this pre-patriarchal world is the bed she occupied as an adolescent, her "cama de soltera" (virgin's bed), and the books she once delighted in, foremost among them "las mujercitas puritanas y arquetípicas de Louisa May Alcott" (p. 30) (Louisa May Alcott's puritanical and archetypal little women).

Like the female hero delineated by Pratt, Tusquets' protagonist remembers the green world as a positive force in her life, for the vegetation beneath her balcony formed an integral part of the fantasy world to which she frequently retreated as a child. Likening the greenery below her to the expansiveness of the sea, she perceived the city and its inhabitants as occupants of the ocean depths. Central to this fantasy world was her magical triangle, whose vertices express the youthful hope and illusion represented by the green world. Though the first of these was only an ordinary movie theater visible from the balcony, it assumed magical proportions in her childish fantasy as a "magnífico palacete encantado" (p. 31) (magnificent, enchanted palace) from which would issue forth the handsome prince of her dreams. The second point on this imaginary triangle was occupied by the most marvelous of shops, an art store replete with "misteriosas cajas polvoriento-hechizadas" (mysterious dust-bewitched boxes) and two "grifos-hembras"

---

[8] Pratt, p. 17.

(female griffins) as its employees. Here too reigned Prince Charming stamped on supple erasers alongside Snow White and the Seven Dwarfs. The third point of the triangle was perhaps the most enticing, for the real world lost all intensity when compared with the infinite possibilities offered in the enormous mirror covering the wall of the ice cream parlor. It was here that the protagonist relinquished reality, immersing herself in the fanciful world of the beautiful siren to whom she paid homage each time she savored the flavor bearing the mermaid's name. Like her heroine, the narrator dreamed of the handsome prince who would someday appear to free her from loneliness and complete her transformation into a woman. A self-styled Ariadne, she longed for the Theseus who would lead her to freedom and fulfillment.

Memories of adolescence also serve as sources of green-world images of hope and expectation. When the protagonist recalls the springtimes of her youth, the sterile spirituality of May, a month dedicated to the cult of the Virgin, is overshadowed by memories of May as a carnal celebration of life. Images of death and stagnation, such as the moribund roses decorating the altars and the stench of fetid water in their vases, are countered by those of life and vitality in which the protagonist and her girlhood friends dream of nuptial chambers filled with exotic flowers and sensuous princes from the Orient. The cold sterility of the chapel with its "tapetes almidonados, bordados y planchados hasta el infinito por manos ásperas y virginales" (alter cloths endlessly starched, embroidered and ironed by rough and virginal hands) forms a sharp contrast with the voluptuous exploration of life characteristic of adolescence: nosotros nos escabullimos, sombras rientes, torpes aprendices de bacantes locas ... recorremos con dedos curiosos, no del todo inocentes, los largos penes amarillos, ásperos, llenos de pelusa ... Nos embriagamos con el polvillo tan dorado y maligno de las flores" (p. 20) (we scurry away, laughing shadows, awkward apprentices of Bacchus' wild priestesses ... we examine with curious, and not entirely innocent, fingers the long, rough, yellow penises, covered with fuzz ... we intoxicate ourselves with the golden and malign dust of the flowers). Not even death itself can dampen this exuberance, for the nun discovered in a white casket one May morning only serves to reaffirm the sense of vital abundance experienced by the girls.

The protagonist's return to the university where she had studied as a young woman likewise evokes images of the green world of lost youth. Thoughts of this period of her life bring to mind the longing for freedom experienced by the students on May mornings when "la esencia misma de las humanas libertades, la plenitud de un existir donde radicaba nuestra esencia ultísima, consistía en algo tan sencillo como salir a la calle y bajar paseando hasta el mar ..." (p. 55) (the very essence of human liberty, the fullness of an existence in which our ultimate essence was rooted, lay in something as simple as going out to the street and strolling down to the sea). More than anything else, this escape to the sea served as a celebration of youth itself, for it was staged in honor of the disgruntled elders who disapprovingly observed the students' boisterous and disrespectful rejection of propriety and responsibility. Similarly, the young people studying in the library where the narrator herself had spent so many hours as a university student recall the exuberance of the youth she once knew, a youthfulness intensified by the disapproving stares of the "viejas momias" (old mummies) and "atildados gatos de Cheshire" (p. 52-53) (fastidious Cheshire cats).

These reminiscences are not, however, simply nostalgic glimpses of a bygone era. Rather, they provide a means by which the protagonist is able to recuperate lost time and re-establish contact with the individual she once was. Though much has changed since her own days as a student, her return to the university as a professor awakens such vivid memories that she experiences a sense of continuity very much like that felt upon returning to her childhood home. May and all of its green-world associations have removed the obstacle of time and precipitated her toward a rediscovery of the past:

> ... es un mes sofocante y extraño en que muchas cosas parecen volver a mí ligadas a recuerdos de exámenes, de flores en la capilla, del brotar incipiente de los brotes tiernísimos ... hoy se enlaza misteriosamente con mayos ya lejanos, y es como si todos estos años. ... no fueran de repente otra cosa que un paréntesis banal y un tanto estúpido ... un sueño del que ahora pudiera finalmente despertar, devuelta a la realidad única ... de mi adolescencia y de mi infancia. (p. 53)
> (It is a strange and suffocating month in which many things seem to return to me linked to memories of exams, flowers in the chapel, the incipient budding of tender shoots ... today is bound mysteriously to now distant Mays and it's as though all these years ... were suddenly nothing more than a banal and somewhat stupid parenthesis ... a dream from which I might now finally awaken, restored to the only reality ... of my adolescence and childhood).

In this special green world recalled by the narrator, nature and fantasy merge to form a place of refuge on the fringes of a reality experienced as unsatisfying. Dominating this reality is the protagonist's mother, "una diosa helénica" (a Hellenic goddess) and "reina bruja" (witch queen) whose ambivalent character is expressed in her comparison to the Greek statue guarding the vestibule of their home. Like the statue with its welcoming manual gesture and contradictorily distant and ethereal facial expression, the protagonist's mother exhibits a dual nature. Memories of her uninhibited, heterodox lifestyle are countered by those of an uncompromising demand for order and perfection and a total inability to relate to her daughter. The narrator perceives her relationship with her mother as having always been one of personal inadequacy, for she could never satisfy her mother's desire for a daughter as beautiful and brilliant as the universe in which she herself revolved: "A la señora le gustaban ... las niñitas rubias, indiscutiblemente anglosajonas, muy arias, herederas de al menos otras veinte generaciones de otras niñitas rubias de su mismo linaje, niñas que lucían sus gorritas de punto, sus deliciosos trajecitos escoceses, en las revistas extranjeras ilustradas" (p. 24) (The Mrs. liked ... little blonde girls who were indisputably Anglo-Saxon, very Aryan and heiresses of at least another twenty generations of little blonde girls of their same lineage, girls who showed off their little knitted bonnets, their precious little Scotch dresses, in the illustrated foreign magazines). Her sense of insufficiency is heightened by her mother's attempts to mold her into the kind of daughter expected of a "diosa rubia de ... manos blancas" (p. 21) (blonde goddess with ... white hands). The numerous trips to hairdressers and dressmakers, ballet and tennis classes are likened to her mother's efforts to renovate the old house, thus underscoring the protagonist's sense of having been treated as an object in need of repair. And like the house, whose hidden stains and disguised moldings refuse to be definitively eliminated by the successive layers of paint and wallpaper, the narrator's imperfections can not be erased by her mother's insistence upon order and beauty. Instead, these pressures for conformity prompt the protagonist's retreat from the brilliance of her mother's world to her own interior reality:

> Creo que la casa vieja y la niña oscura sellamos un pacto en las tinieblas. Inventamos extraños mitos órficos, secretos subterráneos para escapar así a la diosa de la luz, Atenea tronante: introdujimos tenaces el desorden, la angustia, lo ambiguo y mutilado en un universo que se creía o al menos se quería perfecto. Y en esta guarida, en esta gruta hechizada y maléfica y enternecedora, floreció el país de las maravillas y de nunca jamás. (p. 26)

(I believe that the old house and the dark little girl sealed a pact in the shadows. We invented strange Orphic myths, secret subterranean rites, to thus escape the goddess of light, thundering Athena: we tenaciously introduced disorder, anguish, ambiguity and mutilation into a universe which believed itself to be or at least wanted to be perfect. And in this lair, in this bewitched and maleficent and enchanting grotto, flourished Wonder Land and Never Never Land).

The pressures for conformity first experienced by the protagonist in her relationship with her mother are intensified in adolescence when childhood games are replaced by the farce of social expectations and finally then by the full-fledged masquerade of adulthood. The sense of placelessness and inadequacy created by her mother's attempts to force her into an inauthentic role also continues. She remembers very clearly, for example, her deviation from the pattern of behavior expected of girls of her class: "Nada de lo que yo sentía, nada de lo que yo pensaba ... encajaba en aquel mundo isleño y cerrado en el que había nacido .." (p. 193) (Nothing that I felt, nothing that I thought ... fit in with that closed island of a world in which I had been born). This margination from the other members of her class is expressed in adulthood, as well, when she marvels at the vocal tone of her old friend Maite, which readily distinguishes her as a member of Barcelona's upper class. This is only one trait among many others which she never adopted in her progression toward adulthood.

The protagonist's sense of placelessness, of having "flotado siempre en [una] incómoda tierra de nadie" (always floated in an uncomfortable no man's land), is especially acute in interpersonal relationships within her own family. Her mother has remained the "bella dama marmórea" (beautiful, marble lady) that she knew in her childhood, too busy now as always to respond to her daughter's emotional needs with more than a postcard or letter. Compounding this alienation from her mother is her relationship with her daughter Guiomar. A worthy descendent of her grandmother's race of Olympians, Guiomar has inherited not only her grandmother's physical beauty and social poise, but also her remoteness and frigidity. Reflective of these qualities is her scientific profession, which is exercised with antiseptic precision in a large North American university. Having replaced fantasy with numbers and formulas and emotion with empty gestures, Guiomar always maintains a perfect, social and personal equilibrium: "... es una maravilla Guiomar repartiendo besos neutros y precisos, con el grado justísimo de calor y afectuosidad, o de distancia y frío, sin necesidad siquiera de haberlo aprendido, porque ha sabido desenvolverse desde siempre, desde niña, con una naturaleza magnífica, tan olímpica como la de mi madre ..." (p. 113) (Guiomar is a marvel doling out neutral and precise kisses, with the exact degree of warmth and affection, or distance and frigidity, without even having had to learn, because she has always known how to conduct herself, since childhood, with a magnificent naturalness, as Olympic as my mother's). Guiomar's affinity with the "Diosa helénica' (Hellenic goddess) also extends to her relationship with her mother, for it is characterized by a total lack of comprehension for this "niña difícil" (difficult girl) who stands like an "eslabón torcido" (twisted link) between two perfect links on the genealogical chain. The narrator experiences herself as trapped between these two strangers whose love for her is apportioned on the basis of convenience and social propriety. The function of Guiomar and her grandmother as patriarchal guardians of their "madre loca" (crazy mother) and "hija insensata" (foolish daughter) is particularly apparent at the funeral of the oldest link on their genealogical chain, the narrator's grandmother. As the three women march toward the cemetery along with the funeral procession, the protagonist feels that she is being closely watched by her mother and daughter, who are situated on either side of her like "enfermeras" (nurses) or "alguaciles" (bailiffs). Though they apparently fear some form of impropriety on her part, any chance of such an extravagance was stifled long ago by these very watchmen.

One of the social conventions accepted by the narrator was that of marriage to the proper husband. Though celebrated by her mother as an astounding stroke of luck, the protagonist views this relationship as just one more expression of the inauthenticity of her existence. Julio has never represented anything more for her than a stock character in an expensive television commercial, always impeccably dressed with all the right lines, yet totally devoid of substance: "... tampoco Julio existe realmente, más que como institución, una institución a nivel nacional, invención de unos críticos y un público que le necesitan ... y una institución matrimonial — a nivel más social que privado — que inventaron para mí ..." (p. 208) (Julio doesn't really exist either, except as an institution, as a national institution, the invention of some critics and a public that need him ... and as a marital institution — more at a social than a private level — that they invented for me).

The protagonist's return to her childhood home is repeatedly referred to as an attempt to escape a reality experienced as inauthentic in hopes of rediscovering a part of herself abandoned long ago: Her re-establishment of ties with the green world and confrontation with problematic figures from the past thus serve as only a preparation for the accomplishment of the true goal of her quest, the self-realization earlier denied her upon entrance into the patriarchal enclosure. Reflective of this desire for personal transcendence are the many images of transformation presented throughout the novel. Foremost among these is the use of springtime as a leitmotif to underscore the primary action, that of rebirth. The narrator thus expresses her desire to witness the transformation represented by "el momento preciso, ese instante brevísimo y escurridizo en que brotan las hojas ... contra el cielo azul" (p. 18) (the exact moment, that brief and passing instant in which the leaves burst forth ... against the blue sky). Associated with this nature imagery is the role played by the sea as the aqueous source from which all life proceeds. Accordingly, the narrator's penetration into her past is frequently related to a submersion into the ocean depths. It is similarly significant that her final baring of self takes place at sea immediately following a submersion in the ocean, whose aftermath is described as one of absolute peace and contentment. Another recurrent motif is that of the fairy tale mermaid who longed for the handsome prince who would enable her to complete her metamorphosis into a woman. As the narrator relates this story, her own history merges with that of the siren to produce a single tragic outcome. Perhaps most representative of the goal of transformation, however, is the cocoon image used to indicate the narrator's preparation for new life: "cuando se haya tejido el último hilo de seda y el capullo quede cerrado ... volveré a nacer transformada en mariposa ..." (p. 199) (when the last silk thread has been woven and the cocoon is closed ... I will be reborn, transformed into a butterfly).

The narrator's process of transformation is initiated when she meets Clara, a student in her literature class. Though the barrage of fanciful images aroused by a friend's colorful description of the girl as "una aristócrata salvaje y solitaria, que cabalga a pelo sobre corceles pura sangre" (p. 49) (a wild and solitary aristocrat, who rides bareback on pure blooded steeds) is quickly dispelled by the reality of the pale, insignificant girl before her, Clara remains inextricably linked in the narrator's imagination with the green world of the Colombian jungle from which she came. Her designation of Peter Pan as a favorite novel reinforces this association with the magical world of youth. Experiencing this meeting as the "pre-visible final de un primer acto" (foreseeable end of a first act), the narrator begins with Clara a second act in which her student serves as both companion and guide on her journey of self-discovery and affirmation. Clara may thus be viewed as a representative of the green-world lover identified by Pratt, an "ideal, non-patriarchal lover" who "leads the hero away from society and toward her own unconscious depths."[9]

The psychological journey initiated by Clara is expressed in terms of both a spatial penetration and a temporal regression. The lovers embark upon "un complicado ritual ... a través de tres pozos sucesivos de sombra — un pozo dentro de un pozo que está dentro de otro ..." (p. 80) (a complicated ritual ... across three successive wells of shadow — one well within another well within another). Their odyssey is also described as the penetration of a labyrinth and a passage from cave to cave. From a temporal standpoint, the narrator proposes to lead Clara through the labyrinth of time, sharing with her fragments of personal history. The green world's very important role in this recuperation of the past is evident in Tusquets' extensive use of nature imagery to describe their odyssey, for the past is sought "en las ramas de los plátanos y las palmeras del paseo ... entre las olas que rompen en la playa ..." (p. 80) (in the branches of the banana and palm trees along the boulevard ... among the waves that break on the beach).

The concrete goal of this temporal and spatial voyage is the interior patio in the home of the narrator's maternal grandmother. Tusquets' description of this "último pozo" (last well) closely approximates that of the vestibule of the protagonist's former home, for both are presented as places apart from external reality. Isolating themselves in this purified atmosphere among bougainvillea and rustling fields of cane, the lovers recreate a green world in which the freedom and expectation of youth are still possible. In Clara's company the monotony of the narrator's existence is alleviated by a new-found intensity, and she experiences once again the wonder and excitement of adolescence. With this vitality comes a renewal of the erotic energy which characterized the Mays of her girlhood. As she once envisioned nuptial chambers filled with exotic flowers and oriental princes, she now gives full reign to her fantasy amid the lush vegetation of the patio: "... entre las macetas ... he sentado yo a Clara ... Debajo de las buganvillas y las campanillas porque me gustaría que una flor densa, morada, olorosa, vencida, le cayera madura en el regazo o entre el cabello oscuro" (p. 85) (among the flowerpots ... I have seated Clara ... Beneath the bougainvillea and bell-flowers because I would like for a dense, purple, fragrant flower to fall conquered and mature into her lap or among the dark strands of her hair).

Clara's role as auditor and guide facilitates the narrator's plunge into her psychic past in search of the reality hidden beneath the many masks donned

---

[9] Pratt, p. 140.

in her years of participation in the societal farce. At length she discovers a long forgotten aspect of herself which has been preserved intact, safe in its authenticity from the deterioration suffered by others assumed in more recent years. This identity now reappears to replace the many false masks of adulthood:

> ... ningún disfraz de novia, ni de amante, ni de mujer que ha descubierto el amor ... ni de compañera fiel o de madre amantísima, ningún disfraz siquiera de mujer realizada o importante o simplemente feliz. Solo encuentro en el baúl este disfraz agobiante e incómodo ... el disfraz de todas las angustias, de todos los miedos, de toda la tristeza de una infancia ... (pp. 91-92)
>
> (... no mask of a girlfriend, nor of a lover, nor of a woman who has discovered love ... nor of a faithful companion or of a beloved mother, not even the mask of a woman who is fulfilled or important or simply happy. I only find in the trunk this oppressive and uncomfortable mask ... the mask of all the anguish, of all the fears, of all the sadness of a childhood ...)

In this confrontation with the past the narrator discovers that the pain and solitude of her unhappy childhood were never overcome. Her physical maturation was not accompanied by a comparable emotional growth, for this mask overwhelms her now just as it did in her childhood years, "tan pesado que hace que me tambalee y vacile bajo su peso, tan monstruoso que pienso puede arrastrarme en cualquier instante a morir ..." (p. 92) (so heavy that it makes me stumble and sway beneath its weight, so monstrous that I think it can drag me in any moment to my death).

In this exploration of the past, the protagonist experiences for the first time a sense of being understood and accepted for the reality hidden beneath her many social masks. As her relationship with Clara develops on a physical as well as emotional level, the regenerative power of Eros allows the lovers to venture beyond the confines of the patriarchal enclosure to a new personal space. As Elizabeth Ordóñez has noted, one indication of this breach of societal norms is the dissolution of the male/female polarity between active and passive sexuality.[10] The women's mutual recreation of the roles of Beauty and the Beast reflects a movement toward the androgynous state necessary not only for a mature love relationship, but also for

---

[10] Ordóñez, p. 43.

self-realization.[11] Similarly suggestive of a penetration of new space is the narrator's description of Clara's love for her as a power far beyond the narcissistic glorification of self known within the patriarchy. Lowering all of the defensive barriers that have incapacitated them for interpersonal communication, the lovers experience a dissolution of the boundaries of self which is expressed in terms of a symbolic death:

> ... estamos repentinamente al otro lado — mucho más allá — del miedo y la vergüenza, y es evidente y claro que en cualquier instante yo tendré que morir, porque la ternura me ha traspasado como cien alfileres de diamante, la ternura me ha pisoteado y arrollado a su paso como el más terrible de los ejércitos en marcha y me voy deshaciendo, disolviendo, desangrando en palabras ... (p. 158)
> (we are suddenly on the other side of — far beyond — fear and shame, and it is evident and clear that at any moment I will have to die, because tenderness has pierced me like one hundred diamond pins, tenderness has trampled and crushed me at its feet like the most terrible of marching armies and I am melting, dissolving, bleeding away in words ...)

This death of self does not represent, however, a definitive annihilation, but rather an eradication of the old necessary for the construction of a new, transformed personality. Indicative of this psychological rebirth is the new language discovered by the narrator in her relationship with Clara, a language expressive of the tenderness earlier sensed with Guiomar, but never fully realized. Similarly suggestive of a forthcoming metamorphosis is Clara's isolation of her lover from the reality responsible for her disorientation. In much the same way that primitive peoples separated tribal initiates from their former mode of existence prior to incorporation into the new, so Clara constructs a virtual cocoon around the protagonist. Carefully guarding against intrusions from the outside world, she creates an environment in which her lover is strengthened and offered a glimpse of the freedom and fulfillment possible in the future.

Renewed by Clara's unconditional love, the narrator experiences a sensation of wholeness and happiness never known before. Her dignity and self-worth restored, she is at last able to expose the wound responsible for her marginal existence and condemnation to a loveless marriage, "aquella que

---

[11] Pratt, p. 88.

yace oculta y ponzoñosa en lo más hondo de [sus] ciénagas" (the one that lies hidden and poisonous in the deepest of her quagmires), her betrayal by Jorge as an adolescent. The knight in shining armor envisioned in her childhood fantasies, Jorge had come to rescue her from both the antiseptic perfection of a world to which she had never belonged and from the imaginary realm constructed as a refuge from that reality. Like the mythological Theseus, he would free his Ariadne from the depths of the labyrinth and from the Minotaur who had served as her only companion. She would be victorious in her hard fought battle against the narrow world of her parents and the future they had designed for her: "... yo avanzaba al fin con él y él me llevaba por fin hacia la libertad, hacia el encuentro definitivo conmigo misma y con los hombres ... por que avanzábamos hacia unas tierras sin fronteras donde las gentes tenían que ser forzosamente mejores y distintas ..." (p. 196) (I advanced at last with him, and he carried me finally toward freedom, toward the definitive encounter with myself and with man ... because we advanced toward borderless lands where the people had to be better and different). The narrator experienced this period of her life as a joyous release from patriarchal restrictions and from the solitude of her childhood. Reflective of her new-found sense of wholeness was the natural world and the regenerative power of springtime: "... aquel año sí hubo primavera y aprendí a descubrir el momento mágico en que nacen los primeros brotes de los árboles, tiernos y pálidos, aprendí a descifrar la llegada de las primeras golondrinas, y pusimos nombres juntos a árboles y a pájaros ..." (p. 221) (that year there was a spring and I learned to discover that magical moment when the first shoots of the trees are born, tender and pale, I learned to decipher the arrival of the first swallows, and together we named trees and birds). This journey toward a more satisfying existence was never to be completed, however. Like Ariadne abandoned on the island of Naxos and the ice cream parlor mermaid with her half-human body, this new Ariadne was set adrift in the midst of her voyage by the unexplained suicide of her liberator. The hero who had promised to free her from the patriarchal enclosure proved to be only another of its agents, a false green-world lover who led her toward confinement rather than toward liberation.

Though the exposure of the wound responsible for the protagonist's lifelong condemnation to the "tierra de nadie" (no man's land) of a loveless marriage greatly facilitates the healing process initiated by Clara, the final test of this individuation takes the form of a long awaited and much feared phone call and meeting with her husband. Upon leaving the warmth and protection of the green world shared with Clara, the protagonist enters into a reality experienced as alien. Julio's expensive clothing, graying temples and flashy sports car lend the reunion an air of artificiality only matched by his empty rhetoric and the rear seat filled to overflowing with red roses. Her own position within this "spot televisivo" (television spot) is one of awkwardness, the familiar sensation of not knowing exactly what should be said or done. As Julio helps her into the car, her sense of disequilibrium is intensified by the possessive and self-assured manner in which he directs her every movement "como si ... fuera una ancianita o una inválida y no pudiera colocar[se] por [sí] misma piernas y bolso y faldas en su sitio ..." (p. 204) (as if ... she were an old woman or an invalid and couldn't place by herself legs and purse and skirt in their place). As the evening progresses, her desire to halt the absurd representation being staged in her honor is gradually replaced by the inertia that has characterized her thirty years of married life. Incapable of expressing her fundamental indifference toward this man with whom she has spent the entirety of her adult years, she realizes that such an affirmation will perhaps never be possible. Her longing for the opportunity to begin life anew, to "andar por fin sobre las aguas sin que nadie [le] tienda previamente una mano y [le] diga 'ven conmigo,'" (pp. 211-12) (to walk at last on the waters without anyone first holding out their hand saying 'come with me') is countered by her inability to definitively come to terms with what Pratt has referred to as "her feelings about the perfectly nice horrible husband figure."[12]

As Julio opens the car door and helps her in, the protagonist knows that it is, indeed, too late to begin anew. Only a few hours in the company of her husband have reduced her to the condition of helplessness and dependency she has so fought to escape. Incapable of uttering even the feeblest of protests, she allows herself to be driven to the luxurious apartment where her brief flight to freedom will be terminated. Here on a bed resembling that of a movie set, or an operating room, she is definitively separated from the green world and its ideal lover by a representative of the patriarchy whose only model for love is that of rape.[13] Accommodating his listless victim on pillows until the desired effect is achieved, Julio initiates a Hollywood style love scene in which he is the sole participant, a love act whose only object is the narcissistic magnification of self. Like a butterfly sacrificed and added to an already extensive collection, the protagonist's penetration by her husband is expressed in terms of a sacrificial death of self to the patriarchy, a final agonizing submission to a force too powerful to resist:

---

[12] Pratt, p. 142.
[13] Pratt, pp. 24-28.

> ... es mi propia muerte la que cabalga sobre mí, la que me tiene aferrada entre sus piernas sin escape posible, la que me penetra en acometidas sucesivas y brutales, cada vez mas brutales, es mi muerte la que me colma, me inunda, me desborda ... mientras mantengo los ojos fijos en la tapa de la caja implacable que se cerró hace mucho sobre mí ... solo acierto pensar confusamente, tan dolorosamente, en todas las sirenas que recorrerán para siempre las playas en inútil persecución de un alma de mujer ... (p. 216)
> (it is my own death which mounts me, which has me clutched between its legs without any possible means of escape, which penetrates me in successive and brutal assaults, each time more brutal, it is my death which fills me, inundates me, overflows me ... while I keep my eyes fixed on the lid of the implacable box that closed on me long ago ... I am able only to think confusedly, with such sorrow, of all the sirens who will forever search the beaches in useless pursuit of a woman's soul ...)

With her return to the marital fold, Tusquets' protagonist recapitulates the experience of the female hero described by Pratt, for the middle-age hero, like her adolescent counterpart, is seldom successful in her bid for liberation from the patriarchal enclosure. Unable to free herself from what Ordóñez has referred to as "traditional readings of myth and the texts of her unhappy childhood," she remains trapped within the patriarchy and limited to the auxiliary role played by the Ariadnes, Penelopes and Wendys of western society.[14] Here, situated on the margins of both life and death, she relinquishes her futile attempt to realize a dream that no longer exists:

> ...podré volver yo ... a hundirme sin problemas en este duermevela que es mi vida, mi no vida ... mientras un zombie bien amaestrado y moviente me sustituirá con eficacia y hasta con ventaja en las cenas de gala y los estrenos cinematográficos, en la universidad, en mis noches de amor ... y me arrastran felices arriba y abajo sin que a mí me importe nada, sin que a mí me duela ya nada ... (p. 228)
> (I will be able to return ... to immerse myself with no problems in this netherland that is my life, my no life ... while a well-trained and portable zombie will take my place effectively and even to advantage at the formal dinners and movie premieres, at the university, in my nights of

---

[14] Ordóñez, p. 38.

love ... and they will happily drag me up and down without anything mattering to me, without anything hurting me anymore ...)

Montserrat Roig:
A Feminine Perspective and
a Journalistic Slant

Catherine G. Bellver

Since the death of Franco, Spanish women writers have begun to publish with regularity and to show a great diversity in orientation. Spain's youngest women writers set themselves apart from the earlier group of postwar female writers by their cosmopolitanism and their professionalism. Spain's new female narrators form a corps of professional writers who do not write, as has often been scornfully alleged, as a pastime or emergency economic measure, but as a commitment to a career.[1] The field in which many of them engage and earn their first recognition as writers is the journalistic media. While male writers in Spain have long supplemented their income by writing for the press, the existence of numerous female journalists who publish fiction and women narrators who also write for major newspapers and magazines is a new social phenomenon in Spain.

One of the prominent examples of these female narrator-journalists is Montserrat Roig. Born in Barcelona in 1946, Roig graduated in 1968 from the University of Barcelona, where she later taught. Besides being an active print journalist, she has directed a cultural program for Catalan television. She has published three books of interviews, (*Los hechiceros de la palabra,*

---

[1] Although the role of women in Spanish society is changing, the general perception of the female writer is still guided by sexism. In her introduction to *Doce relatos de mujeres* (Madrid: Alianza, 1982), pp. 11-12, Ymelda Navajo states that male critics and sometimes female critics refer to female narrations with scorn. For many, writing by women is still a pastime for idle housewives and frustrated old maids.

1975, *Personatges*, 1979, and *Personatges, segona sèrie*, 1980), a documentary on Catalans in Nazi concentration camps (*Els catalans als camps nazis*, 1978), a report on Leningrad during World War II (*Mi viaje al bloqueo*, 1982), and a book of feminist essays (*¿Tiempo de mujer?*, 1980). Between 1970 and 1982 she also wrote in Catalan a collection of short stories and four novels, all of which appeared in Spanish translation within the four year span of 1980-1983.[2]

Firstly it is of paramount importance that we acknowledge the diversity that exists among female writers. Critics can no longer assert that literature by women is predetermined by a supposed common female mentality, certain appropriately feminine themes, and a particular feminine style, because as the number of women writers increases and as feminist critics challenge stereotype-bound literary analyses, the divergence among female writers becomes more apparent. An objective reading of female texts reveals that changing sociopolitical times and different personal experiences within the same time frame produce differing modes of writing. It is true, as Elizabeth Ordóñez points out, that the reading of female texts ought to focus "upon the possibilities of difference in the female intertext" for, because cultural context and intertext are predominantly authored, shaped and defined by males, works by females have often been considered aberrations or not considered at all.[3] But we must also take into account Annette Kolodny's suggestion that "what we have not fully acknowledged is that the variations among individual women may be as great as those between women and men — and in some cases, perhaps, the variations may be greater within the same sex than between two particular writers of different sexes."[4] A study of Montserrat Roig's fiction illustrates this well, for while her work embraces some concerns found

---

[2] These are her fictional works to date: *Molta roba i poc sabó ... i tan neta que la volen* (Barcelona: Editorial Selecta, 1971), published in Spanish as *Aprendizaje sentimental* (Barcelona: Argos Vergara, 1981); *Ramona, adéu* (Barcelona: Edicions 62, 1972), published in Spanish as *Ramona, adiós* (Barcelona: Argos Vergara, 1980); *El temps de les cireres* (Barcelona: Edicions 62, 1977), published in Spanish as *Tiempo de cerezas* (Barcelona: Argos Vergara, 1980); *L'hora violeta* (Barcelona: Edicions 62, 1980), published in Spanish as *La hora violeta* (Barcelona: Argos Vergara, 1982); and *L'òpera quotidiana* (Barcelona: Planeta, 1982), published in Spanish as *La òpera cotidiana* (Barcelona: Planeta, 1983). All references to Roig's fiction have been taken from these editions and will be indicated in the text by page numbers.

[3] Elizabeth J. Ordóñez, "Reading Contemporary Spanish Narrative by Women," *Anales de la Literatura Española Contemporánea*, 7, no. 2 (1982), pp. 239-40.

[4] "Some Notes on Defining a 'Feminist Literary Criticism,'" *Critical Inquiry*, 2, no. 1 (Autumn 1975) p. 79.

in the fiction of her female contemporaries, it displays a writing style different from most of them. Although coinciding to a certain degree with the autobiographic orientation and the themes traditionally considered characteristic of the woman writer, Roig's works chronicle the emergence of a new Spanish woman, one who begins to question women's traditional role, work outside the home, and participate in political activities. As for her style, far from showing the "delicateness" supposedly peculiar to a woman's disposition, it exhibits the simplicity, sturdiness and unencumbered syntax common to a journalist's prose. The communication media in which Roig works, as we will see, also influences some of her choices of themes and her attitude toward her fictional world.

The autobiographical mode so often assumed to be inherent in women writers and therefore favored by them has been criticized as an indication of self-centeredness and literary inmaturity. Yet, at the same time, for some the autobiographical is desirable in women writers. Antonio de Hoyos, for example, reads literature by women with the hope of finding insight into the mysteries of the feminine soul: "Siempre que aparece un libro escrito por una mujer, cabe la esperanza de dar con el secreto que revele ciertas zonas femeninas difícil de conocer ... Una literatura creada por mujeres que deje paso a la intimidad de pensamiento ... será una experiencia y una ayuda para comprender la limitada noción de la femineidad."[5] (Every time a book written by a woman appears, there is a hope of finding the secret that will reveal certain unfamiliar feminine zones. A literature created by women that unlocks their intimate thoughts will be an experience and an aid to understanding the limited notion of femininity.) Rather than to attack or defend the autobiographical preference of women writers, our purpose here is to establish Montserrat Roig's deviation from the standard autobiographical mode. To be sure, portions of her narrative material are from familiar geographical places, social environments, and professional experiences. The university world of the third Ramona of *Ramona, adéu* and the writing activities of Norma and her feminist discussions with her friend Natàlia in *L'hora violeta* no doubt parallel Roig's own experiences and concerns. Perhaps Norma is simply a mask of the author, as Janet Pérez maintains, but her novels are not autobiographies, for they are not her life story.[6] They are not existen-

---

[5] Antonio de Hoyos, *Ocho escritores actuales* (Murcia: Aula de Cultura, 1954), pp. 157-8. The translation of this citation and all others appearing in parentheses in this text are my own.

[6] Janet Pérez, review of Montserrat Roig, *L'hora violeta* (Barcelona: Edicions 62, 1980), *World Literature Today*, 55, no. 4 (Autumn 1981), pp. 658-9.

tial vehicles of self-revelation, as were the novels of writers such as Unamuno or Baroja, nor are they instruments of psychological exorcism, as *El cuarto de atrás* is for a somewhat older female contemporary, Carmen Martín Gaite.

Fiction for Roig the Journalist is a means of documenting the features of the world around her, particularly as they relate to the psychological struggles of women. Her effective mix of the sociological and the psychological has won her critical praise. Writing of *Ramona, adeu*, C.B. Cadenas concludes that Roig does not fall into the excesses either of the sociological novel or the psychological novel because of her capacity to transmit general substance through particulars, her ability to record the exterior world through memory and language, and her efforts to make the reader not feel detached from that realm in which the everyday becomes history.[7] In *Ramona, adéu* Roig projects the narrative line of the novel upon a temporal grid of three successive generations of women named Ramona — a grandmother married in 1894, a mother who matured during the Civil War, and a granddaughter belonging to the 1960s. The author explores the psychological constant of frustration in love in the lives of these three women and their varying degree of rebellion against the social conventions of their day. Both sociological and psychological factors are present in the novel, but it is the sociological element that provides the conditioning circumstances that account for the third Ramona's break with her ancestors' reluctant accommodations to the will of men and family.

The essential words of the titles of most of her works — the "adéu" of *Ramona, adéu*, "temps" of *El temps de les cireres*, and "hora" of *L'hora violeta* — connote succession, change, history. Her novels represent an attempt to write the fictional biography of an interrelated network of characters belonging to the Catalan bourgeoisie and living during a span of ninety years. In short, her novels constitute the saga of one family group or, as one critic has suggested, the countersaga, for, while in the traditional saga the role assigned to women is generally secondary, in Roig's novels the females are the central focus.[8] Even in *L'òpera quotidiana*, novel in which Horaci Duc reaches the status of major character, the work is narrated to a great extent from the point of view of Patrícia Miralpeix. In addition, Duc's wife, María, is portrayed more sympathetically by the author than he is. Roig's novels ought to be called countersagas also because they represent a pronounced effort to

---

[7] C.B. Cadenas, "Historia de tres mujeres," *Nueva Estafeta*, no. 18 (May 1980), p. 77.

[8] Cadenas, p. 76.

vindicate women and show them as silently heroic in their battle with the passivity their environment imposes on them and with the frustration that this tension inflicts upon them. Roig reconfirms this underlying saga form by providing us, in *L'hora violeta*, with a geneological chart of the two major interconnected families of her novels — the Miralpeix and the Ventura-Claret families —, but unlike the traditional family tree, hers follows the maternal lines. In this way, Roig creates a matrilineal society within the realm of her invented world.

Just as women provide the basis for the ancestral structure in this created society, they supply the point of view, the thematic substance, and the dominant interest. It has often been noted that most of the major characters created by women writers are female. Montserrat Roig is no exception. The men in her novels, as one critic has said, form the screen on which the women project themselves[9] or, as another has said, they stand for the elusive, masculine other half.[10] Unlike the female other in works by men, however, her men do not serve as avenues of self-fulfillment, but, on the contrary, present obstacles to it.

All of Roig's female characters share a comparable female experience. This is not to say that they do not possess a distinctive narrative personality. The non-conventional Kati is different from the abnegated Judit; the idle "grande dame" Ramona of the turn-of-the-century contrasts with the active professional women of today. But while these women are fully developed fictional entities, they are also paradigms of women of their social group and of all women. We ought not go as far as David Ross Gerling and see the women of *L'hora violeta* as a single collective female protagonist, for they are not a single abstract being, but a collective community of differing females who, despite the advance of successive generations, share similar experiences of frustration in love and unfulfillment in life.[11] For example, Natàlia of *L'hora violeta*, by reflecting upon the intimate story of her mother, comes to realize that Judit was not altogether the reprehensible victim she had always thought and that she herself inevitably takes on the passive stance women have always assumed. Nàtalia becomes part of the Penelope syndrome she and her friend Norma have discussed: "Ara hauria d'esperar, i no sabia què. Esperar, destí passiu de les dones (no li servien de res, hauria volgut dir a la

---

[9] Cadenas, p. 77.
[10] David Ross Gerling, "Review of Montserrat Roig, *La hora violeta*," *Anales de la Literatura Española Contemporánea*, 8 (1983), p. 244.
[11] Gerling, p. 244.

Norma, tots els mítings i llibres sobre feminisme. Ara, l'única diferència és que ho sabia, que no li servien de res). Calia esperar, esperar davant del telèfon, mirant de fit a fit l'aparell, com si tingués vida pròpia." (p. 225) (Now she would have to wait., and she did not quite know what she was waiting for. Waiting, the passive destiny of women /she wanted to tell Norma that all those books and feminist meetings were utterly useless. Now the only difference was that she knew they were useless/. She would have to wait, wait for a phone call, stare at the telephone, as if it were a living thing.)

Because she examines the social structure that oppresses women, Montserrat Roig can be considered part of the history of social literature in Spain, but her works differ from the social novels of the 1950s. These encompass a critical viewpoint, a consciousness of national social problems and a sense of collectivity; but the problems treated in them are circumstantial questions of working conditions in a specific region or of repression under a particular political regime. Montserrat Roig, on the other hand, explores problems arising from deep-rooted attitudes and firmly established conventions that do not necessarily change with an improvement in economic and political conditions. Like the social novelist of the 1950s, Roig tends to sympathize with leftist political ideologies, but in her novels she reveals a sense of disillusionment with Marxist political promises. She paints for us a somber picture of a country that enjoys new liberties, both political and sexual, but in which women are still bound by passivity, emotional dependency, and sexism.

Roig's novels differ in another way from the social novels of the 1950s. In the latter, the sense of class struggle is shared among the inhabitants of the fictional world but not generally by the author. Even in the case of Isabel Alvarez de Toledo, a noteworthy female exponent of social realism, we find an aristocrat looking at the downtrodden from a superior social position that detaches her from the empirical impact of the conditions she deplores. Montserrat Roig, on the other hand, suffers some of the marginality of her characters. In her prologue to *Aprendizaje sentimental*, she documents the derision she met when she decided to pursue writing as a career: "¡Una señorita que escribe! ¡No me diga! Usted, con esas piernas, ¿como se atreve a liarse en una proeza que no le corresponde?" (p. 10). (A "young lady" who writes? Don't tell me! With those legs, how do you dare get involved in a feat so improper for you?) Writing, then, becomes for Roig an expression of solidarity with her own group and a challenge to the denigration of women. She becomes the spokesperson of the collective group she depicts and to which she belongs.[12] It is precisely in this spirit of communality among women and not in specific details that the autobiographical quality of Roig's novels resides.

The central theme Roig treats in her novels is the one long considered characteristic of literature by women: love. Love assumes a variety of forms in her works. There is love that is but a mercenary means of exchange and love that is pure fantasy, love inflamed into jealousy and love diluted by routine, love as passion and patience, and love as sacrifice and endurance. However, what we find most often is not the theme of love itself but subordinant themes implying its loss or failure: unrequited love, insufficient love, unhappy marriages and the meaninglessness of daily existence, a desire for freedom from the oppression of love and a longing for the security of love. Her novels are essentially a gallery of women whose lives and conversations revolve around love or the frustration, tedium, insecurity and alienation caused by it. Montserrat Roig seems to define love as an all-consuming passion known primarily to women that devastates yet gives meaning to life. Kati, the woman of experience, who in the 1930s defied conventions by treating sex casually as men often do, was transformed by love. Unwilling to accept a mediocre life without the intensity of love, she commits suicide when her lover is killed in war. This radical refusal of a life without love is contrasted to her married friend Judit's gradual withdrawal from life. Most of Roig's other married women unsuccessfully seek escape from loneliness and frustrated love in fantasy, affairs, or time-consuming, banal activities. Those who leave their husbands or lovers are faced with another type of loneliness implicit in autonomy. Feminism, as Norma and Natàlia discover, does not reconcile the modern independence of professional women with their need for love. Roig's novels, then, are a series of case studies of the impossibility of love as something permanent, stable and eternal on any level or in any historical period. Whether married or unmarried, whether from a past generation or not, whether a professional woman or a housewife, her characters are united in their failure to find lasting love.

Roig's constant focus on the preoccupation of her female characters with love presents a rather traditional view of the feminine psyche. Less typical are some of her youngest women who do begin to show signs of positive

---

[12] Although to lesser extremes than in the nineteenth century, women writers still reflect the literal reality of their own confinement in the constraints they depict in their ficton. We find, then, a continuation of the phenomenon Sandra M. Gilbert and Susan Gubar trace in their *The Madwoman in the Attic* (New Haven: Yale, 1979).

rebellion against the impasse caused by failed love. For example, the third Ramona of *Ramona, adéu*, unlike her mother and grandmother, frees herself from her unsatisfying relationship with a man. She breaks the silence maintained by her predecessors and utters the symbolic farewell of the book's title. This break with tradition is extenuated throughout Roig's novels by her choice of age-group for her characters. Whereas in the novels written by Spanish women born in the 1920s the heroine was often an adolescent, in the narrations written by women like Roig, born in the 1940s, she is more often middle-aged. As the Spanish female emerges from the enclosure of a domestic setting, her knowledge of life extends beyond the altar rail; and as the fictional woman ceases to marry or marries without living happily ever after, the Cinderella myth begins to crumble.

What sets Montserrat Roig apart the most from previous Spanish women writers is the interest and frankness with which she treats sexuality and related taboo motifs. Spanish women writers have scarcely included eroticism in their works until recently.[13] Increased social freedom in Spain since the last years of Franco has manifested itself in an openness toward sexuality among both male and female writers. The distinguishing note among recent women writers who treat sexuality has been their striking challenge of deep-rooted Spanish beliefs on the "feminine being": her presumed passivity, her unlimited maternal abnegation, her incapacity for sexual pleasure, her ineptness in careers. Montserrat Roig disputes the restrictions placed upon women by traditional social norms regarding sex, recognizes the sexual needs of women, considers homosexuality, and explores sexuality as a way to combat tedium. Only with radical defiance can a person like Kati treat sex casually and only within an increasingly feminist mental structure does a person like the youngest Ramona and later Agnes break with Jordi. It is important to note that in Roig's novels sexual liberation does not eliminate disappointment, failed love, and great loneliness for her characters. While on an individual level sexual freedom does not eliminate frustration, on a social level, the very inclusion of sexuality in narrations by women indicates a certain social liberation. If it is true, as Michel Foucault has said, that men have

---

[13] Joaquín Caro Romero in his *Antología de la poesía erótica de nuestro tiempo* (Paris: Ruedo Ibérico, 1973), p. 5, points this out and adds that Spanish women writers have produced even less erotic literature than Latin American ones. Quoting Joaquín Marco, he gives as reasons for the scarcity of erotic poetry in Spain the pervasiveness of Catholic education in Spain and the various social institutions that have been set up over the centuries to repress eroticism.

reacted against sexual repression by talking about sex,[14] then the attention given to sexuality in recent novels by women must be taken as a sign of the same reaction. In her later books Roig is more explicit in her description of erotic scenes, and the variety of sexual preferences adopted by her characters increases. She describes sexual relationships with a straightforward naturalness that excludes lewdness, and she treats homosexuaitiy, not as an issue of debate, but merely as another fragment in the social mosaic she assembles. This "testimonial" orientation reflects Roig's background as a journalist and confers on her fiction a quality of contemporary chronicle.

The aforementioned sociological quality is borne out further by Roig's attention to certain social questions relating to sex: abortion, birth control, and gynecology. In this regard, Roig's novels contrast markedly with those of some of her contemporaries, for example, Esther Tusquets. In Tusquets' works the outside world — historical events, narrative anecdote, and social circumstances — are but an indistinct backdrop before which her characters explore their sexuality and submerge themselves into the secret channels of their psyche. Montserrat Roig, the reporter-novelist, does not focus on the psychological turmoil engendered by the myths imprinted on the female subconscious but on the social or circumstancial inconveniences, restrictions and pain that those myths cause. Her concern is less for a woman's knowledge of herself as a person than for her inability to function freely as an individual in a society conditioned and dominated by patriarchal norms. In her novels, erotic adventures are never, as in Tusquets' fictional world, a blissful, even though temporary, dream time. Never veiling and thereby mythifying sexuality with archetypes, metaphors and literary allusion as Esther Tusquets does, the reporter-novelist intensifies the sour contours of the world she paints with the very directness, terseness and matter-of-fact tone of her journalistic language.

Roig's journalistic activities no doubt also account for the timeliness and topicality of many of the themes she includes in her fiction. No longer can the woman novelist be criticized for shunning the "descorazonante realidad actual," (disheartening current reality) because she does include in her fiction references to current political issues and social questions.[15] Roig uses her fiction to record the crisis in which leftist politics finds itself in post-Franco

---

[14] Michel Foucault, *The History of Sexuality. Volume I: An Introduction* (New York: Vintage Books, 1980), p. 94.

[15] This is the position held by Olga Prjevalinsky Ferrer, "Las novelistas españolas de hoy," *Cuadernos Americanos*, 20, no. 118 (1962), p. 223.

Spain. She indicates that the legalization of the Communist party in Spain seems to have diffused the intensity of commitment of party members, disclosed the contradictions and inauthenticity of the motives of many militants, and highlighted an ideological disintegration paralleling the broken human relationships so prevalent in her novels. Rational and cautious, Roig approaches political liberation with the same sense of reservation she does sexual freedom. It is apparent to her that the death of a dictator does not in itself erase all political dilemmas and does in fact give rise to a new set of problems.

Monserrat Roig incorporates political events in her novels, often making them the temporal skeleton that supports the body of other narration. In *Ramona, adéu,* it is the Civil War that serves as a structural frame by both opening and closing the novel and as a point of psychological reference for some of the female characters who experienced during that time rare moments of emotional intensity and of liberation from patriarchal dominion. In *El temps de les cireres,* Natàlia consciously correlates her departure from Spain to the demonstrations on behalf of the Asturian strikers and the arrest of the political dissident Grimau and her return to Spain to the death of the anarchist Puig Antich. Although Montserrat Roig weaves political events into the fabric of her prose, the women of her novels are divorced from political action until the postwar period, and, even then, they remain peripheral to active participation. Natàlia accompanies Emilio in some political demonstrations, but it is he who is imprisoned for his activities and Communist affiliation. The youngest Ramona attends political meetings not only out of ideological conviction but to be with her boyfriend, Jordi, a militant student leader. This placement of women in the position of spectator of political events, of course, reflects the traditional subordinate political role to which women have been confined. Only an alert feminist woman like Norma begins to notice the discrepancy in political roles between men and women and their differing perception of politics: "Aquella nit, en Ferran va entrar cridant a casa. No era el seu costum, i em va estranyar. Hem guanyat!, va fer. No sé si va ser aleshores quan em vaig adonar per primera vegada que la seva lluita ja no era la meva ... per a en Ferran tot era qüestió de termes i paraules. Jo li volia parlar de la meva visita a en Germinal i de la història del barquer." (p. 149) (The other night Ferran came into the house shouting. He didn't usually do that, so it surprised me. We've won, he said to me. I don't know if it was at that moment that I realized that his struggle was no longer mine ... for Ferran everything was a matter of terms and words. I wanted to talk to him about my visit to Germinal and the story about the boatman.)

Montserrat Roig's novels are filled with feminist preoccupations and thematics. Many of her female characters are women who have professionally entered the man's world as journalists, novelists, photographers, doctors and artists, but they are shown throughout her novels to be psychologically different from men. This last point becomes an issue of debate in *L'hora violeta*, which in many sections constitutes the exposition of two divergent feminist points of view as espoused by its protagonists. Natàlia, having considered women the designers of their own victimization, has, throughout her life, unconsciously admired and even attempted to assume features of the male personality. Norma, on the other hand, embraces with enthusiasm the total female identity of professional woman, mother, and wife. Since each in the end must come to terms with her emotional dependency on men, the author leaves us with the thought that, despite differing attitudes toward womanhood and the increased freedom women have in today's world, women universally share a basic subservience to love.

In spite of this message of communality among women, Roig's writing technique deviates from that delicate and meticulous style so often deemed characteristically feminine and, therefore, unacceptable. Yet, by the same token, any coincidences with traditionally male styles of writing are also seen as inappropriate and equally anomalous. Long-honored gender bound stereotypes make it difficult for male critics to accept a vigorous style in a female writer as inherently her own. For instance, Valbuena Prat, unable to reconcile the "femenino" and "varonil" evident in Santa Teresa, constantly counterposes these elements in his comments on her. He equates the "femenino" with delicateness and the "varonil" with "dominio": "En la vida y en la prosa de Teresa se perciben ecos de un carácter que inspira confianza, atrae y termina por dominar. Sensiblidad de contraste, posee un delicado espíritu femenino a la vez que una potencia de dominio verdaderamente varonil.[16] (In the life and prose of Teresa, there can be perceived echoes of a character that inspires trust, attracts, and eventually dominates. A sensibility of contrast, she possesses a delicate feminine spirit and at the same time a truly virile power of dominion.) Unwilling to accept that this mystical and unpretentious writer was also an effective founder of convents and a person keenly aware of the public world of malicious court intrigues, he pardons her strength by implying it merely veils her hidden femininity: "Bajo el ropaje varonil de la monja andariega, la voz femenina más delicada de unas entra-

---

[16] Angel Valbuena Prat, *Historia de la literatura española* (Barcelona: Editorial Gustavo Gili, 1963), vol. I, p. 673.

ñas transverberadas de espiritual maternidad."[17] (Beneath the virile garb of the travelling nun, the most delicate feminine voice of mystical feelings of spiritual maternity.) This digression is necessary to show that Montserrat Roig's style is not "varonil," as Valbuena Prat states, but that a writer's cultural context and professional training inevitably manifest themselves in the writings of women as well as men. The journalistic qualities of Roig's prose — terseness, objectivity, abruptness — are not, then, an artificial imposition of male attributes but a natural consequence of her own particular experiences.

To begin with, Montserrat Roig treats her fictional material much in the same way a reporter lays out news items in a newspaper or an interviewer presents a human interest story on television. She treats numerous social issues moving quickly from one item to another. Roig is an observer of the contemporary scene interested more in recording what she sees than in pausing for analysis or for studied refinement of her verbal style. Along with this distinctive attitude toward the material of her fiction, we find an attitude toward the vehicle of writing that also reflects her journalistic training.[18] Montserrat Roig emphasizes the referential or informative function of language whereby words are a direct medium for transmitting meaning. Consequently, her fiction is devoid of the many literary allusions, the symbolism, and self-conscious stance present in some of her contemporaries.

Roig's overriding attitude toward her text is that of the serious, objective and detached chronicler. Her seriousness sets her apart from her contemporary male journalists, like the humorous Francisco Umbral, whose professed motivation for writing is self-revelation, or like Manuel Vicent, who sardonically mocks the foibles and neuroses of our times without challenging society's myths.[19] Whether evoking the past or referring to today, Roig paints a series of representative portraits of women who cope with, succumb to, or reject social myths. This preference for human portraiture to some extent confirms her training in television interviewing, just as rapid and disjointed treatment of events corroborates the terse and abrupt style of a

---

[17] Valbuena Prat, p. 684.

[18] The direction of influence may, of course, on occasion be reversed. Azorín brought to his newspaper articles the earmark of his lyrical, impressionistic fiction.

[19] José Angel Fernández Roca, "Crónica y la novela en *La ninfas* de Umbral," *Cuadernos Hispanoamericanos*, no. 373 (1981), p. 110, observes that Umbral's typical chronicle always has an autobiographic base. Umbral himself has said in *Las ninfas* (Barcelona: Destino, 1976), p. 107, that "el hombre está repasando siempre el libro de su vida."

newspaper writer. In *Ramona, adéu*, Roig interweaves three distinct historical periods, *El temps de les cireres* contains numerous flashbacks, and in *L'hora violeta*, the author jumps freely from the Civil War to different years of the postwar period and from places both in and out of Spain. What we find, much like in a human interest documentary, is a flickering montage of events and faces the author chooses to focus upon in her attempt to explore the human drama beneath the surface of historical fact. The journalist's sense of objectivity obliges Roig to ask questions rather than answer them. She exposes cooly the personal problems of her characters and some of those of the period in which they live, without hyperbole of deformation and never proposing solutions. Whether treating sexuality, politics, or feminism, she balances enthusiasm with disenchantment.

Within her montage effect, Roig often structures the individual episodic elements of her human chronicle along the lines of an interview or eyewitness scheme. For example, despite the editors' notice that *L'òpera quotidiana* contains a series of arias, cavatinas and duets, the book is basically composed of a series of dramatic monologues that remind us of an interview, in which one party speaks endlessly but no true communication takes place because both parties do not share mutual feelings. Even Roig's frequent recourse to a diary format suggests one active, revealing voice overheard by a curious, questioning onlooker (the reader). Where we see the closest correlation between fictional narration and the journalistic interview is in Roig's incorporation, in her character Norma's interviews, of information she herself gathered when preparing her documentary book on Catalans in Nazi concentration camps. Roig goes beyond the interpolation of facts to interweave the drama of some of the survivors of these camps into the conversations and lives of her fictional creations. This treatment of real events through literary form to a great extent meets the criteria of "New Journalism," Tom Wolfe's terminology for the application of specific devices of realistic fiction to material gathered by exhaustive reportage.[20]

"New Journalism" demands that the devices of scene-by-scene construction, the recording of dialogue, status details, and a point of view other than the author's own be applied to the exterior world actually observed by the author or his contemporaries. Roig's historical perspective and her many

---

[20] Tom Wolfe explains this new form in "The New Journalism" in *The New Journalism*, eds. Tom Wolfe and E.W. Johnson (New York: Harper and Row, 1979), pp. 389-99. For an outline of the discussion on the "New Journalism" theory see John Hellman, "The Nature and Modes of the New Journalism: A Theory," *Genre*, 13, no. 4 (Winter, 1980), pp. 517-29.

invented events prevent her fiction from being classified as "New Journalism." However, she does employ many of its recommended devices of eyewitness reportage, particularly in the initial pages of *Ramona, adéu*. In these pages, Roig reconstructs one day in the Spanish Civil War through the eyes of Ramona, the mother, and with exact references to dates and elements of the actual world. The journalist's dependence on quotations to authenticate facts and eliminate her own inner voice from the writing leads Roig to an excessive and awkward use of indirect discourse. By crowding a number of themes and narrative threads in one short chapter without stopping to develop them or making connections among them, Roig reveals an underlying desire to transfer to her fictional world some of the compactness of style and the condensation of materials for which a reporter strives. These elements serve to imbue her fiction with movement and a sense of nervous urgency that help convey the agitation and instability of the scene she depicts.

Another journalistic feature Roig transfers to her fiction is a reliance on colloquial language and foreign words, especially English ones. In her works we find such idiomatic expressions as "no la podia veure gens ni mica," "deixar-la verde," and "la ballàvem magra." The words she uses are simple, everyday ones, and primarily nouns and verbs. Even Roig's most descriptive passages contain a minimum of adjectives; and those that are used are not unusual: "un riu glaçat que travessa una vall, les roques d'un espadat tenebrós, unes barques amb xarxes i el mar que bramula al fons, unes donzelles entre coloms de color negre, una noia amb el càntir trencat i una tempesta que s'acosta, un jardí sinestre i ple de desmais, un castell misteriós mig amagat per les enfiladisses i els emparrats" (*Ramona, adéu*, pp. 78-79) (An icy river that crosses a valley, the rocks of a dark cliff, boats with nets and the sea roaring in the background, young maidens among black doves, a girl with a broken water jug and an approaching storm, a sinister garden full of weeping willows, a mysterious castle half hidden by ivy and arbors.)

Montserrat Roig's incorporation of Spanish words into novels appearing originally in Catalan does not attest to her journalistic background but to her bilingualism and the predominance of Spanish as the primary language of Spain. What does however provide evidence of her training as a reporter is her use of numerous anglicisms. After studying three different Spanish publications, John England and J.L. Caramés Lage have concluded that the more liberal the publication, the more unrestricted the use of anglicisms. They found that *Cambio 16* includes anglicisms not only in advertisements, sports articles, and less serious reports but also in editorials and political articles and uses them so profusely that often a feeling of confusion and tedium is produced. More than providing information, these words create an impression of cosmopolitanism and modernity.[21] Montserrat Roig inserts an ample number of anglicisms into her novels. The snatches of conversation in English and words like "cream tea" and "scones," in *El temps de les cireres*, can be said to evoke the England Natàlia is leaving; but, other English words like "hippy," "baby-sitter," "tupperware" and terms like "bluejeans," "living-room," and "hamsters" that have Spanish equivalents demonstrate the desire to be up-to-date that England and Caramés Lage study.

The following excerpt from *El temps de les cireres* can serve as a concluding illustration of the rhythm, the structure, and the language characteristic of Montserrat Roig's style and particularly of the terseness and abruptness derived from her journalistic training.

> La Sílvia arribà. Què t'ha passat?, el rostre candorós, què has fet? En veure-la, la Natàlia se'n va penedir. M'ho promets, que no diràs res a Lluís? La Sílvia, però, què ...? m'ho jures?, repetí la Natàlia. T'ho juro. Si no, féu la Natàlia, si li dius, és que no em vols ajudar. Es clar que sí, que et vull ajudar!, gairebé cridà la Sílvia. He avortat i no em trobo bé. Em fa molt de mal el ventre i deixo anar uns coàguls de sang enormes. Oh, va fer la Sílvia tapant-se la boca. La Natàlia li donà el telèfon del ginecòleg i la Sílvia va trucar. (p. 137)
>
> (Sílvia arrived. What's wrong with you?, her innocent look, what have you done? When she saw her, Natàlia regretted having spoken. Will you promise me you won't say anything to Lluís? And Sílvia, but what...? Swear to me you won't, Natàlia repeated, I swear to you. If you tell him, Natàlia said, it means you don't want to help me. Of course I want to help you, Sílvia nearly shouted. I've had an abortion and I don t feel well. My stomach hurts and enormous clots of blood are coming out. Oh!, said Sílvia, covering her mouth. Natàlia gave her the gynecologist's number, and Sílvia called.)

Roig focuses her interest more on narrative events than on psychological analysis, moving quickly from item to item with a brusqueness and quickness that project the urgency of her characters and, by extension, reflect the fast-moving, disjointed, cluttered modern world. Her sentences are short, the

---

[21] John England and J.L. Caramés Lage, "El uso y abuso de anglicismos en la prensa española de hoy," *Arbor*, 100, no. 390 (June 1978), pp. 77-89.

lexicon simple, the syntax uncomplicated, and the general tone conversational. She achieves a cool objectivity by the meager use of adjectives and the avoidance of abstract terms. Her unadorned and unencumbered prose moves swiftly and effectively as she rushes to capture the fleeting moment and human gesture.

Because women are entering fields unknown to them in the past, their works exhibit manners of writing not previously associated with them. Montserrat Roig's involvement in the communication media has had an undeniable impact on her approach to fictional writing. It has shaped her voice, influenced her choice of materials, determined the construction of her novels, and governed her use of vocabulary. A study of Roig's fiction reveals that while many women writers may share certain common features, particularly thematic ones, their styles reflect their varying experiences and literary training. In addition, Roig's works attest to the adaptability of a non-fictional style to fictional writing and to the compatibility between author and woman. With the growth of feminism, Spanish women writers have begun to demythify traditional conventions, particularly marriage and romantic love. What Roig fails to resolve in her fiction is the dilemma of those women who free themselves from former social constraints but who still endure an emotional dependence on love for their well-being. The Cinderella myth may be crumbling, but the Penelope syndrome remains. For Roig, the recent changes in the institution of marriage, in the traditional role of women, and in old moral codes are self-evident, but psychologically women still are more committed to love than men. In her collection of feminist essays ¿*Tiempo de mujer?*, Roig affirms that women surrender themselves more completely to love than men, who always maintain a psychic division within themselves. There are women today, she says, who have begun to have a partial, masculine idea of love, women who are cerebral and less vital. Her conclusion is, however, that these women save themselves more but live less.[22] Thus, we learn that beneath the pain of her female characters' psychological frustration there lies in Roig s fiction an implicit celebration of women's capacity for total love. Her portrayal of the marginal part women play in social and political events is meant to call attention to the subordination of women while, at the same time, recording the reality of our times, for Roig never abandons her perspective as chronicler of the contemporary scene when she embraces the feminine dimension of today's world. She writes

---

[22] Montserrat Roig, ¿*Tiempo de mujer?* (Barcelona: Plaza y Janés, 1980), p. 286.

from a woman's point of view, but being a reporter, her fiction is based on her experiences and inclinations as a journalist.

BIBLIOGRAPHY

I. MAJOR WORKS BY AUTHORS STUDIED IN ESSAYS

Galvarriato, Eulalia. *Cinco sombras*. Barcelona: Destino, 1947.
Gómez Ojea, Carmen. *Otras mujeres y Fabia*. Barcelona: Argos Vergara, 1982.
Laforet, Carmen. *La insolación*. Barcelona: Planeta, 1963.
_____. *La isla y los demonios*. Barcelona: Destino, 1952.
_____. *La llamada*. Barcelona: Destino, 1954.
_____. *La muerta*. Madrid: Ediciones Rumbos, 1952.
_____. *La mujer nueva*. Barcelona: Destino, 1955.
_____. *Nada*. Barcelona: Destino, 1945.
_____. *La niña y otros relatos*. Madrid: Magisterio Español, 1970.
Martín Gaite, Carmen. *Las ataduras*. Barcelona: Destino, 1960.
_____. *El balneario*. Madrid: Afrodisio Aguado, 1945.
_____. *El cuarto de atrás*. Barcelona: Destino, 1978.
_____. *Cuentos completos*. Madrid: Alianza, 1978.
_____. *Entre visillos*. Barcelona: Destino, 1958.
_____. *Fragmentos de interior*. Barcelona: Destino, 1976.
_____. *Retahílas*. Barcelona: Destino, 1974.
_____. *Ritmo lento*. Barcelona: Seix Barral, 1963.
Matute, Ana María. *A la mitad del camino*. Barcelona: Rocas, 1961.
_____. *Los Abel*. Barcelona: Destino, 1948.
_____. *Algunos muchachos*. Barcelona: Destino, 1968.
_____. *El arrepentido*. Barcelona: Rocas, 1961.
_____. *En esta tierra*. Barcelona: Exito, 1955.

———. *Fiesta al noroeste*. Barcelona: Pareja y Borrás, 1959.
———. *Los hijos muertos*. Barcelona: Planeta, 1958.
———. *Historias de la Artámila*. Barcelona: Destino, 1961.
———. *Libro de juegos para los niños de los otros*. Barcelona: Lumen, 1961. (essays and short stories)
———. *Los niños tontos*. Madrid: Arion, 1956.
———. *Pequeño teatro*. Barcelona: Planeta, 1954.
———. *Primera memoria*. Barcelona: Destino, 1960.
———. *El río*. Barcelona: Argos, 1963. (personal essays).
———. *Los soldados lloran de noche*. Barcelona: Destino, 1964.
———. *El tiempo*. Barcelona: Mateu, 1957.
———. *La torre vigía*. Barcelona: Lumen, 1971.
———. *La trampa*. Barcelona: Destino, 1969.
———. *Tres y un sueño*. Barcelona: Destino, 1961.
Medio, Dolores. *Andrés*. Oviedo: R. Grandio, 1967.
———. *Atrapados en la ratonera: Memorias de una novelista*. Madrid: Alce, 1980.
———. *El bachanco*. Madrid: Magisterio Español, 1974.
———. *Bibiana*. Madrid: Bullón, 1963.
———. *Compás de espera*. Barcelona: Ediciones G.P., 1954.
———. *Diario de una maestra*. Barcelona: Destino, 1961.
———. *El fabuloso imperio de Juan sin Tierra*. Barcelona: Plaza y Janés, 1981.
———. *Farsa de verano*. Madrid: Espasa Calpe, 1973.
———. *Funcionario público*. Barcelona: Destino, 1956.
———. *Mañana. Cinco novelas*. Madrid: Cid, 1954.
———. *Nosotros, los Rivero*. Barcelona: Destino, 1953.
———. *La otra circunstancia*. Barcelona: Destino, 1972.
———. *El pez sigue flotando*. Barcelona: Destino, 1959.
———. *El señor García*. Madrid: Alfaguara, 1966.
———. *El urogallo*. Gijon: NOEGA, 1982.
Moix, Ana María. *Baladas del dulce Jim*. Barcelona: Saturno, 1969.
———. *Ese chico pelirrojo a quien veo cada día*. Barcelona: Lumen, 1971.
———. *Julia*. Barcelona: Seix Barral, 1970.
———. *No time for flowers y otras historias*. Barcelona: Lumen, 1971/72.
———. *Walter ¿por qué te fuiste?* Barcelona: Barral Editores, 1973.
Montero, Rosa. *Cinco años de País*. Madrid: Debate, 1979. (interviews)

──────────. *Crónica del desamor*. Madrid: Debate, 1979.
──────────. *España para ti ... para siempre*. Madrid: A.Q. Ediciones, 1976. (interviews)
──────────. *La función Delta*. Madrid: Debate, 1981.
──────────. *Te trataré como a una reina*. Barcelona: Seix Barral, 1983.
Oliver, Maria-Antònia. *Crineres de foc*. Barcelona: Laia, 1985.
──────────. *Cròniques de la molt anomenada ciutat de Montcarrà*. Barcelona: Edicions 62, 1972.
──────────. *Cròniques d'un mig estiu*. Barcelona: Club Editor, 1970.
──────────. *Figues d'un altre paner*. Palma de Mallorca: Moll, 1979.
──────────. *Punt d'arròs*. Barcelona: Galba, 1979.
──────────. *El vaixell d'iràs i no tornaràs*. Barcelona: Laia, 1976.
──────────. *Vegetal i Muller qui cerca espill*. Barcelona: La llar del llibre, 1982. (TV screenplays)
Ortiz, Lourdes. *Comunicación crítica*. Madrid: Pablo del Río, 1977. (literary criticism)
──────────. *En días como estos*. Madrid: Akal, 1981.
──────────. *Luz de la memoria*. Madrid: Akal, 1976.
──────────. *Las murallas de Jérico*. Madrid: Peralta, 1980. (play)
──────────. *Picadura mortal*. Madrid: Sedmay, 1979.
──────────. *Urraca*. Barcelona: Puntual, 1982.
Puértolas, Soledad. *El bandido doblemente armado*. Madrid: Legasa, 1980.
──────────. *Una enfermedad moral*. Madrid: Trieste ,1982. (short stories)
Quiroga, Elena. *Algo pasa en la calle*. Barcelona: Destino, 1954.
──────────. *Carta a Cadaqués*. Santander: Bedia, 1961.
──────────. *La enferma*. Barcelona-Madrid-México: Noguer, 1955.
──────────. *Escribo tu nombre*. Barcelona-Madrid: Noguer, 1965.
──────────. *Plácida, la joven y otras narraciones*. Madrid: Prensa Española, 1956.
──────────. *Presente profundo*. Barcelona: Destino, 1973.
──────────. *La sangre*. Barcelona: Destino, 1952.
──────────. *La soledad sonora*. Madrid: Espasa-Calpe, 1949.
──────────. *Tristura*. Barcelona-Madrid: Noguer, 1960.
──────────. *La última corrida*. Barcelona: Noguer, 1958.
──────────. *Viento del norte*. Barcelona: Destino, 1951.
Riera, Carme. *Epitelis tendríssims*. Barcelona: Edicions 62, 1981.
──────────. *Jo pos per testimoni les gavines,* Barcelona: Laia, 1977.
──────────. *Palabra de mujer, bajo el signo de una memoria impenitente*. Barcelona: Laia, 1980.

———. *Una primavera per a Domènico Guarini*. Barcelona: Edicions 62, 1981.

———. *Una primavera para Domènico Guarini*, trans. Luisa Cotoner. Barcelona: Ediciones Norte, 1981.

———. *Te deix, amor, la mar com a penyora*. Barcelona: Laia, 1975.

Rodoreda, Mercè. *Aloma*. Barcelona: Edicions 62, 1969.

———. *El carrer de les Camelies*. Barcelona: Club dels Novelistes, 1966.

———. *Jardí vora el mar*. Barcelona: Club dels Novelistes, 1967.

———. *La meva Cristina i altres contes*. Barcelona: Edicions 62, 1967.

———. *My Christina and Other Stories*, trans. and with an introduction by David H. Rosenthal. Port Townsend, WA: Graywolf Press, 1984.

———. *Mirall trencat*. Barcelona: Club Editor, 1974.

———. *La Plaça del Diamant*. Barcelona: Club dels Novelistes, 1962.

———. *La Plaza del Diamante*, trans. Enrique Sordo. Barcelona: EDHASA, 1965.

———. *The Pigeon Girl*, trans. Eda O'Shield. London: Deutsch, 1967.

———. *Time of the Doves*, trans. and with an introduction by David Rosenthal. New York: Taplinger, 1983.

———. *Semblava de seda i altres contes*. Barcelona: Edicions 62, 1978.

———. *Quanta, quanta guerra*. Barcelona: Club Editor, 1980.

———. *Viatges i flors*. Barcelona: Edicions 62, 1980.

———. *Vint-i-dos contes*. Barcelona: Selecta, 1957.

Roig, Montserrat. *L'hora violeta*. Barcelona: Edicions 62, 1980.

———. *La hora violeta*. trans. Enrique Sordo. Barcelona: Argos Vergara, 1980.

———. *Molta roba i poc sabó*. Barcelona: Edicions 62, 1971.

———. *Aprendizaje sentimental*. trans. Mercedes Nogués. Barcelona: Argos Vergara, 1971.

———. *L'òpera quotidiana* Barcelona: Planeta, 1982.

———. *La ópera cotidiana*. trans. Enrique Sordo. Barcelona: Planeta, 1983.

———. *Ramona, adéu*. Barcelona: Edicions 62, 1976.

_____. *Ramona, adiós.* trans. Joaquim Sempere. Barcelona: Argos Vergara, 1980.
_____. *El temps de les cireres.* Barcelona: Edicions 62, 1977.
_____. *Tiempo de cerezas.* trans. Enrique Sordo. Barcelona: Argos Vergara, 1981.
_____. Salisachs, Mercedes. *Adagio confidencial.* Barcelona: Planeta, 1973.
_____. *Carretera intermedia.* Barcelona: Luis de Caralt, 1956.
_____. *El declive y la cuesta.* Barcelona: Planeta, 1962.
_____. *La estación de las hojas amarillas.* Barcelona: Planeta, 1963.
_____. *La gangrena.* Barcelona: Planeta, 1975.
_____. *Los que se quedan.* Barcelona: Juventud, 1942.
_____. *Más allá de los raíles.* Barcelona: Luis de Caralt, 1957.
_____. *Una mujer llega al pueblo.* Barcelona: Planeta, 1957.
_____. *Pasos conocidos: Dos novelas y nueve relatos.* Barcelona: Pareja y Borras, 1958.
_____. *La presencia.* Barcelona: Argos Vergara, 1979.
_____. *Primera mañana, última mañana.* Barcelona: Luis de Caralt, 1955.
_____. *El proyecto y otros relatos.* Barcelona: Planeta, 1978.
_____. *La sinfonía de las moscas.* Barcelona: Planeta, 1982.
_____. *La última aventura.* Barcelona: Planeta, 1967.
_____. *Vendimia interrumpida.* Barcelona: Planeta, 1960.
_____. *Viaje a Sodoma.* Barcelona: Planeta, 1977.
_____. *El volumen de la ausencia.* Barcelona: Planeta, 1983.
Soriano, Elena. *Caza menor.* Madrid: La Nave, 1951.
_____. *Caza menor.* Madrid: Prensa Espanola, 1976.
_____. *Mujer y hombre.* Madrid: Calleja, 1955. Contains: *La playa de los locos, Espejismos* and *Medea 55.*
Tusquets, Esther. *El amor es un juego solitario.* Barcelona: Lumen, 1979.
_____. *El mismo mar de todos los veranos.* Barcelona: Lumen, 1979.
_____. *Siete miradas en un mismo paisaje.* Barcelona: Lumen, 1981.
_____. *Varada tras el último naufragio.* Barcelona: Lumen, 1980.
Valentí, Helena. *L'amor adult.* Barcelona: Edicions 62, 1977.
_____. *La solitud d'Anna.* Barcelona: Edicions 62, 1981.

II. CRITICAL STUDIES

Arnau, Carme. *Introducció a la narrativa de Mercè Rodoreda.* Barcelona: Edicions 62, 1979.
Arnau, Carme. "La obra de Mercè Rodoreda." *Cuadernos Hispanoamericanos,* no. 383 (May 1982), pp. 239-57.
Atlee, A.F. Michael. "El enigma de Ana María Matute." *Explicación de Textos Literarios,* XIII, no. 1 (1984-85), pp. 289-57.
Badía, Lola. "*Solitud,* novel.la." *Quaderns Crema,* 8 (1984), pp. 27-35.
Bellver, Catherine G. "Carmen Martín Gaite as a Social Critic." *Letras Femeninas,* VI, no. 2, (1980), pp. 3-16.
Bellver, Catherine G. "The Language of Eroticism in the Novels of Esther Tusquets." *Anales de la Literatura Española Contemporanea,* IX, (1984), pp. 13-27.
Bellver, Catherine G. "Two New Women Writers from Spain." *Letras Femeninas,* VIII, no. 2 (1982), pp. 3-7.
Bieder, Maryellen. "Cataclysm and Rebirth: Journey to the Edge of the Maelstrom: Mercè Rodoreda's *Quanta, quanta guerra ... .*" *Actes del Tercer Col.loqui d'Estudis Catalans a Nord America.* Barcelona: Publicaciones de l'Abadia de Montserrat (1983), pp. 227-237.
Bieder, Maryellen. "The Woman in the Garden: The Problem of Identity in the Novels of Mercè Rodoreda." *Actes del Segon Colloqui d'Estudis Catalans a Nord America.* Barcelona: Publicacions de l'Abadia de Montserrat (1982), pp. 253-64.
Bigorda, J. "El cuarto de atrás o el desvelo de unos recuerdos." *El Correo Catalán,* (25 June, 1978).
Bloomquist, Gregori. "Notes per a una lectura de *Solitud.*" *Els marges,* 34 (January 1975), pp. 104-07.
Brent, Albert. "The Novels of Elena Quiroga." *Hispania,* 42 (1959), pp. 210-13.
Brown, Joan Lipman. "The Nonconformist Character as Social Critic in the Novels of Carmen Martín Gaite." *Kentucky Romance Quarterly,* XXVIII, no. 2, (1981), pp. 165-76.
Brown, Joan Lipman. *Secrets from the Back Room: The Fiction of Carmen Martín Gaite.* University, MS: Romance Monographs, 1985.
Brown, Joan Lipman. "A Fantastic Memoir: Technique and History in *El cuarto de atrás.*" *Anales de la Novela Española Contemporánea,* VI (1981), pp. 13-20.
Brown, Joan Lipman. "*Tiempo de silencio* and *Ritmo lento*: Pioneers of the

New Social Novel in Spain." *Hispanic Review*, 50, no. 1, (Winter 1982), pp. 61-73.

Butler de Foley, Isabel. "Hacia un estudio del tiempo en la obra narrativa de Carmen Martín Gaite." *Insula*, XXXIX, nos. 452-453 (July-August 1984), p. 18.

Callejo, Alfonso "Corporeidad y escaparates en *La Plaza del Diamante* de Mercè Rodoreda." *Butlletí de la NACS*, no. 16, (1983), pp. 14-17.

Castellanos, Jordi. "*Solitud*, novella modernista." *Els Marges*, 25 (1982), pp. 45-70.

Cerezales, Agustín. *Carmen Laforet*. Madrid: Ministerio de Cultura, 1982.

Chown, Linda E. "American Critics and Spanish Women Novelists." *Journal of Women in Culture and Society*, 9, no. 1 (Autumn 1983), pp. 91-107.

Claraso, Mercè. "The Angle of Vision in the Novels of Mercè Rodoreda." *Bulletin of Hispanic Studies*, no. 57 (1980), pp. 143-52.

Cordero, Mercedes Hilda. *La novelística de Elena Quiroga; La problematica social en 'Algo pasa en la calle'*. Ann Arbor: Dissertation Abstracts International, 1976.

Cotoner, Luisa. "Una primavera per a Domenico Guarini de Carme Riera." *Mirall de glaç: Quaderns de literatura*, (Spring-Summer, 1982), pp. 52-57.

DeCoster, Cyrus C. "Carmen Laforet: A Tentative Evaluation." *Hispania*, XL (1957), pp. 187-91.

Domingo, José. "Narrativa española." *Insula*, 253 (December 1967), p. 5.

Durán Manuel. "Carmen Martín Gaite: *Retahílas, El cuarto de atrás*, y el diálogo sin fin." *Revista Iberoamericana*, XLVII, no. 116-117 (1981), pp. 233-40.

El Saffar, Ruth. "Structural and Thematic Tactics of Suppression in Carmen Laforet's *Nada*." *Symposium*, 28 (1974), pp. 119-29.

Espadas, Elizabeth. "The Short Fiction of Carmen Martín Gaite." *Letras Femeninas*, IV, no. 1 (1978), pp. 3-19.

Fagundo, Ana María. "Presencia de la mujer novelista en la literatura española." *Letras Femeninas*, IX, no. 1 (1983), pp. 3-10.

Falcón, Lidia. "El patrimonio imperecedero del feminismo." *Vindicación feminista*, no. 12 (1 June 1977), pp. 6-7.

Feal Deibe, Carlos. "*Nada* de Carmen Laforet: La iniciación de una adolescente." *The Analysis of Hispanic Texts: Current Trends in Methodology*, ed. Mary Ann Beck et al. Jamaica, NY: Bilingual Press, 1976.

Flores-Jenkins, Raquel Galbis. *La mujer como individuo y como tipo en la novelística de Ana María Matute*. Ann Arbor: Dissertation Abstracts International, 1980.

Formica, Mercedes. "Spain." trans. Judith Arnon. in *Women in the Modern World*. Edited by Raphael Patai. New York: The Free Press, 1967.

Forrest, Gene Steven. "El diálogo circunstancial en *La Plaza del Diamante*." *Revista de Estudios Hispánicos*, 12 (1978), pp. 15-24.

Gabancho, Patricia. *La rateta encara escombra l'escaleta*. Barcelona: Edicions 62, 1982.

Galerstein, Carolyn L. "*Bibiana:* A Plea for the Liberation of Spanish Women." *Letras Femeninas*, VIII, no. 1 (1982), pp. 3-8.

Galerstein, Carolyn.. "Carmen Laforet and the Spanish Spinster." *Revista de Estudios Hispánicos*, XI, no. 2 (Mayo 1977), pp. 303-15.

Gautier, Marie-Lise Gazarian. "Conversación con Carmen Martín Gaite en Nueva York." *Insula*, XXXVI, no. 411 (February 1981), pp. 1, 10-11.

Glenn, Kathleen M. "Animal Imagery in *Nada*." *Revista de Estudios Hispánicos*, XI, no. 3 (October 1977), pp. 381-94.

Hadjopoulos, Theresa Mary. *Four Women Novelists of Postwar Spain: Matute, Laforet, Quiroga and Medio*. Ann Arbor: Dissertation Abstracts International, 1974.

Illanes Adaro, Graciela. *La novelística de Carmen Laforet*. Madrid: Gredos, 1971.

Jones, Margaret, E.W. "Dialectical Movement as Feminist Technique in the Works of Carmen Laforet." *Studies in Honor of Gerald E. Wade*. Madrid: José Porrúa Turanzas, 1979.

Jones, Margaret E.W. *Dolores Medio*. New York: Twayne, 1974.

Jones, Margaret, E.W. *The Literary World of Ana María Matute*. Lexington, KY: The University Press of Kentucky, 1970.

Jones, Margaret E.W. "Las novelistas españolas contemporáneas ante la crítica." *Letras Femeninas*, IX, no. 1 (1983), pp. 22-34.

Johnson, Roberta. *Carmen Laforet*. New York: Twayne, 1981.

Lamar Morris, Celita. "Carmen Laforet's *Nada* as an Expression of Woman's Self-Determination." *Letras Femeninas*, I (1975), pp. 40-47.

Levine, Linda Gould and Gloria Waldman. *Feminismo ante el franquismo*. Miami: Ediciones Universal, 1980.

Lucio, Francisco. "La soledad, tema central en los últimos relatos de Mercè Rodoreda." *Cuadernos Hispanoamericanos*, no. 242 (1970), pp. 455-68.

Marks, Martha Alford. "Elena Quiroga's Yo Voice and the Schism between Reality and Illusion." *Anales de la Narrativa Española Contemporánea*, V (1981), pp. 39-55.

Matamoro, Blas. "Carmen Martín Gaite: El viaje al cuarto de atrás." *Cuadernos Hispanoamericanos*, no. 351 (1979), pp. 581-605.

Mateu, William F. *The New Spanish Feminism in the Writings of Carmen Laforet*. Ann Arbor: Dissertation Abstracts International, 1983.

Mayoral, Jedina. "Una lucha nunca acabada." *Cuadernos Hispanoamericanos*, no. 69 (1967), pp. 553-56.

McNerney, Kathleen. "La identitat a *La Plaça del Diamant*: Supressió i recerca." *Actas del Quart Col.loqui d'Estudis Catalans a Nord-Amèrica*. Barcelona: l'Abadia de Montserrat, 1985, pp. 295-302.

Medina, Hector. "Conversación con Carmen Martín Gaite." *Anales de la Literatura Española Contemporánea*, VIII (1983), pp. 183-94.

Miller, Beth, ed. and introduction. *Women in Hispanic Literature: Icons and Fallen Idols*. Berkeley: University of California Press, 1983.

Myers, Eunice D. "Estación, ida y vuelta: Rosa Chacel's Apprenticeship Novel." *Hispanic Journal*, 4 (Spring 1983), pp. 77-84.

Myers, Eunice D. "Four Female Novelists and Spanish Children's Fiction." *Letras Femeninas*, X, no. 2, (Fall 1984), pp. 40-49.

Myers, Eunice D. "Modern Man's Quest for Identity in Rosa Chacel's *La sinrazón*." *Perspectives on Contemporary Literature*, 8 (1982), pp. 85-90.

Nelson, Esther W. "Review of Carmen Martín Gaite, *Las ataduras*." *Anales de la Narrativa Española Contemporánea*, 4 (1979), pp. 193-95.

Newberry, Wilma. "Acquatic Imagery in Carmen Laforet's *Nada*." *Letras Femeninas*, X, no. 2 (Fall 1984), pp. 20-27.

Ordóñez, Elizabeth. "*Nada*: Initiation into Bourgeois Patriarchy." *The Analysis of Hispanic Texts: Current Trends in Methodology*, ed. Lisa E. Davis and Isabel C. Taran. Jamaica, NY: Bilingual Press, 1976.

Ordóñez, Elizabeth. "The Decoding and Encoding of Sex Roles in Carmen Martín Gaite's *Retahílas*." *Kentucky Romance Quarterly*, XXVII (1980), pp. 237-44.

Ordóñez, Elizabeth. "A Quest for Matrilineal Roots and Mythopoesis: Esther Tusquets' *El mismo mar de todos los veranos*." *Crítica Hispánica*, 6 (1984), pp. 37-46.

Ordóñez, Elizabeth J. "Reading Contemporary Spanish Narrative by

Women." *Anales de la Literatura Española Contemporánea,* VII, no. 2 (1982), pp. 237-251.

Ortega, José. "La frustración femenina en *Los mercaderes* de Ana María Matute." *Hispanófila,* no. 54 (1975), pp. 31-38.

Oyarzún, Luis A. "Eroticism and Feminism in Spanish Literature after Franco: *Los amores diurnos* de Francisco Umbral and *Crónica del desamor* de Rosa Montero." *Mid-Hudson Language Studies,* VI (1981), pp. 135-44.

Pérez (Díaz), Janet W. *Ana María Matute.* New York: Twayne, 1971.

Pérez. (Díaz), Janet W. "Three New Works of Dolores Medio." *Romance Notes,* no. 11 (1969), pp. 244-50.

Pérez (Díaz), Janet Winecoff. "The Autobiographical Element in the Works of Ana María Matute." *Kentucky Romance Quarterly,* no. 15 (1968), pp. 139-48.

Pérez (Díaz), Janet. ed. *Novelistas femeninas de la postguerra española.* Madrid: Porrúa, 1983.

Pérez, Janet. "Variantes del arquetipo femenino en la narrativa de Ana María Matute." *Letras Femeninas,* X, no. 2 (Fall 1984), pp. 38-39.

Pérez (Winecoff), Janet. "Fictionalized Autobiography in the Novels of Dolores Medio." *Kentucky Foreign Language Quarterly,* XIII, no. 3 (1966), pp. 170-78.

Pessarrodona, Marta. "Les dones a l'obra de Mercè Rodoreda." *Serra d'Or,* XXV, no. 290 (November 1983), pp. 17-19.

Pont, Jaume. "Carme Riera y Guillén Frontera: Signos de la narrativa mallorquina." *Insula,* XXXIV, no. 388 (March 1979), pp. 3-4.

Prjevalinsky Ferrer, Olga. "Las novelistas españolas de hoy." *Cuadernos Americanos,* CXVIII, no. 5 (September-October 1961), pp. 211-23.

Ramos, Alicia. "Conversación con Carmen Martín Gaite." *Hispanic Journal,* I, no. 2 (1980), pp. 117-24.

Rodríguez, Pedro. "Elena Quiroga veinte años después." *El Siglo* (Bogotá) (30 May 1971), p. 2.

Roma, Rosa. *Ana María Matute.* Madrid: EPESA, 1971.

Saludes, Anna. "Mercè Rodoreda, periodista." *Revista del centro de lectura de Reus,* 241 (December 1972), pp. 1325-26.

Schwartz, Ronald. *Spain's New Wave Novelists 1950-1974.* Metuchen, NJ: Scarecrow Press, 1976. Chapter 5: "Quiroga and *Algo pasa en la calle* (1974)" and Chapter 9: "Matute and *Primera memoria* (1960)."

Servodidio, Mirella and Marcia L. Welles, eds. *From Fiction to Metafiction:*

    Essays in Honor of Carmen Martín Gaite. Lincoln. NE: Society for Spanish and Spanish-American Literature, 1983.
Shelby, James Townsend. *Alienation in the Novels of Ana María Matute.* Ann Arbor: Dissertation Abstracts Internationai, 1976.
Sobré, Josep Miguel. "L'artifici de *La Plaça del Diamant*, un estudi lingüistic." *In Memoriam Carles Riba: 1959-1969.* Barcelona: University of Barcelona -Ariel, 1973.
Vida, Jeronia. "Feminismo: La revolución pendiente." *Opción, Revista de la Mujer Liberada,* 7 (June, 1977), pp. 29-41.
Wyers, Frances. "A Woman's Voices: Mercè Rodoreda's *La Plaça del Diamant.*" *Kentucky Romance Quarterly,* XXX, no. 3 (1983), pp. 301-09.
Zatlin Boring, Phyllis. "Carmen Martín Gaite, Feminist Author." *Revista de Estudios Hispánicos,* XI, no. 3 (October 1977), pp. 323-38.
Zatlin, Phyllis. "Divorce in Franco Spain: Elena Quiroga's *Algo pasa en la calle.*" *Mosaic,* XVII, no. 1 (1984), pp. 129-38.
Zatlin, Phyllis. "La aparición de nuevas corrientes femeninas en la novela española de postguerra." *Letras Femeninas,* IX, no. 1 (1983), pp. 35-42.

III. OTHER WORKS REFERENCED IN ESSAYS

Abel, Elizabeth, ed. *Writing and Sexual Difference.* Chicago: University of Chicago Press, 1982.
Axthelm, Peter. *The Modern Confessional Novel.* New Haven: Yale University Press, 1967.
Barthes, Roland. *The Pleasure of the Text,* trans. by Richard Miller. New York: Hill & Wang, 1975.
Beauvoir, Simone de. *The Coming of Age,* trans. Patrick O'Brian. New York: Warner, 1973.
Boulding, Elisa. *The Underside of History: A View of Women Through Time.* Boulder, CO: Westview Press, 1976.
Bridenthal, Renate and Claudia Koonz. *Becoming Visible: Women in European History.* Boston: Houghton Mifflin, 1977.
Briffault, Robert. *The Mothers.* New York: MacMillan, 1927.
Cadenas, C.B. "Historia de tres mujeres." *Nueva Estafeta,* no. 18 (May 1980), pp. 76-77.

Caro Romero, Joaquín. *Antología de la poesía erótica de nuestro tiempo*. Paris: Ruedo Ibérico, 1973.

Carroll, Berenice A., ed. *Liberating Women's History*. Champaign-Urbana: University of Illinois Press, 1976.

Chandernagor, Françoise. *L'Allée du Roi*. Paris: Julliard, 1981.

Chopin, Kate. *The Awakening*. New York: Avon, 1972.

Ciplijauskaité, Biruté. *Los noventayochentistas y la historia*. Madrid: Porrúa Turanzas, 1981.

Cixous, Helene. "The Laugh of the Medusa." *New French Feminisms: An Anthology*, ed. Elaine Marks and Isabelle de Courtivron. Amherst: University of Massachusetts Press, 1980.

Columbia Dictionary of Modern European Writers. New York: Columbia University Press, 1980.

Coward, Rosalind. *Patriarchal Precedents: Sexuality and Social Relations*. Boston: Routledge and Kegan Paul, 1983.

Crowley, Ernest. *The Mystic Rose*. New York: Meridian Books, 1960.

De la Rada y Delgado, Juan de Dios. *Mujeres célebres de España y Portugal*. Buenos Aires: Espasa Calpe, 1954.

Diccionario de Literatura Española. Madrid: Revista de Occidente, 1972.

England, John and J.L. Caramés Lage. "El uso y abuso de anglicismos en la prensa española de hoy." *Arbor*, 100, no. 390 (June, 1978), pp. 77-89.

Fernández Roca, José Angel. "Crónica y la novela en *Las ninfas* de Umbral." *Cuadernos Hispanoamericanos*, no. 373 (1981), pp. 109-127.

Flores de Setien, Eugenio. *Memoria de las reinas católicas de España*. Madrid: Aguilar, 1945.

Foucault, Michel. *The Archaeology of Knowledge*, trans. by A.M. Sheridan Smith. New York: Harper & Row, 1972.

Foucault, Michel. *The History of Sexuality. Volume 1: An Introduction*. New York: Vintage Books, 1980.

Foulkes, A.P. *Literature and Propaganda*. London and New York: Methuen, 1983.

Gallop, Jane. *The Daughter's Seduction: Feminism and Psychoanalysis*. Ithaca, NY: Cornell Univ. Press, 1982.

García, Evelyne. "Lectura: N. Fem. Sing. ¿Lee y escribe la mujer en forma diferente al hombre?" *Quimera*, 23 (September 1982), pp. 54-57.

Gardiner, Judith Kegan. "On Female Identity and Writing by Women."

Elizabeth Abel, ed. *Writing and Sexual Difference.* Chicago: University of Chicago Press, 1982.

Gerling, David Ross. "Review of Montserrat Roig, *La hora violeta.*" *Anales de la Literatura Española Contemporánea,* 8 (1983), pp. 243-245.

Gilbert, Sandra M. and Susan Gubar. *The Madwoman in the Attic: The Woman Writer and the Nineteenth-Century Literary Imagination.* New Haven and London: Yale University Press, 1979.

Gilbert, Sandra. "What Do Feminist Critics Want?; or, A Postcard from the Volcano." *ADE Bulletin* (Winter 1980), p. 19.

Gombrich, E.H. "Botticelli's Mythologies: A Study in the Neoplatonic Symbolism of his Circle." *Journal of the Warburg and Courtauld Institutes,* 9 (1945), pp. 7-60.

Guillén, Nicolás. "El apellido." *Campo Abierto,* ed. Mary Jane Treacy and Nancy Abraham Hall. Boston: Houghton Mifflin, 1984.

Hamburger, Kate. *Die Logik der Dichtung.* Stuttgart: Ernst Klett, 1957.

Heilburn, Carolyn G. "Discovering the Lost Lives of Women." *The New York Times Book Review,* June 24, 1984.

Hellman, John. "The Nature and Modes of the New Journalism: A Theory." *Genre,* 13, no. 4 (Winter 1980), pp. 517-29.

Hoyos, Antonio de. *Ocho escritores actuales.* Murcia: Aula de Cultura, 1954.

Irvin, Helen Deiss. "Gea in Georgia: A Mythic Dimension in *Gone With the Wind.*" *Recasting: Gone With the Wind in American Culture,* ed. Darden A. Pyron. Miami: University Press of Florida, 1983.

Iser, Wolfang. *The Act of Reading: A Theory of Aesthetic Response.* Baltimore: The Johns Hopkins University Press, 1978.

Jacobus, Mary. "The Difference of View." *Women Writing and Writing About Women,* ed. Mary Jacobus. London: Croom Helm, 1979.

Janeway, Elizabeth. *Powers of the Weak.* New York: Knopf, 1980.

Kolodny, Annette. "Some Notes on Defining a 'Feminist Literary Criticism.'" *Critical Inquiry,* 2, no. 1 (Autumn 1975).

Kristeva, Julia. *Desire in Language: A Semiotic Approach to Literature and Art,* ed. Leon S. Roudiez. New York: Columbia Univ. Press, 1980.

Lafuente, Modesto. *Historia general de España.* Barcelona: Montaner y Simón, 1889.

Lerner, Gerda. *The Majority Finds Its Past: Placing Women in History.* New York and Oxford: Oxford University Press, 1979.

Lukacs, Gyorgi. *Le Roman historique.* Paris: Payot, 1972.

Miron, E.L. *The Queens of Aragon: Their Lives and Times*. New York: Kennikat Press, 1970.

Morán, Fernando. *Novela y semidesarrollo*. Madrid: Taurus, 1971.

Morson, Gary Saul. "Who Speaks for Bakhtin?: A Dialogic Introduction." *Critical Inquiry*, 10, no. 2 (December 1983), p. 236.

Moss, Zoe. "It Hurts To Be Alive and Obsolete: The Ageing Woman." *Sisterhood Is Powerful*, ed. Robin Morgan. New York: Vintage, 1970.

Navajo, Ymelda. *Doce relatos de mujeres*. Madrid: Alianza, 1983.

Ordoñéz, Elizabeth. "Narrative Texts by Ethnic Women: Rereading the Past, Reshaping the Future." *MELUS*, 9 (1982), p. 26.

Ortega y Gasset, José. *The Revolt of the Masses*, trans. New York: Norton, 1957.

Peréz, Janet. "Some Desiderata in Studies in Twentieth Century Spanish Fiction." *Siglo Veinte/Twentieth Century*, 1, no. 2 (Spring 1984), pp. 4-6.

Pratt, Annis. *Archetypal Patterns in Women's Fiction*. Bloomington: Indiana Univ. Press, 1981.

Reilly, Bernard F. *The Kingdom of Leon-Castilla Under Queen Urraca: 1109-1126*. Princeton, NJ: Princeton Univ. Press, 1982.

Rich, Adrienne. *On Lies, Secrets and Silence*. New York: Norton, 1979.

Riera, Carme. "Literatura femenina: ¿Un lenguaje prestado?" *Quimera*, 18 (April 1982), pp. 9-12.

Sánchez Arnosi, Milagros. "El mundo de los libros." *Insula*, 37, no. 431 (October 1982), p. 8.

Sargent, Lyman Tower. Future Females. Bowling Green, OH: Bowling Green Univ. Press, 1981.

Sarton, May. *Journal of a Solitude*. New York: W.W. Norton, 1973.

Schulenburg, Jane Tibbets. "Clio's European Daughters: Myopic Modes of Perception." *The Prism of Sex: Essays in the Sociology of Knowledge*, ed. Julia A. Sherman and Evelyn T. Beck. Madison, WI: The Univ. of Wisconsin Press, 1977.

Shahar, Shulamith. *The Fourth Estate*, trans. Chaya Galai. London: Metheun, 1983.

Showalter, Elaine. "Feminist Criticism in the Wilderness." *Critical Inquiry*, 8, no. 2 (1981), pp. 179-205.

Spacks, Patricia Meyer. *The Female Imagination*. New York: Avon, 1972.

Spacks, Patricia Meyer. *Imagining a Self: Autobiography and Novel in Eighteenth-Century England*. Cambridge, MA and London: Harvard University Press, 1976.

Spivak, Gayatri Chakrovorty. "Finding Feminist Readings: Dante-Yeats." *American Criticism in the Poststructuralist Age*, ed. Ira Konigsberg. Ann Arbor: Univ. of Michigan Studies in the Humanities, 1981.

Stimpson, Catherine. "Feminism and Feminist Criticism." *Massachusetts Review*, 24, no. 2, pp. 272-288.

Traba, Marta. "Hipótesis sobre una escritura diferente." *Quimera*, 13 (November 1981), pp. 9-11.

Umbral, Francisco. *Las ninfas*. Barcelona: Destino, 1976.

Valbuena Prat, Angel. *Historia de la literatura española*. Barcelona: Gustavo Gili, 1963.

Villegas, Juan. *La estructura mítica del héroe*. Barcelona: Planeta, 1973.

Walker, Barbara G. *The Woman's Encyclopedia of Myths and Secrets*. San Francisco: Harper & Row, 1983.

Wolfe, Tom. "The New Journalism." *The New Journalism*, eds. Tom Wolfe and E.W. Johnson. New York: Harper & Row, 1979.

White, Hayden. "The Value of Narrativity in the Representation of Reality." *Critical Inquiry*, 7, no. 1 (Autumn 1980), pp. 5-27.

Woolf, Virginia. *A Room of One's Own*. London: Hogarth Press, 1929.

Yourcenar, Margarite. *Mémoires d'Hadrien*. Paris: Plon, 1951.

Feminine Concerns in Contemporary Spanish Fiction by Women

List of Contributors

CATHERINE BELLVER is Professor of Spanish at the University of Nevada, Las Vegas. She is author of "The Language of Eroticism in the Novels of Esther Tusquets," *Anales de la Literatura Española Contemporánea*, XI (1984), "Carmen Martín Gaite as a Social Critic," *Letras Femeninas*, VI, no. 2 (1980), and, more recently, "Division, Duplication, and Doubling in Ana María Moix," in *Nuevos novísimos*, Ricardo Landeira and Luis González del Valle, eds.

JOAN LIPMAN BROWN is Associate Professor of Spanish at the University of Delaware and author of *Secrets From the Backroom: The Fiction of Carmen Martín Gaite* (University of Mississippi Press, 1984), "Tiempo de silencio and Ritmo lento. Pioneers of the New Social Novel in Spain," *Hispanic Review*, 50, no. 1 (1982), and "A Fantastic Memoir: Technique and History in *El cuarto de atrás*," *Anales de la Novela Española Contemporánea*, VI (1981).

BIRUTÉ CIPLIJAUSKAITÉ is John Bascom Professor of Spanish at the University of Wisconsin, Madison and a permanent member of the University's Institute for Research in the Humanities. Author of numerous books and articles on Spanish and World literatures, Professor Ciplijauslaité's most recent work includes, *La mujer insatisfecha: El adulterio en la novela realista*

(Edhasa, 1984) and *La novela femenina contemporánea (1970-1985)*, soon to be published by Anthropos.

CAROLINE GALERSTEIN in Associate Professor of Comparative Literature at the University of Texas at Dallas and editor of *Women Writers of Spain: An Annotated Bio-bibliographical Guide* (Greenwood Press, 1986). Her critical studies include "Carmen Laforet and the Spanish Spinster," *Revista de Estudios Hispánicos* (May 1977), "Bibiana: A Plea for the Liberation of Spanish Women," *Letras Femeninas*, VIII, No. 1 (1982), and, more recently, "The Spanish Civil War: The View of Women Novelists," *Letras Femeninas*, X, no. 2 (1984).

ROBERTA JOHNSON is Associate Professor of Spanish at Scripps College and author of several books and articles on modern Spanish literatura from Pío Baroja to Esther Tusquets. She is recognized for her work on Gabriel Miró. Among her more well-known studies on women writers is *Carmen Laforet* (Twayne, 1981).

LUCY LEE-BONANNO is Assistant Professor of Spanish at Northeast Missouri State University. She received her Ph.D from the University of Kentucky.

ROBERTO MANTEIGA is Associate Professor of Hispanic Studies at the University of Rhode Island. He is author of *The Poetry of Rafael Alberti: A Visual Approach* (Tamesis Books, 1978), editor of *Critical Approaches to the Writings of Juan Benet* (University Press of New England, 1984), and has published numerous articles on 20th Century Spanish theater, poetry and narrative. Among his studies on women writers is the soon to be published "El triunfo del Minotauro: Ambigüedad y razón en *El mismo mar de todos los veranos* de Esther Tusquets" (*Letras Femeninas*).

KATHLEEN MCNERNEY is Associate Professor of Spanish at West Virginia University. She is editor for non-Castilian authors for *Women Writers of Spain: An Annotated Bio-bibliographical Guide* (Greenwood Press, 1986), and author of several books and articles on Catalan Studies and Women Studies. Her most recent works include *On Our Own Behalf: Women's Tales of Catalonia* (University of Nebraska Press) and *Understanding García Márquez* (South Carolina University Press, forthcoming).

EUNICE MYERS is Associate Professor of Spanish at Wichita State University. She is Co-Director of the Wichita State University Conference on Foreign Literature, editor of the conference's *Selected Papers*, and author of several studies on women writers, including "Estación, ida y vuelta. Rosa Chacel's Apprenticeship Novel," *Hispanic Journal*, 4 (1983), "Narcissism and the Quest for Identity in Rosa Chacel's *La sinrazón*," *Perspectives on Contemporary Literature*, 8 (1982), and "Four Female Novelists and Spanish Children's Fiction," *Letras Femeninas*, X, no. 2 (1984).

ELIZABETH ORDÓÑEZ is Associate Professor of Spanish at the University of Texas at Arlington and author of numerous articles on the works of Hispanic women writers, including "The Decoding and Encoding of Sex Roles in Carmen Martín Gaite's *Retahílas*," *Kentucky Romance Quarterly*, 27 (1980), "Reading Contemporary Spanish Narrative by Women," *Anales de la Narrativa Española Contemporánea*, VII (1982), and "A Quest for Matrilineal Roots and Mythopoesis: Esther Tusquet's *El mismo mar de todos los veranos*," *Crítica Hispánica*, 6 (1984).

JANET PÉREZ is Professor of Spanish at Texas Tech University. She is editor or co-editor of several journals, including the recent and successful *Monograph Review*, and author of numerous books and articles on 20th Century Spanish Fiction. Among her works on women writers are *Ana María Matute* (Twayne, 1969) and *Novelistas femeninas de la postguerra española* (Porrúa, 1983).

Scripta humanistica
Directed by
BRUNO M. DAMIANI
The Catholic University of America
COMPREHENSIVE LIST OF PUBLICATIONS*

1. Everett W. Hesse, The "Comedia" and Points of View. $24.50
2. Marta Ana Diz, Patronio y Lucanor: la lectura inteligente "en el tiempo que es turbio." Prólogo de John Esten Keller. $26.00
3. James F. Jones, Jr., The Story of a Fair Greek of Yesteryear. A Translation from the French of Antoine-François Prévost's L'Histoire d'une Grecque moderne. With Introduction and Selected Bibliography. $30.00
4. Colette H. Winn, Jean de Sponde: Les sonnets de la mort ou La Poétique de l'accoutumance. Préface par Frédéric Deloffre. $22.50
5. Jack Weiner, "En busca de la justicia social: estudio sobre el teatro español del Siglo de Oro." $24.50
6. Paul A. Gaeng, Collapse and Reorganization of the Latin Nominal Flection as Reflected in Epigraphic Sources. Written with the assistance of Jeffrey T. Chamberlin. $24.00
7. Edna Aizenberg, The Aleph Weaver: Biblical, Kabbalistic, and Judaic Elements in Borges. $25.00
8. Michael G. Paulson and Tamara Alvarez-Detrell, Cervantes, Hardy, and "La fuerza de la sangre." $25.50
9. Rouben Charles Cholakian, Deflection/Reflection in the Lyric Poetry of Charles d'Orléans: A Psychosemiotic Reading. $25.00
10. Kent P. Ljungquist, The Grand and the Fair: Poe's Landscape Aesthetics and Pictorial Techniques. $27.50
11. D.W. McPheeters, Estudios humanísticos sobre la "Celestina." $20.00
12. Vittorio Felaco, The Poetry and Selected Prose of Camillo Sbarbaro. Edited and Translated by Vittorio Felaco. With a Preface by Franco Fido. $25.00
13. María del C. Candau de Cevallos, Historia de la lengua española. $33.00
14. Renaissance and Golden Age Studies in Honor of D.W. McPheeters. Ed. Bruno M. Damiani. $25.00
15. Bernardo Antonio González, Parábolas de identidad: Realidad interior y estrategia narrativa en tres novelistas de postguerra. $28.00
16. Carmelo Gariano, La Edad Media (Aproximación Alfonsina). $30.00
17. Gabriella Ibieta, Tradition and Renewal in "La gloria de don Ramiro". $27.50
18. Estudios literarios en honor de Gustavo Correa. Eds. Charles Faulhaber, Richard Kinkade, T.A. Perry. Preface by Manuel Durán. $25.00
19. George Yost, Pieracci and Shelly: An Italian Ur-Cenci. $27.50
20. Zelda Irene Brooks, The Poetry of Gabriel Celaya. $26.00
21. La relación o naufragios de Alvar Núñez Cabeza de Vaca, eds. Martin A. Favata y José B. Fernández. $27.50

22.	Pamela S. Brakhage, *The Theology of "La Lozana andaluza."*	$27.50
23.	Jorge Checa, *Gracián y la imaginación arquitectónica.*	$28.00
24.	Gloria Gálvez Lira, *Maria Luisa Bombal: Realidad y Fantasía.*	$28.50
25.	Susana Hernández Araico, *Ironía y tragedia en Calderón.*	$25.00
26.	Philip J. Spartano, *Giacomo Zanella: Poet, Essayist, and Critic of the "Risorgimento."* Preface by Roberto Severino.	$24.00
27.	E. Kate Stewart, *Arthur Sherburne Hardy: Man of American Letters.* Preface by Louis Budd.	$28.50
28.	Giovanni Boccaccio, *The Decameron.* English Adaptation by Carmelo Gariano.	$30.00
29.	Giacomo A. Striuli, "Alienation in Giuseppe Berto".	$26.50
30.	Barbara Mujica, *Iberian Pastoral Characters.* Preface by Frederick A. de Armas.	$33.00
31.	Susan Niehoff McCrary, *"'El último godo' and the Dynamics of the Urdrama."* Preface by John E. Keller.	$27.50
32.	*En torno al hombre y a sus monstruos: Ensayos críticos sobre la novelística de Carlos Rojas,* editados por Cecilia Castro Lee y C. Christopher Soufas, Jr.	$31.50
33.	J. Thomas O'Connell, *Mount Zion Field.*	$24.50
34.	Francisco Delicado, *Portrait of Lozana: The Lusty Andalusian Woman.* Translation, introduction and notes by Bruno M. Damiani.	$39.50
35.	Elizabeth Sullam, *Out of Bounds.* Foreword by Michael G. Cooke.	$23.50
36.	Sergio Corsi, *Il "modus digressivus" nella "Divina Commedia"*	$28.75
37.	Juan Bautista Avalle-Arce, *Lecturas (Del temprano Renacimiento a Valle Inclán).*	$28.50
38.	Rosendo Díaz-Peterson, *Las novelas de Unamuno.* Prólogo de Antonio Carreño.	$30.00
39.	Jeanne Ambrose, *Syntaxe Comparative Français-Anglais.*	$29.50
40.	Nancy Marino, *La serranilla española: notas para su historia e interpretación.*	$28.75.
41.	Carolyn Kreiter-Kurylo, *Contrary Visions.* Preface by Peter Klappert.	$24.50
42.	Giorgio Perissinotto, *Reconquista y literatura medieval: Cuatro Ensayos.*	$29.50
43.	Rick Wilson, *Between a Rock and a Heart Place.*	$25.00
44.	*Feminine Concerns in Contemporary Spanish Fiction by Women.* Edited by Roberto C. Manteiga, Carolyn Galerstein and Kathleen McNerney.	$35.00

Forthcoming

- Carlo Di Maio, *Antifeminism in Selected Works of Enrique Jardiel Poncela*. $20.50
- Juan de Mena, *Coplas de los siete pecados mortales: Second and Third Continuations*. Ed. Gladys Rivera. $25.50
- Salvatore Calomino, *From Verse to Prose: The Barlaam and Josaphat Legend in Fifteenth-Century Germany*. $28.00
- Darlene Lorenz-González, *A Phonemic Description of the Andalusian Dialect Spoken in Almogía, Málaga — Spain*. $25.00
- Maricel Presilla, *The Politics of Death in the «Cantigas de Santa María.»* Preface by John E. Keller. Introduction by Norman F. Cantor. $27.50
- *Studies in Honor of Elias Rivers*, eds. Bruno M. Damiani and Ruth El Saffar. $25.00
- Godwin Okebaram Uwah, *Pirandellism and Samuel Beckett's Plays*. $28.00

BOOK ORDERS

* Clothbound. All book orders, except library orders, must be prepaid and addressed to **Scripta Humanistica**, 1383 Kersey Lane, Potomac, Maryland 20854. Manuscripts to be considered for publication should be sent to the same address.